Statistics Workbook

1998

Robert Lakeland & Carl Nugent

NuLake Texts
Innovative publisher of educational text books

Acknowledgments

The authors appreciate the constructive criticism with which the 1996 statistics students of Wanganui High School and Nga Tawa School shaped this production. We also acknowledge the support and encouragement from our fellow staff members.

Special thanks to:

Margaret Pearson for the time spent proof reading this book.

First published 1997

Reprinted June 1997

1998 edition printed in January 1998

NuLake Texts

P.O. Box 103, Wanganui

Fax   (06) 348 0194, (06) 344 6166

Phone   (06) 344 6066, (025) 240 3641

email   feedback@nulake.co.nz

Web Site   http://www.nulake.co.nz

Typeset by the authors.

Printed by Perry Print, Wanganui

How to use this book

Icons are used throughout this book to alert the student as to the function of each section.

 Notes. At the beginning of each section all the relevant notes are summarised. Please accent these (see section on learning styles) as your teacher presents the material.

 Additional Material. The class teacher may cover additional points or an alternative approach. Space is left so that a student can integrate additional material or examples.

 Note Well. Points that should be well understood or committed to memory are signposted. This is the sort of material that you could put on flip cards.

 Bright Ideas. Where the authors have found an innovative approach for a particular concept they have indicated this.

 Examples. Straight forward examples of the concept being explained.

 Solution. For each example. Go through these carefully as they contain teaching points.

 Problems. These straight forward problems are designed to reinforce the concept being explained. The student will need to attempt additional problems from a text book.

 Answers. Space for the student to attempt the problem.

Rounding

Answers are usually rounded to the appropriate degree of accuracy. If the question involves given measurements then the answer can not be stated more accurately than these. If the calculation involves multiplication (or division) then the least number of significant figures is used. If the calculation involves addition (or subtraction) then the least number of decimal places is used. Usually the calculation involves both and the authors have selected the degree of accuracy they think is appropriate. The maximum accuracy expected is 4 significant figures.

Contents

Introduction

This workbook has been written by two experienced teachers as an additional aid to teachers and students in the study of Bursary Mathematics with Statistics. It is more than just a notebook with extra space to write in. It is, as its name suggests, a *Statistics Workbook*.

We envisage students purchasing their *Statistics Workbook* at the beginning of the year and using it in class primarily as their note book. It is hoped that because students have notes for each topic in advance, more time can be spent by the teacher in teaching the concepts and investigating examples and problems. As the teacher explains the concepts the students would endorse their notes with relevant points (see notes on learning styles). It is designed to complement the teacher and to allow more time for the teacher to teach, rather than dictate notes.

There are worked examples for each concept with space for key points to be highlighted by the teacher. Each concept is followed by four to six questions, some of which are partially done, to help students grasp the solving procedure and setting out. The answers in the back usually include some of the setting out required to solve these examples so students will get feedback as to the correct approach.

Syllabus

This year will be the third year of a new syllabus for Mathematics with Statistics . Details of the syllabus are included with the relevant section. Not all concepts covered in the *Workbook* are specifically mentioned in the syllabus (eg. Display of Data) but where the authors considered it appropriate these have been included. In addition to the specific objectives, the syllabus does require candidates to have knowledge and understanding of the Sixth Form prescription.

Graphics Calculators

The authors recommend students use a graphical calculator to help with Equations (particularly Simultaneous equations), Graphs, Statistics and Normal Probability. Both of us have made good use of the Casio CFX 9850 G and the Texas Instruments TI 83. These calculators will enable a student to concentrate on interpretation rather than calculations. These calculators are allowed in the Bursary Mathematics with Statistics examination.

Feedback

Thank you for the feedback we have received. We particularly enjoyed the letters from students who obviously had gained in confidence from using the book. We have kept the same basic structure of

- Plenty of white space so students could tailor the *Workbook* as they like (see Customising the Workbook - learning styles).

- Full notes so the student can concentrate on the lesson and catch up missed work.

We welcome feedback and suggestions on the layout or content. We have not only written this guide but we have done the layout and publishing which means we are now in an ideal position to adapt to your ideas as well as respond to changes in the prescription and the transition to unit standards.

If you wish to make comments or check if you have found an error then have a look at our web site at http://www.nulake.co.nz where any errors that have been found are listed and from which you can email us comments or questions.

Statistical Project

There is no common approach to the 20% internally assessed component of the Mathematics with Statistics prescription. We welcome feedback as to how we can help students with the project. Two pieces of advice we can offer are

- Make sure you are answering the question being asked. Ask for interpretation and feedback on your approach. If possible get the marking scheme so you can check that your approach is going to be rewarded with marks.

- Use a statistical package to decrease the time spent number crunching and increase the time spent interpreting.

Robert Lakeland & Carl Nugent

Customising the Workbook for your own learning style

When we learn, we use a number of different learning styles. The main ones are Visual, Auditory, and Kinaesthetic. Most people have one of these learning styles as the predominant or more effective style. Remember back to your last formal statistics lesson and concentrate on what you remember. If you remember

- what the teacher was doing and the layout of the material on the board. What everything looked like then you are probably a predominantly visual learner.

- what the teacher said. The little tips that were suggested by the teacher as they explained the concept. Then you are probably an auditory learner. When you are doing mathematics problems you may hear a voice in your brain telling you the next step.

- how you felt or what you were doing (playing with a pen?) then you are probably a kinaesthetic learner.

We all use all the learning styles but to different degrees. An excellent introduction to learning is Christine Ward & Jan Daley's book *"Learning to Learn"*. If you know how you learn most effectively then you can customise your Workbook for your preferred style.

Visual Learners

You remember with pictures. It is important that you see what the teacher is doing rather than getting notes down. If you can read the notes in the *Workbook* prior to the lesson. Underline or accent mark important points in your *Workbook* as your teacher explains the concept. If the teacher does a different diagram then copy that in the space provided along side. At the end of a topic, draw a mind map of the content to be used for revision prior to exams. Keep your mind map on your bedroom wall for a week or so.

Visual learners would concentrate on the presentation of the page. They would watch what the teacher was doing and make sure the points demonstrated are illustrated in their workbook.

Auditory Learners

You remember what people said or a voice tells you the next step (internal dialogue). As the teacher explains the concept, draw out and complete speech balloons at the relevant place in the notes in your Workbook. Listen carefully and just add the tips or explanations that are missing. At home when you are going over your work or attempting examples, speak out loud. Have some slow baroque music playing in the background when you work.

Auditory learners would listen carefully to the points being made by their teacher. They would draw out speech balloons from the notes in their Workbook to explain concepts or steps in calculations.

Kinaesthetic Learners

You remember what you were doing so it is important that you copy down all relevant material even when you have already got adequate notes. Go over the notes in the Workbook rewriting them in your own words in the space provided. It is important that you copy out diagrams and complete notes made by your teacher. Add emotional words "I feel this is true because ..." (or smiley faces) to your own work.

Kinaesthetic Learners need to physically do something with the material in order to remember it. Emotional comments in their notes help.

Study Skills

Below are some guide lines to studying for examinations. Each student is different in his or her approach to study. This page highlights some important principles and ideas that we believe are the basis to a good revision programme and successful exam performance.

Positive Affirmations

Too many students have the wrong mental attitude prior to beginning revision for exams and the exam itself. How often do you hear students mutter statements such as "I don't understand this subject". "I've never been any good at mathematics". These sort of statements form the wrong mental picture in your subconscious - defeating much of the hard work in terms of study that may have taken place.

Be positive in your approach to study and the exam itself. Believe in yourself. Continually repeating statements such as *"My knowledge of Statistics has improved throughout the year." "Since purchasing the Statistic Workbook I am confident that I can do well"*, will form the right mental picture. These positive affirmations together with a good revision programme WILL make a difference.

Organisation

The basis of any good revision programme is organisation. Beginning to study for an exam the night before, is NOT being well organised. Prepare a timetable for your studying - starting early enough so that you can comfortably cover the work.

People study and achieve better when they have small targets or objectives to meet. Prepare your study plan so that each night you are achieving some small objective or target. It may be the section on Time Series or a certain number of pages or similar.

Break up your study time into hour long blocks or similar. Reward yourself when you have completed an hour, by taking a fifteen minute break.

Use your study time productively, by actively working, ie. taking brief notes, or highlighting pertinent points, or attempting problems. Just sitting and reading your note book, for most people, is ineffective study.

Physical Environment

Where you study is very important.   To make the best of your study time ensure the room you are working in

- is free from distractions and noise.
- has a suitable desk and a comfortable chair.
- is heated in winter and has good ventilation in summer.
- has good light.
- can be left undisturbed from study time to study time.
- is an environment you feel comfortable studying in.

Summary

Examinations are a stressful time for most people. If you have studied hard and are well prepared for the exam you are less likely to feel the symptoms of stress. Give yourself the chance to do the best you can, by preparing thoroughly. There is nothing worse, on receiving your result and the return of your paper than knowing that you could have passed, or done considerably better, if only you had done more revision.

Good luck

1.0 Statistics

Introduction

In this section we introduce the measures of central tendency and spread and distinguish between sample and population statistics. We look at the Central Limit Theorem and confidence intervals and their role and function in statistics.

Prescription

Calculate and interpret sample statistics
- **measures of centre and spread**
- **deriving the identity** $\sum (x - \bar{x})^2 = \sum x^2 - n(\bar{x})^2$

Explain the meaning of the sampling distribution of the mean and the sampling distribution of a proportion

Explain the difference between sample statistics and population parameters
- **calculating the sample size required for a given precision estimate of a population parameter**

Explain and use the Central Limit Theorem

Calculate point and interval (confidence interval) estimates for a population parameter, and explain the meaning of confidence intervals
- **the mean of a population**
- **a population proportion**
- **the difference between the means of two populations (using independent samples from those populations)**
- **interpreting 'margin of error' in survey reports and opinion polls.**

1.1 Measures of Central Tendency

Prescription

Explain the difference between sample statistics and population parameters
- **measures of centre**

Measures of Central Tendency

Statistics deals with the analysis of **data** (numbers) from samples, surveys, models, tests etc. From our sample statistics we estimate the corresponding population statistics.

Statistical data can be either **discrete** or **continuous**.

Discrete data occurs most commonly in 'counting' processes - discrete data can only take on isolated values, eg. the number of cars past a certain point, the number of marbles in a hat.

Continuous data assumes any value can be obtained within an interval, eg. lengths, masses, weights and times.

Continuous data can frequently be represented discretely because of rounding, eg. the time taken to complete a phone call, rounded to the nearest minute, is discrete data.

Measures of Central Tendency

There are three measures of central tendency or **'averages'** that you should already be familiar with, namely the mean, mode and median.

Each of these 'averages' summarises the data with a single number and theoretically gives us information on the 'middle' or 'centre' of the sample or population.

$$\text{Mean} = \frac{\text{sum of all the numbers}}{\text{total number of numbers}}$$

Median = middle number when all the numbers are ranked in order

Mode = the number that occurs more often than any other

Each of the three averages has advantages and disadvantages.

The **mean** is easy to calculate because it has a formula, but it is affected by extreme values.

The **median** is unaffected by extreme values, but it is more difficult to calculate, because the data has to be ordered first.

The **mode**, while useful to manufacturers who want to identify the most common size, etc. is not always typical of a population as a whole.

Of all the 'averages' the mean is the one that we will use more than any other, for it is an integral part of statistical theory.

Sample Mean

Consider the sample numbers $x_1, x_2, x_3, x_4, ..., x_n$

The sample mean which we denote by the symbol $\bar{x}$, (x bar) is given by

$$\bar{x} = \frac{x_1 + x_2 + x_3 + x_4 + ... + x_n}{n}$$

$$= \frac{\sum_{i=1}^{n} x_i}{n}$$

$$= \frac{\sum x}{n} \quad \text{(often written like this)}$$

We designate the population mean with the symbol μ.

Sample Mean cont...

Consider the sample data

x	1	2	3	4
f	2	4	3	1

where 'x' are the sample numbers and 'f' represents the frequency. (ie. the number of times 'x' occurs)

The sample mean in this situation can best be represented by the formula

$$\bar{x} = \frac{\sum fx}{n}$$

so

$$\bar{x} = \frac{(2 \times 1) + (4 \times 2) + (3 \times 3) + (1 \times 4)}{10}$$

$$= 2.3$$

Your calculator will have the mean function built into it. Use it to calculate the mean, in the example below.

This is the formula for the sample mean in your tables.

Example 1

Below are the length of 20 Billington Early plum tree leaves to the nearest mm.
80, 73, 76, 84, 72, 56, 98, 66, 76, 84, 78, 76, 48, 93, 76, 69, 87, 70, 71, 75

a) State whether the data is discrete or continuous and why.

b) Find the mode, median and mean of the data.

Solution

a) The data is discrete for it has been rounded to the nearest mm.

b) Mode   = 76 (it occurs more often than any other number)

Arranging the numbers from smallest to largest we obtain

48, 56, 66, 69, 70, 71, 72, 73, 75, 76, 76, 76, 76, 78, 80, 84, 84, 87, 93, 98
                                        ↑
                                     Median

The median lies between the 10th and the 11th numbers

∴   Median   = 76

       Mean   = $\frac{1508}{20}$ (sum of the numbers divided by the number of numbers)

       Mean   = 75.4 mm (1dp)

1.2 Measures of Spread

Prescription

- measures of spread
- deriving the identity $\sum (x - \bar{x})^2 = \sum x^2 - n(\bar{x})^2$

Measures of Spread

To describe or identify a set of data we need more than just the mean. We need to look at a measure of spread of the data.

If $\bar{x}$ is the mean of 'n' sample numbers $x_1, x_2, x_3, x_4, ..., x_n$ then $(x_1 - \bar{x}), (x_2 - \bar{x}), ..., (x_n - \bar{x})$ are called the deviations from the mean,

and $(x_1 - \bar{x})^2 + (x_2 - \bar{x})^2 + ... + (x_n - \bar{x})^2$ are the sum of the deviations squared.

The **variance** of 'n' sample numbers is defined as

$$s^2 = \frac{(x_1 - \bar{x})^2 + (x_2 - \bar{x})^2 + ... + (x_n - \bar{x})^2}{n}$$

$$= \frac{\sum_{i=1}^{n} (x_i - \bar{x})^2}{n}$$

$$= \frac{\sum (x_i - \bar{x})^2}{n}$$

and the **standard deviation** of 'n' sample numbers is defined as

$$s = \sqrt{\text{variance}}$$

$$= \sqrt{\frac{\sum (x_i - \bar{x})^2}{n}}$$

Essentially the standard deviation is the average spread of the numbers from the mean. The mean is subtracted from each number to get a spread and then squared to prevent the positive and negative values cancelling each other out when they are added together. The sum is then divided by 'n' to obtain the 'average' and then square rooted to remove the effect of the squaring.

Note Well

Make sure you can use the standard deviation function on your calculator to calculate the standard deviation of individual terms and of samples with frequencies greater than one. Note the difference between the σ_n and σ_{n-1} buttons on your calculator.

Extra Notes

Note Well

We designate the population standard deviation with the symbol σ.

Note Well

The formulae for the sample standard deviation and population standard deviation have different divisors. The sample standard deviation is divided by $n - 1$ while the population standard deviation is divided by n (see note page 17).

The present Bursary examination Examiner does NOT require candidates to use the $n - 1$ divisor at all. The authors do not agree with this approach but early problems in the workbook will also only use the n divisor. Later problems finding confidence intervals will use the $n - 1$ divisor.

Measures of Spread cont...

The formula for the standard deviation we have just defined is cumbersome and awkward to calculate. We are therefore interested in representing the standard deviation in a simpler form.

Let us consider the sum of the squares of deviations from the mean.

$$\sum (x - \bar{x})^2 = \sum [(x - \bar{x})(x - \bar{x})]$$

$$= \sum (x^2 - 2x\bar{x} + (\bar{x})^2)$$

$$= \sum x^2 - 2\bar{x}\sum x + n(\bar{x})^2$$

$$= \sum x^2 - 2\bar{x}(n\bar{x}) + n(\bar{x})^2$$

$$= \sum x^2 - n(\bar{x})^2$$

Hence the variance can now be written as

$$s^2 = \frac{\sum x^2 - n(\bar{x})^2}{n}$$

or

$$s^2 = \frac{1}{n}\sum x^2 - (\bar{x})^2$$

or

$$s^2 = \frac{\sum fx^2 - \frac{\left(\sum fx\right)^2}{n}}{n}, \text{ where 'f' is the frequency}$$

and the standard deviation as

$$s = \sqrt{\frac{\sum fx^2 - \frac{\left(\sum fx\right)^2}{n}}{n}}$$

Extra Notes

Note Well

Make sure you can derive this identity as it is specifically mentioned in the syllabus.

Note Well

This is the formula for the variance in your tables.

Example 2

Below is the data presented in Example 1 - the length to the nearest mm of 20 Billington Early plum tree leaves.

80, 73, 76, 84, 72, 56, 98, 66, 76, 84, 78, 76, 48, 93, 76, 69, 87, 70, 71, 75

Calculate the standard deviation by using the formula given in the notes above. Confirm your answer by using your calculator.

Solution

$$\sum fx^2 = 1 \times 80^2 + 1 \times 73^2 + 1 \times 76^2 + 1 \times 84^2 + ...+ 1 \times 75^2 = 116158$$

$$\left(\sum fx\right)^2 = \left(1 \times 80 + 1 \times 73 + 1 \times 76 + 1 \times 84 + ...+ 1 \times 75\right)^2 = 2274064$$

$$s = \sqrt{\frac{116158 - \frac{2274064}{20}}{20}}$$

$$s = 11.1 \text{ mm (1dp)}$$

Problems

1. Find the mean and standard deviation for each of the sets of data in the table below. Show all working.

	$\sum fx^2$	$\sum fx$	n
a)	1254	80	9
b)	3879	140	11

a) _____

_____

_____

_____

b) _____

_____

_____

_____

2. Find the mean and standard deviation of the following distributions. Use your calculator.

a) 4, 7, 8, 9, 11, 2, 5

b) 42, 47, 50, 52, 55, 60, 63, 67, 71, 75, 83, 87, 97, 99

a) _____

_____

_____

_____

b) _____

_____

_____

_____

3. Find the mean and standard deviation of the data showing the shoe sizes of 133 kindergarten pupils.

Size	9	9.5	10	10.5	11
Number	12	28	42	36	15

_____

_____

_____

_____

_____

Problems continued

4. Find the mean and standard deviation of the data showing the age of 122 people when they died.

Age	0 - < 15	15 - < 30	30 - < 45	45 - < 60	60 - < 75
Number	8	36	18	22	38

5. For the set of data 6.8, 3.7, 2.5, 1.9, 8.8, 9.3, 2.5, 7.8, 3.6, 4.4, 5.1, 9.8, find the mean and standard deviation.

6. Of 500 secondary school pupils, whose mean height is 1.65 m, 140 of them are girls. If the mean height of the 140 girls is 1.54 m, what is the mean height of the boys.

Problems continued

7. If 150 numbers has a mean of 26.32 and a standard deviation of 4.5.

a) What is the variance of the numbers.

b) If each of the numbers had 8 added to them, what would be the new mean and standard deviation.

c) If each of the numbers was multiplied by 3, what would be the new mean and standard deviation.

d) If each of the numbers was multiplied by 5 and then 1 subtracted from it, what would be the new mean and standard deviation.

Answer

a) _____

_____

_____

_____

_____

_____

Answer

b) _____

_____

_____

_____

_____

Answer

c) _____

_____

_____

_____

_____

Answer

d) _____

_____

_____

_____

_____

Sample versus Population

One of the main functions of statistics is to calculate population parameters. It is unrealistic, costly and in most cases impractical to survey an entire **population**.

Therefore we take **samples** and calculate the parameters from these hoping they reflect the **population** as a whole.

In order to identify whether population or sample parameters have been calculated we use a different notation for sample and population.

For a sample we use

$$\text{mean} \quad = \bar{x}$$

standard deviation $\quad = s$

$$\text{variance} \quad = s^2$$

For a population we use

$$\text{mean} \quad = \mu$$

standard deviation $\quad = \sigma$

$$\text{variance} \quad = \sigma^2$$

In addition to this when calculating the sample variance or sample standard deviation we divide by $n - 1$ as opposed to dividing by n when we are working with the population.

The advantage of using the $n - 1$ divisor when dealing with a sample is that it gives a better estimate of the population parameter when n is small. As the sample size becomes larger the difference between the sample and population standard deviations becomes less.

As a rule - if the question indicates that the list of numbers given are a sample then we should divide by $n - 1$ when calculating the variance and standard deviation.

If the numbers are described as a population then it is sufficient to use the divisor n, for we are dealing with the population as a whole.

In most practical situations we will be using a sample. If it is to be an unbiased sample then it will be of a reasonable size ie. $n > 30$. In such situations when n is large the difference between the standard deviation calculated with an n divisor and an $n - 1$ divisor is negligible.

In such instances what is important is that the appropriate notation is used in order to portray to the reader whether the data was from a sample or the entire population.

Note Well

The present Bursary examiner in Mathematics with Statistics does not require candidates to use the $n - 1$ divisor.

The authors do not accept this and have used the $n - 1$ divisor when sample statistics are used to make predictions about a population (confidence intervals).

Extra Notes

1.3 Distribution of the Sample Mean

Prescription

- the meaning of the sampling distribution of the mean and the sampling distribution of a proportion
- calculating the sample size required for a given precision estimate of a population parameter

Sample Mean versus Population Mean

Consider a population which is made up of the numbers 0, 1, 2 and 3.

If we were to take all the possible samples of size 2 (n = 2) from this population we would have

Sample	$\bar{x}$	Sample	$\bar{x}$
0,0	0	2,0	1
0,1	0.5	2,1	1.5
0,2	1	2,2	2
0,3	1.5	2,3	2.5
1,0	0.5	3,0	1.5
1,1	1	3,1	2
1,2	1.5	3,2	2.5
1,3	2	3,3	3

Each sample mean $\bar{x}$, on its own, is an estimate of the population mean. Obviously, the larger the sample we take, the more accurate estimate of the population mean we would get. Remember in our example above we have only taken samples of size 2.

Instead of taking just one sample as our estimate of the population, if we took a collection of samples and found the mean of the sample means, we would expect to obtain a better estimate of the population mean.

In the above example the population mean μ is

$$\mu = \frac{0+1+2+3}{4}$$

$$= 1.5$$

The mean of the sample means which we denote by $E(\bar{X})$ is

$$E(\bar{X}) = (0 + 0.5 + 1 + 1.5 + 0.5 + 1 + 1.5 + 2 + 1$$

$$+ 1.5 + 2 + 2.5 + 1.5 + 2 + 2.5 + 3)/16$$

$$= 1.5$$

Therefore we can assume that

$$E(\bar{X}) = \mu$$

ie. the mean of the sample means is equal to the population mean.

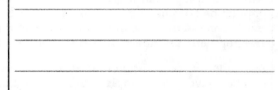

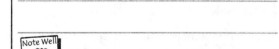

This is an important result and appears in your tables.

Variance of the Sample Means versus the Population Variance

For the population 0, 1, 2 and 3 from the previous page we can calculate.

Variance of the population	= 1.25
Standard deviation of the population	= 1.118
Variance of our sample means	= 0.625
Standard deviation of our sample means	= 0.791

The variance of the sample means is related to the population variance by

$$\text{Variance of sample means} = \frac{\text{Variance population}}{\text{sample size}}$$

$$\text{ie.} \quad \text{Var}(\overline{X}) = \frac{\sigma^2}{n}$$

so in this example

$$\text{Var}(\overline{X}) = \frac{1.25}{2}$$
$$= 0.625$$

Similarly with the standard deviation

$$\text{sd}(\overline{X}) = \frac{\sigma}{\sqrt{n}}$$

(known as the standard error of the mean OR the standard deviation of the sample means)

so in this example $\quad \text{sd}(\overline{X}) = \frac{1.118}{\sqrt{2}}$
$$= 0.791$$

Distribution of the Sample Proportion

A similar approach is used to find the relationship between a sample proportion and a population proportion.

If a sample of size n has x successes then the proportion

$$p = \frac{x}{n}$$

is the best estimate of the population proportion π.

The mean of the sample proportions is

$$E(p) = \pi$$

The variance of the sample proportions is related to the population variance by

$$\text{Variance of sample proportions} = \frac{\text{Variance pop. proportion}}{\text{sample size}}$$

$$\text{ie.} \quad \text{Var}(p) = \frac{\pi(1 - \pi)}{n}$$

Similarly with the standard deviation

$$\text{sd}(p) = \sqrt{\frac{\pi(1 - \pi)}{n}}$$

(the standard error of proportion)

These are important results and appear in your tables.

These are important results and appear in your tables.

Just as the mean of each sample taken is likely to differ, so does the value of p from sample to sample. Hence we have a sampling distribution for the proportion p and the distribution of p is approximately normal.

Example 3

A large population of test results yields a mean $\mu = 20$ and standard deviation $\sigma = 6$. If samples of size 4 are randomly drawn from the population.

a) What is the expected value of the sample means.
b) What is the standard deviation of the sample means.

Solution

a) The expected value of the sample means is equal to the population mean.

$$\therefore \ E(\overline{X}) = 20$$

b) The standard deviation of the sample means is calculated using the formula $sd(\overline{X}) = \dfrac{\sigma}{\sqrt{n}}$

$$\therefore \ sd(\overline{X}) = \dfrac{6}{\sqrt{4}}$$
$$= 3$$

Example 4

In New Zealand the standard deviation of the number of children in a family is 0.5. A researcher wants to estimate the number of children so that the standard deviation of this estimate is 0.1 or better. How many families should be in the sample.

Solution

Using the formula $sd(\overline{X}) = \dfrac{\sigma}{\sqrt{n}}$. We know $\sigma = 0.5$

Therefore
$$\dfrac{0.5}{\sqrt{n}} = 0.1$$
$$\therefore \ 0.5 = 0.1\sqrt{n}$$
$$\therefore \ 0.25 = 0.01n \ \text{(squaring both sides)}$$
$$\therefore n = 25$$

Example 5

If 30% of a population favours a certain electoral candidate and a sample of 150 voters is taken.

a) What is the expected value of the sample proportion.
b) What is the variance of the sample proportion.

Solution

a) The expected value of the sample proportion is equal to π

$$\therefore \ E(p) = 0.3$$

b) The variance of the sample proportion is calculated using the formula $Var(p) = \dfrac{\pi(1 - \pi)}{n}$

$$\therefore \ Var(p) = \dfrac{0.3(1 - 0.3)}{150} = 0.0014$$

Problems

8. Complete the table using the relationships $E(\overline{X}) = \mu$ and $Var(\overline{X}) = \frac{\sigma^2}{n}$. Space is provided below the table for your working.

	μ	σ	n	$E(\overline{X})$	$Var(\overline{X})$	$sd(\overline{X})$
a)	40	6	16			
b)			35	47	9.1	
c)	613	132				33
d)		1.9		87		0.05

a) _____

_____

_____

b) _____

_____

_____

c) _____

_____

_____

d) _____

_____

_____

9. A large population of test results yields a mean $\mu = 43$ and standard deviation $\sigma = 5.47$. If samples of size 8 are randomly drawn from the population.
   a) What is the expected value of the sample means.
   b) What is the standard deviation of the sample means.

a) _____

_____

_____

_____

b) _____

_____

_____

_____

Problems continued

10. An experiment is conducted by tossing a fair die 240 times.

   a)   What is the expected number of 3's that will appear.

   b)   What is the standard deviation of the proportion of 3's appearing.

a) _____   b) _____

_____   _____

_____   _____

_____   _____

11. It is known that 15 per cent of a certain cooker will have an electrical fault before the guarantee has expired. If samples of size 100 are randomly selected.

   a)   Find the expected mean number of cookers that will need replacing in the sample.

   b)   What is the variance of the proportion of cookers that will need replacing.

a) _____   b) _____

_____   _____

_____   _____

_____   _____

_____   _____

12. A sample of size 87 is used in an experiment and the standard deviation of the sample means is 14.5. What would we need to increase the sample size to, if we wished to reduce the standard deviation of the sample means to 8.2.

_____

_____

_____

_____

_____

_____

1.4 Distribution of the Difference between Two Sample Means

Prescription

- the distribution of the difference between the means of two populations

Distribution of the Difference between Two Sample Means

Sometimes we need to investigate the difference between the means of two populations eg. the kill rate of one fly spray compared to another. If $\overline{x}_1$ and $\overline{x}_2$ are the means of random samples from each of the two populations then obviously they will vary from sample to sample as will their difference $\overline{x}_1 - \overline{x}_2$.

From section 1.3 in this chapter we obtained the following two results

$$E(\overline{X}) = \mu \quad \text{and} \quad Var(\overline{X}) = \frac{\sigma^2}{n}$$

Therefore it is reasonable to expect that if we have two independent populations, with means μ_1 and μ_2 and standard deviations σ_1 and σ_2, and samples of size n_1 and n_2 are taken from these respective populations, then we obtain the following results for the difference of two means.

$$E(\overline{X}_1 - \overline{X}_2) = \mu_1 - \mu_2$$

$$\text{and } Var(\overline{X}_1 - \overline{X}_2) = \frac{\sigma_1^2}{n_1} + \frac{\sigma_2^2}{n_2}$$

$$\text{and } sd(\overline{X}_1 - \overline{X}_2) = \sqrt{\frac{\sigma_1^2}{n_1} + \frac{\sigma_2^2}{n_2}}$$

We subtract the means but add the variances and standard deviations.

Extra Notes

Just as the mean of each sample will vary so will their difference. Hence we have a sampling distribution for $\overline{X}_1 - \overline{X}_2$.

Note Well
These are important results and appear in your tables.

Example 6

For two normal and independent populations we know the means are 85.4 and 64.3 respectively and the standard deviations 8.7 and 6.4. If a sample of 64 is drawn from the first population and a sample of 36 from the second population.

a) What is the expected value of the difference between the sample means.

b) What is the standard deviation of the difference between the sample means.

Solution

a) The expected value of the difference between the sample means is given by

$$E(\overline{X}_1 - \overline{X}_2) = 85.4 - 64.3$$
$$= 21.1$$

b) The standard deviation of the difference between the sample means is given by

$$sd(\overline{X}_1 - \overline{X}_2) = \sqrt{\frac{8.7^2}{64} + \frac{6.4^2}{36}}$$
$$= 1.5$$

Problems

13. A manufacturer produces two types of light bulbs. A sample of 100 Type I light bulbs are found to have a mean life of 1600 hours with standard deviation of 120 hours. A sample of 121 Type II light bulbs are found to have a mean life of 1350 hours with standard deviation 80 hours.

   a) What assumptions do you have to make about the distributions.

   b) What is the expected value of the difference between the sample means.

   c) What is the variance of the difference between the sample means.

   d) What is the standard deviation of the difference between the sample means.

a) _____

b) _____

c) _____

d) _____

14. Two machines are set to fill 500 ml cartons with milk. A sample of size 50 was taken from machine A and the mean contents filled was found to be 504 ml with standard deviation of 3 ml. A sample of size 62 was taken from machine B and the mean contents filled was 510 ml with a standard deviation of 8 ml. Assuming that the filling of the cartons is normally distributed and machine A is independent of machine B.

   a) What is the expected value of the difference between the sample means.

   b) What is the variance of the difference between the sample means.

a) _____

b) _____

1.5 The Central Limit Theorem

Prescription

- the Central Limit Theorem

The Central Limit Theorem

We have found that when we look at the means of random samples of size 'n' from a population with mean μ and variance σ^2 they themselves will have a distribution. This distribution has mean μ and variance $\frac{\sigma^2}{n}$.

The shape of this distribution is dependent upon the shape of the original distribution.

When we introduced the distribution of the sample means we looked at an example with samples of size 2.

If we looked at results for differing samples sizes we would see that the larger the sample size the closer the distribution would get to the Normal shape.

Therefore in summary we assume that the distribution of $\overline{X}$ is approximately Normally distributed with mean μ and standard deviation $\frac{\sigma}{\sqrt{n}}$. This result is known as the **Central Limit Theorem** and is formally stated as follows.

If all possible random samples of size 'n' are drawn with replacement from a finite population of size 'N' with mean μ and standard deviation σ then the sampling distribution of the mean will be approximately normally distributed with mean μ and standard deviation $\frac{\sigma}{\sqrt{n}}$.

Therefore

$$z = \frac{\overline{X} - \mu}{\sigma/\sqrt{n}}$$

is the value of the standard normal variable, known as the **Central Limit Theorem**.

If when dealing with the normal distribution the problem involves only population parameters we use the standard normal variable $z = \frac{x - \mu}{\sigma}$. If mention is made of "samples of specific sizes being drawn from a population" we MUST use the Central Limit Theorem.

It is expected that Section 3.8 on the Normal curve would have been completed before attempting this section.

Example 7

A sample of size 36 is taken from a population which is normally distributed and has a mean of 39 and a standard deviation of 11. Find the probability that the sample mean

a)   is less than 35

b)   is greater than 37

c)   is between 36 and 43

Solution

To standardise we use the formula $z = \dfrac{\overline{X} - \mu}{\sigma/\sqrt{n}}$

a) To find $P(\overline{X} < 35)$

Standardising $= P(Z < \dfrac{35 - 39}{11/\sqrt{36}})$

Simplifying $= P(Z < -2.182)$

$= 0.5 - P(0 < Z < 2.182)$

Using tables $= 0.5 - 0.4855$

$= 0.0145$

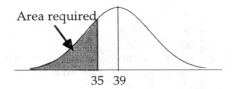

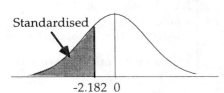

b) To find $P(\overline{X} > 37)$

Standardising $= P(Z > \dfrac{37 - 39}{11/\sqrt{36}})$

Simplifying $= P(Z > -1.091)$

$= 0.5 + P(0 < Z < 1.091)$

Using tables $= 0.5 + 0.3623$

$= 0.8623$

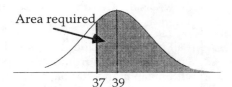

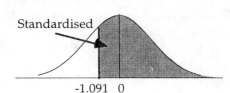

c) To find $P(36 < \overline{X} < 43)$

Standardising $= P(\dfrac{36 - 39}{11/\sqrt{36}} < Z < \dfrac{43 - 39}{11/\sqrt{36}})$

Simplifying $= P(-1.636 < Z < 2.182)$

$= P(0 < Z < 1.636) + P(0 < Z < 2.182)$

Using tables $= 0.4490 + 0.4855$

$= 0.9345$

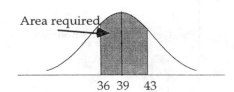

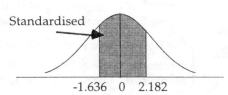

Problems

15.   Chezzel packets are filled by machine. The weights of the packets are found to be normally distributed with mean 120g and standard deviation 10g. A random sample of 20 packets of chezzels are selected from the production line.

Find the probability that the sample mean

a)   weighs more than 125g.

b)   weighs less than 112g.

c)   weighs between 118g and 127g.

a)	Normal curves
$P(\overline{X} > 125)$	
Standardise	
Simplify	
Use tables	
b) $P(\overline{X} < 112)$	
Standardise	
Simplify	
Use tables	
c) $P(118 < \overline{X} < 127)$	
Standardise	
Simplify	
Use tables	

16.   A random sample of 81 car insurance policies is taken from the files of an insurance company. It is claimed that the mean coverage per policy is $12,000, with a standard deviation of $8000.

Find the probability that the sample mean

   a)   will exceed $13,000.

   b)   will be less than $9,800.

   c)   will be between $13,000 and $15,000.

   d)   will not exceed $12,750

a)

b)

c)

d)

Normal curves

17.   A coke dispensing machine is set to discharge on average 150 ml of coke per cup, with a standard
       deviation of 12 ml. When testing the machine a random sample of 20 cups is taken. Find the
       probability that the sample mean

       a)   will be less than 145 ml.

       b)   will be either less than 142 ml or greater than 153 ml.

a) | Normal curves

b)

18.   The weights of jaffas are normally distributed with mean 12.2 g and standard deviation 1.7 g.
       Find the probability that a random sample of 27 of these jaffas will have a sample mean between
       11.7 g and 12.1 g.

                                                                    | Normal curves

1.6 Confidence Intervals - Mean

Prescription

Calculate point and interval (confidence interval) estimates for a population parameter, and explain the meaning of confidence intervals
- confidence intervals for the mean of a population

Confidence Intervals - Mean

In statistics we are primarily concerned with identifying population parameters. It is unlikely that we can measure or test the whole population to find these parameters. Hence we obtain samples and use the sample parameters as estimates for the population parameters. But how reliable are these estimators?

If we use our sample mean as an estimate of the population mean it is obvious that different samples will produce different estimates for the population mean.

The solution lies in giving an interval rather than a specific value as an estimator of the population mean. We base our interval on our sample statistics. Such an interval is called a **Confidence Interval**.

A 95% confidence interval for μ is given by two limits (a lower and an upper one). Consider the diagram below.

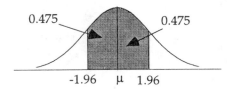

We can write, using our knowledge of the Central Limit Theorem and the standardised normal curve.

$$P(-1.96 < Z < 1.96) = 0.95$$

$$\therefore P(-1.96 < \frac{\bar{x} - \mu}{\sigma/\sqrt{n}} < 1.96) = 0.95$$

$$\therefore P(-1.96\frac{\sigma}{\sqrt{n}} < \bar{x} - \mu < 1.96\frac{\sigma}{\sqrt{n}}) = 0.95$$

$$\therefore P(\bar{x} - 1.96\frac{\sigma}{\sqrt{n}} < \mu < \bar{x} + 1.96\frac{\sigma}{\sqrt{n}}) = 0.95$$

$$\therefore \bar{x} - 1.96\frac{\sigma}{\sqrt{n}} < \mu < \bar{x} + 1.96\frac{\sigma}{\sqrt{n}} \quad \text{is a 95\% confidence interval for } \mu$$

Similarly we can find a 99% confidence interval for μ by using

$$\bar{x} - 2.58\frac{\sigma}{\sqrt{n}} < \mu < \bar{x} + 2.58\frac{\sigma}{\sqrt{n}}$$

A confidence interval does NOT mean that there is a probability of 0.95 that μ lies in the designated interval, instead it says that 95% of such confidence intervals will contain the population mean.

When finding a confidence interval, we use the population parameter σ. If we do not know the value of σ then we can use the sample standard deviation s, instead, (provided the sample is of a reasonable size).

Usual practice is to take either a 95% or 99% confidence interval although other intervals are possible.

Example 8

An electronics company manufactures circuit boards whose life is normally distributed with a standard deviation of 70 hours.
If a random sample of 49 circuit boards have a mean life of 410 hours.

a) Find a 95 % confidence interval for the lifetime of circuit boards manufactured by this company.

b) Find a 99% confidence interval for the lifetime of circuit boards manufactured by this company.

Solution

a) Using

$$\bar{x} - 1.96\frac{\sigma}{\sqrt{n}} < \mu < \bar{x} + 1.96\frac{\sigma}{\sqrt{n}}$$

$$\therefore 410 - 1.96\frac{70}{\sqrt{49}} < \mu < 410 + 1.96\frac{70}{\sqrt{49}}$$

$$\therefore 410 - 19.6 < \mu < 410 + 19.6$$

$$\therefore 390.4 < \mu < 429.6$$

b) Using

$$\bar{x} - 2.58\frac{\sigma}{\sqrt{n}} < \mu < \bar{x} + 2.58\frac{\dot{\sigma}}{\sqrt{n}}$$

$$\therefore 410 - 2.58\frac{70}{\sqrt{49}} < \mu < 410 + 2.58\frac{70}{\sqrt{49}}$$

$$\therefore 410 - 25.8 < \mu < 410 + 25.8$$

$$\therefore 384.2 < \mu < 435.8$$

Example 9

The time taken for an individual to walk to work is to be estimated. On 15 occasions the time was recorded (in minutes). The results were
18, 17, 15, 20, 16, 14, 19, 13, 17, 16, 14, 15, 20, 18, 19

a) Find the sample mean and sample standard deviation.

b) Assuming a normal distribution and that the sample is sufficiently large, calculate a 95% confidence interval for μ, the mean time to walk to work.

Solution

a) Using the calculator we find $\bar{x} = 16.73$ (2 dp) and s = 2.25 (2dp) (using n – 1 divisor for the standard deviation)

b) Using

$$\bar{x} - 1.96\frac{\sigma}{\sqrt{n}} < \mu < \bar{x} + 1.96\frac{\sigma}{\sqrt{n}}$$

$$\therefore 16.73 - 1.96\frac{2.25}{\sqrt{15}} < \mu < 16.73 + 1.96\frac{2.25}{\sqrt{15}}$$

$$\therefore 16.73 - 1.14 < \mu < 16.73 + 1.14$$

$$\therefore 15.59 < \mu < 17.87$$

(using 2.25 as our estimator of the population standard deviation)

Problems

19.   A light bulb manufacturer makes light bulbs whose life is normally distributed with a standard
       deviation of 45 hours. If a random sample of 100 light bulbs have a mean life of 300 hours.

   a) Find a 95% confidence interval for the mean life of light bulbs manufactured by this
        company.

   b) Find a 99% confidence interval for the mean life of light bulbs manufactured by this
        company.

a) _____   b) _____

_____   _____

_____   _____

20.   The mean weekly wage of students working in a particular supermarket is to be estimated. A
       sample of 25 students was taken and their mean wage was found to be $68 with a standard
       deviation of $10.

       Assuming a normal distribution and that the sample is sufficiently large find a 95% confidence
       interval for the mean weekly wage of students working in the supermarket.

_____

_____

_____

21.   The fuel economy of a particular model of car is to be estimated. A sample of 20 cars, of the
       designated model, is taken and their petrol consumption recorded (litres per 100 km). The results
       were

       9.2, 8.6, 7.9, 10.4, 6.6, 11.3, 7.8, 9.5, 9.1, 8.9, 10.2, 7.7, 6.9, 8.2, 9.7, 10.0, 8.1, 7.9, 9.3, 7.7

       Assuming a normal distribution and that the sample is sufficiently large find a 99% confidence
       interval for the mean petrol consumption of this particular model of car.

_____

_____

_____

22. The waiting time at a particular doctor's surgery is to be estimated. The waiting time of a sample of 20 of the doctor's patients is recorded (in minutes). The results were

8.7, 5.9, 10.6, 4.3, 13.5, 4.1, 5.9, 8.6, 2.1, 18.3, 7.5, 11.3, 6.1, 9.2, 7.4, 3.6, 4.7, 6.3, 4.1, 5.4

Assuming a normal distribution and that the sample is sufficiently large find a 95% confidence interval for the mean waiting time at the doctor's surgery.

23. A machine is designed to slice bread into slices of a certain width. The standard deviation of the widths of slices is known to be 2 mm. A random sample of 200 slices of bread have a mean width of 8.5 mm.

Assuming a normal distribution find a 90% confidence interval for the mean width of sliced bread.

24. A battery manufacturer claims that their batteries have a mean life of at least 25 hours. Assuming that the standard deviation of the life of the batteries is 2.5 hours and that a random sample of 50 batteries had a mean life of 27 hours

a) Find a 99% confidence interval for the mean life of the batteries.

b) Does this result support the claim made by the manufacturer.

a)

b)

1.7 Confidence Intervals - Proportion

Prescription

- confidence intervals for a population proportion

Confidence Intervals - Proportion

We have already dealt with the sampling distribution of the random variable p (proportion) and we found that

$$E(p) = \pi$$

and $\quad Var(p) = \dfrac{\pi(1-\pi)}{n}$

and $\quad sd(p) = \sqrt{\dfrac{\pi(1-\pi)}{n}}$

Hence if n is sufficiently large and π is not too close to 0 or 1 then the distribution of the sample proportion p is approximately normally distributed with mean π and standard deviation $\sqrt{\dfrac{\pi(1-\pi)}{n}}$

Therefore in the same way that we found a confidence interval for the population mean μ, we can find a confidence interval for the population proportion π.

Instead of using $\dfrac{\sigma}{\sqrt{n}}$ (the standard error of the mean) we use $\sqrt{\dfrac{\pi(1-\pi)}{n}}$ (the standard error of proportion).

A 95% confidence interval for the population proportion π is written

$$p - 1.96\sqrt{\dfrac{\pi(1-\pi)}{n}} < \pi < p + 1.96\sqrt{\dfrac{\pi(1-\pi)}{n}}$$

Similarly we can find a 99% confidence interval for π by using

$$p - 2.58\sqrt{\dfrac{\pi(1-\pi)}{n}} < \pi < p + 2.58\sqrt{\dfrac{\pi(1-\pi)}{n}}$$

In most situations π is unknown, therefore we can use p instead.

Thus a 95% confidence interval for π is given by

$$p - 1.96\sqrt{\dfrac{p(1-p)}{n}} < \pi < p + 1.96\sqrt{\dfrac{p(1-p)}{n}}$$

and a 99% confidence interval for π is given by

$$p - 2.58\sqrt{\dfrac{p(1-p)}{n}} < \pi < p + 2.58\sqrt{\dfrac{p(1-p)}{n}}$$

A confidence interval does NOT mean that there is a probability of 0.95 that π lies in the designated interval, instead it says that 95% of such confidence intervals will contain the population proportion.

Example 10

A survey of 100 households showed that 42% had Sky television. Find a 95% confidence interval for π, the proportion of all households that have Sky television.

Solution

Using
$$p - 1.96\sqrt{\frac{p(1-p)}{n}} < \pi < p + 1.96\sqrt{\frac{p(1-p)}{n}}$$

$$\therefore 0.42 - 1.96\sqrt{\frac{0.42(1-0.42)}{100}} < \pi < 0.42 + 1.96\sqrt{\frac{0.42(1-0.42)}{100}}$$

$$\therefore 0.42 - 1.96(0.0494) < \pi < 0.42 + 1.96(0.0494)$$

$$\therefore 0.32 < \pi < 0.52$$

Example 11

In a sample of 58 voters 26 are found to support a particular political party. Find a 99% confidence interval for π, the proportion of all voters supporting this particular party.

Solution

Using
$$p - 2.58\sqrt{\frac{p(1-p)}{n}} < \pi < p + 2.58\sqrt{\frac{p(1-p)}{n}}$$

$$\therefore 0.45 - 2.58\sqrt{\frac{0.45(1-0.45)}{58}} < \pi < 0.45 + 2.58\sqrt{\frac{0.45(1-0.45)}{58}}$$

$$\therefore 0.45 - 2.58(0.0653) < \pi < 0.45 + 2.58(0.0653)$$

$$\therefore 0.28 < \pi < 0.62$$

Problems

25. An kiwi fruit grower finds that 15 out of 120 fruit are not fit for export.

a) Find a 95% confidence interval for the proportion of all kiwi fruit which are not fit for export.

b) Find a 99% confidence interval for the proportion of all kiwi fruit which are not fit for export.

a) _____

_____

_____

_____

_____

b) _____

_____

_____

_____

_____

26. In a sample of 210 people with high blood pressure a particular drug is found to be effective for 150 of them. Construct a 95% confidence interval for π, the proportion of all patients who use this particular drug for high blood pressure.

Answer

27. In a random sample of 450 home owners it was found that 390 of them had more than one mortgage on their property. Calculate a 90% confidence interval for the proportion of home owners who have more than one mortgage.

Answer

28. A six sided die is tossed 300 times, and a 6 appears uppermost 75 times.

   a) Find a 99% confidence interval for the proportion of times the 6 will appear.

   b) With an unbiased die what proportion of 6's would you expect.

   c) Is the die biased or unbiased. Why?

Answer

a)

b)

c)

1.8 Confidence Intervals - Difference between Two Means

Prescription

- confidence intervals for the difference between the means of two populations (using independent samples from those populations)

Confidence Intervals for the Difference between Two Means

We have already dealt with the sampling distribution of the difference of two means and we found that

$$E(\overline{X}_1 - \overline{X}_2) = \mu_1 - \mu_2$$

and $Var(\overline{X}_1 - \overline{X}_2) = \dfrac{\sigma_1^2}{n_1} + \dfrac{\sigma_2^2}{n_2}$

and $sd(\overline{X}_1 - \overline{X}_2) = \sqrt{\dfrac{\sigma_1^2}{n_1} + \dfrac{\sigma_2^2}{n_2}}$

Hence if n_1 and n_2 are sufficiently large samples and are taken from populations with means μ_1, μ_2 and standard deviations σ_1 and σ_2 then the distribution $\overline{X}_1 - \overline{X}_2$ will be normal if the original populations are normal.

Therefore in the same way that we found a confidence interval for the population mean μ, we can find a confidence interval for the difference of two means, $\mu_1 - \mu_2$.

Instead of using $\dfrac{\sigma}{\sqrt{n}}$ (the standard error of the mean) we use $\sqrt{\dfrac{\sigma_1^2}{n_1} + \dfrac{\sigma_2^2}{n_2}}$

A 95% confidence interval for the difference of two means is written

$$(\overline{x}_1 - \overline{x}_2) - 1.96\sqrt{\dfrac{\sigma_1^2}{n_1} + \dfrac{\sigma_2^2}{n_2}} < \mu_1 - \mu_2$$

$$< (\overline{x}_1 - \overline{x}_2) + 1.96\sqrt{\dfrac{\sigma_1^2}{n_1} + \dfrac{\sigma_2^2}{n_2}}$$

Similarly we can find a 99% confidence interval for the difference of two means by using

$$(\overline{x}_1 - \overline{x}_2) - 2.58\sqrt{\dfrac{\sigma_1^2}{n_1} + \dfrac{\sigma_2^2}{n_2}} < \mu_1 - \mu_2$$

$$< (\overline{x}_1 - \overline{x}_2) + 2.58\sqrt{\dfrac{\sigma_1^2}{n_1} + \dfrac{\sigma_2^2}{n_2}}$$

The two samples taken from the populations must be independent of one another.

When finding a confidence interval for the difference of two means we use the population parameter σ_1 and σ_2. If we do not know the value of σ_1 and σ_2, we can use the sample standard deviations instead (provided the samples are of a reasonable size).

A confidence interval does NOT mean that there is a probability of 0.95 that $\mu_1 - \mu_2$ lies in the designated interval, instead it says that 95% of such confidence intervals will contain the difference between the population means.

Example 12   When a sample of the weights of 50 fourth form boys and 50 fourth form girls is taken, the fourth form boys mean weight is found to be 52 kg with a standard deviation of 8 kg and the fourth form girls mean weight is found to be 42 kg with a standard deviation of 6 kg. Assuming that weight is normally distributed find a 95% confidence interval for the difference of the two means.

Solution

$$\text{Using} \quad (\bar{x}_1 - \bar{x}_2) - 1.96\sqrt{\frac{\sigma_1^2}{n_1} + \frac{\sigma_2^2}{n_2}} < \mu_1 - \mu_2 < (\bar{x}_1 - \bar{x}_2) + 1.96\sqrt{\frac{\sigma_1^2}{n_1} + \frac{\sigma_2^2}{n_2}}$$

$$\therefore (52 - 42) - 1.96\sqrt{\frac{8^2}{50} + \frac{6^2}{50}} < \mu_1 - \mu_2 < (52 - 42) + 1.96\sqrt{\frac{8^2}{50} + \frac{6^2}{50}}$$

$$\therefore 10 - 1.96(1.414) < \mu_1 - \mu_2 < 10 + 1.96(1.414)$$

$$\therefore 7.2 < \mu_1 - \mu_2 < 12.8 \qquad \text{(1dp)}$$

Example 13   A publishing company believes it sells more books on a Monday than on a Wednesday. Assume its sales are normally distributed and the samples independent. A sample of 20 Mondays gives a mean number of books sold of 50 with standard deviation 6. A sample of 25 Wednesdays gives a mean number of books sold of 58 with standard deviation 8. Find a 99% confidence interval for the difference between the mean of Wednesdays sales and the mean of Mondays sales.

Solution

$$\text{Using} \quad (\bar{x}_1 - \bar{x}_2) - 2.58\sqrt{\frac{\sigma_1^2}{n_1} + \frac{\sigma_2^2}{n_2}} < \mu_1 - \mu_2 < (\bar{x}_1 - \bar{x}_2) + 2.58\sqrt{\frac{\sigma_1^2}{n_1} + \frac{\sigma_2^2}{n_2}}$$

$$\therefore (58 - 50) - 2.58\sqrt{\frac{8^2}{25} + \frac{6^2}{20}} < \mu_1 - \mu_2 < (58 - 50) + 2.58\sqrt{\frac{8^2}{25} + \frac{6^2}{20}}$$

$$\therefore 8 - 2.58(2.088) < \mu_1 - \mu_2 < 8 + 2.58(2.088)$$

$$\therefore 2.6 < \mu_1 - \mu_2 < 13.4 \qquad \text{(1dp)}$$

Problems

29.   An orchardist grows two types of apples Gala and Braeburn. She finds when she takes a sample of 200 Gala apples and 150 Braeburn apples that the Gala's have a mean weight of 270 g and a standard deviation of 30 g whereas the Braeburns have a mean weight of 200 g and standard deviation of 25 g. Assuming the weight of apples is normally distributed and the samples are independent find a 95% confidence interval for the difference between the mean weight of the two types of apples.

30. A woman travels to work one of two routes. Route one, over a sample of 20 days yields a mean time of 25 minutes with standard deviation 3 minutes. Route two, over a sample of 32 days yields a mean time of 16 minutes with standard deviation 5 minutes. Assuming the time taken to travel to work is normally distributed and the two samples are independent of one another. Find a 99% confidence interval for the mean difference in travelling time to work.

31. A manufacturer of batteries produces two types, the *standard* and the *long life*. Two samples of size 30 are taken. The mean life of the sample of *standard* batteries is found to be 35 hours with standard deviation 5 hours. The mean life of the sample of *long life* batteries is 42 hours with standard deviation 3 hours.

a) Find a 95% confidence interval for $\mu_1 - \mu_2$.

b) State any assumptions you would have to make.

c) Does your answer suggest there is a real difference between the two types of batteries.

a)

b)

c)

1.9 Sample Size

Prescription

- calculating the sample size required for a given precision estimate of a population parameter

Sample Size

Often our estimate of the population mean or proportion is required to be of a certain level of accuracy. To improve our level of accuracy we need to increase our sample size, but to what extent.

Our best value estimate of the mean or proportion of the population is the midpoint of the confidence interval we have calculated.

Our maximum error, if we assume that our best estimate is the midpoint of the interval, is the amount from the midpoint to the endpoint ie. $1.96\frac{\sigma}{\sqrt{n}}$ in the case of a 95% confidence interval for μ and $1.96\sqrt{\frac{p(1-p)}{n}}$ in the case of a 95% confidence interval for π.

Therefore, if we require our degree of accuracy for μ to be less than a certain value v, we write

$$1.96\frac{\sigma}{\sqrt{n}} < v \quad \text{(for a 95% confidence interval)}$$

and $\quad 2.58\frac{\sigma}{\sqrt{n}} < v \quad$ (for a 99% confidence interval)

and if we require our degree of accuracy for π to be less that a certain value v, we write

$$1.96\sqrt{\frac{p(1-p)}{n}} < v \quad \text{(for a 95% confidence interval)}$$

and

$$2.58\sqrt{\frac{p(1-p)}{n}} < v \quad \text{(for a 99% confidence interval)}$$

We solve the inequality for n, to find the required sample size, remembering to round appropriately.

Example 14

A greengrocer wishes to check that the scales she uses to weigh customers purchases are accurate. She knows that the standard deviation of measurement is 4 g. She wishes to be 95% confident that the scales are accurate to within 0.5 g of the correct setting. What sample size does she need to take to do this.

Solution

Using $1.96\dfrac{\sigma}{\sqrt{n}} < 0.5$

$\therefore 1.96\dfrac{4}{\sqrt{n}} < 0.5$

$\therefore \dfrac{61.4656}{n} < 0.25$ squaring both sides

$\therefore 61.4656 < 0.25n$ cross multiplying

$\therefore 0.25n > 61.4656$ reversing the inequality

$n > \dfrac{61.4656}{0.25}$

$n > 245.9$

minimum sample size required is 246 (rounding up)

Example 15

Previous research has shown that 42% of households have Sky television. How large a sample would need to be taken to be 99% confident that the sample proportion is within 4% of the true percentage.

Solution

Using $2.58\sqrt{\dfrac{p(1-p)}{n}} < 0.04$

$\therefore 2.58\sqrt{\dfrac{0.42(1-0.42)}{n}} < 0.04$

$\therefore 2.58\sqrt{\dfrac{0.42 \times 0.58}{n}} < 0.04$

$\therefore \dfrac{6.6564 \times 0.2436}{n} < 0.0016$ squaring both sides

$\therefore 1.6215 < 0.0016n$ cross multiplying

$\therefore 0.0016n > 1.6215$ reversing the inequality

$n > \dfrac{1.6215}{0.0016}$

$n > 1013.4$

minimum sample size required is 1014 (rounding up)

Problems

32.   Previous research has shown that 70% of people with high blood pressure are under excessive stress from their job. How large a sample would need to be taken to be 95% confident that the sample proportion is within 5% of the true percentage.

33.   The weekly wage of students working in a particular supermarket has a standard deviation of $10. How large a sample is it necessary to take to be 99% confident of estimating the mean weekly wage to within $3 of the true amount.

34.   Previous surveys have indicated that 18% of golfers are left-handers. How large a sample is needed to be taken to be 90% confident that the sample proportion is within 2% of the true value.

35. Laboratory rats are known to have a variance of weight equal to 400 g. How large a sample is it necessary to take to be 96% confident of estimating the mean weight of rats to within 15 g.

36. Past opinion polls have shown that 87% of home owners have more than one mortgage. How large a sample is needed to be taken to be 98% confident that the sample proportion is within 4% of the true value.

37. Light bulbs produced by a certain company have a standard deviation of life of 45 hours. How large a sample is it necessary to take to be 93% confident of estimating the mean life of light bulbs to within 20 hours of the true value.

2.0 Time Series

Introduction

When real data varies over time it often appears initially to have no pattern or predictability.

Figure 1

Time Series analysis attempts to find any pattern or trend so predictions can be made.

Prescription

Investigate a process which produces time series data

- planning the investigation
- graphing data and smoothing it using moving averages
- identifying patterns, including assignable and inherent variability
- commenting on the features and making predictions

Notes: Candidates should

- know that time series data may include a trend component, a cyclic component, a seasonal component and a random error component and be able to describe the meaning of each of these components.

- be able to apply an additive model to analyse time series data which contain a trend, a seasonal component and an error component and be aware of the limitations of this model for some data types. The candidates will not be expected to apply the multiplicative model in the examination but should be aware of its existence. This does not preclude candidates from using the multiplicative model in the internally assessed component of the course.

- be able to smooth time series data using moving averages with an odd or an even number of terms.

- be able to estimate seasonal effects from data.

- be able to seasonally adjust data in a time series and interpret results.

- be able to predict (forecast) future values in a time series.

- note that specific knowledge of index series is not required.

2.1 Time Series Patterns

In investigating a Time Series we are attempting to identify patterns as well as smooth out the effects of variations which obscure these patterns.

We use Time Series analysis in an attempt to make future predictions about the data.

If a business is able to make predictions about turnover for each month, then it can reflect on the effectiveness of an advertising campaign or make decisions on ordering of supplies or staff numbers.

If a school is able to recognise the attendance patterns of its students, then it can reflect on the success of different initiatives to keep students in the classroom.

 The characteristics of a Time Series we are concerned with are

a) The overall trend.

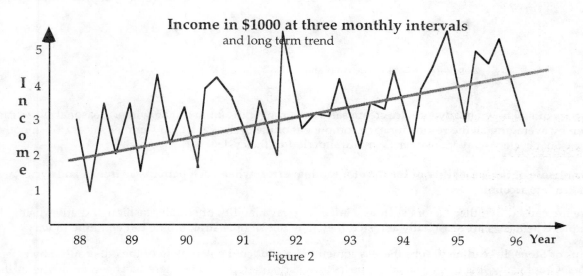

Income in $1000 at three monthly intervals
and long term trend

Figure 2

The overall trend is identified by smoothing out the graph using a technique called moving averages. Ideally it produces a recognisable trend (eg. a straight line or curve). In reality the variability of the data means you usually obtain an approximation of any trend.

b) Any long term cycles (greater than seasonal).

This is where you get an underlying pattern of the data as it increases and decreases over a longer period. Share prices for example may have a seasonal cycle over a year as they increase close to their dividend date and decrease once the dividend is paid. In addition, some people believe there is a long term cycle of about seven years as confidence grows and wanes.

c) Any seasonal cycle or short term cycle.

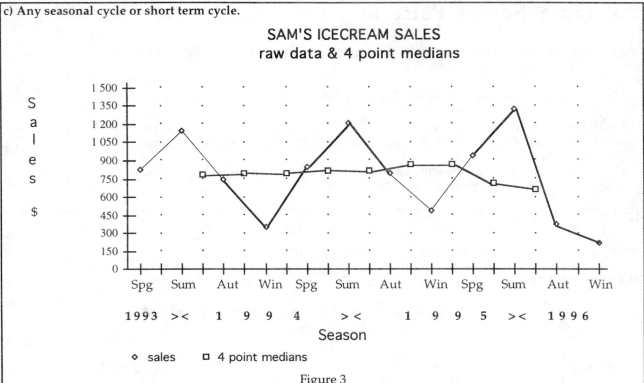

Figure 3

These are often known in advance. Ice cream sales are stronger in summer than winter. Seasonal cycles can be shown by averaging all the results for each component of the cycle (eg. all the summer sales). To smooth out the seasonal cycle you average over the natural period of the cycle.

d) A measure of the variability of the data (or random error) when such patterns as trends and cycles are taken into account.

These are caused by other factors such as competition, availability of supply, fashion and advertising. For example, when sales are seasonally adjusted they may not sit on a straight line but continue to vary.

Ramps or Steps. In reading graphs there is sometimes a sudden displacement of the data caused by external factors. Graphically this displacement appears as a slide or step. Maybe there has been an article in the newspaper about bacteria in ice cream or a competing shop has opened up down the road.

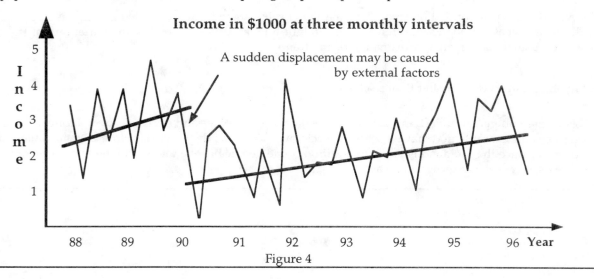

Figure 4

2.2 Planning an Investigation

Prescription

Investigate a process which produces time series data

- **planning the investigation**

Identifying a Suitable Time Series

The characteristics of a suitable time series are

- a distinct seasonal cycle.

or • where a long term trend is suspected but it is masked by variability of the data.

You will need at least 12 pieces of data (3 or more cycles) taken at regular intervals. The data is often readily available.

Seasonal cycles are usually predictable. You would not expect wage rates to be seasonal but the level of unemployment would be.

Suitable Time Series

National Statistics. Statistics collected by *Statistics New Zealand* and published monthly in *Key Statistics* (available at your local library) or the *Statspack*, which your school may have, contain national statistics on

- **Consumer Price Index.** This shows the relative buying power of the consumers dollar over a number of categories. Be careful not to use the seasonally adjusted figures.

- **Unemployment.** There is generally a higher level of unemployment in March than in November. See if you can identify long term trends.

- **Overseas Trade.** NZ sells a lot of primary produce which is generally produced seasonally. Imports too have a seasonal component (consumer purchases at Christmas). Sometimes it is possible to identify ramps or steps in trade where there have been major price changes.

The advantage of *Key Statistics* is that you can find a longer time period by using several issues or an interesting period (eg. post stock market crash).

Suitable Time Series cont...

- **Building Permits.** These often vary more than the health of the economy would indicate. Can you find any long term cycles as well as trends.

- **School Statistics.** If your school will release them, the attendance patterns often show a weekly cycle as well as a cycle for each of the four terms. Are more people absent on Friday or in the winter terms?

Local Statistics. The local Councils or Utilities are often prepared to release suitable statistics on

- **Traffic Patterns.** Road usage at particular intersections show strong daily patterns.

- **Building Permits.** You could see if local building permits have the same patterns as national statistics. Do building permits follow a yearly cycle?

- **Power or Water Consumption.** The figures for consumption show strong daily patterns. Sometimes it is possible to speculate as to the causes of peaks, troughs or ramps (News on TV)

Business Activity. Often businesses (particularly malls) keep pedestrian counts which show strong seasonal patterns. Often businesses turnover show the same patterns but they may be reluctant to release these for commercial reasons.

Approaches to Analysis

In selecting the statistics for analysis you would choose data you would expect to contain cycles or trends. Examine the raw data and construct a line graph to see if you can identify any seasonal cycle. If you can, then the length of the seasonal cycle will determine the number of points you are going to smooth or average over.

Moving Averages

You will use moving averages to smooth out the variability of the data.

Moving Medians are easier to use, particularly for odd numbers of pieces of data. The odd extreme value has no effect on the smoothed data. The disadvantage is that regular highs (or lows) will often not contribute to the median. See Example 2.

Moving Means are almost as easy to calculate. All data contributes to the mean, so extreme data causes the moving mean to fluctuate.

2.3 Smoothing Techniques - Moving Medians (odd)

Prescription

Investigate a process which produces time series data

- graphing data and smoothing it using moving averages

Notes: Candidates should

- be able to smooth time series data using moving averages with an odd or an even number of terms.

Moving Medians - with an odd number of cycles

If we have an odd number of pieces of data it is easy to find the median as it will be the middle piece of data when the data is in rank order. For example for the data

3.2, 1.1, 3.6, 2.3, 3.6, 2.4, 4.3, 2.5, 3.4,

If we are smoothing over a **three point interval** we take the first three pieces of data 3.2, 1.1, 3.6 and arrange them in rank order 1.1, 3.2, 3.6 . The median is then 3.2 . This result becomes the smoothed result corresponding to position two, the middle position of our first three pieces of data.

Raw data 3.2, 1.1, 3.6, 2.3, 3.6, 2.4, 4.3, 2.5, 3.4,
Smoothed   3.2

This process is repeated using 1.1, 3.6 and 2.3 . Note two of this set were used in calculating the median for the first set. We then find the median of these three pieces of data. The median here is 2.3.

Raw data 3.2, 1.1, 3.6, 2.3, 3.6, 2.4, 4.3, 2.5, 3.4,
Smoothed   3.2, 2.3

We repeat the process for each set of three consecutive pieces of data. The first and last interval will therefore not have a smoothed result.

If we were smoothing over a **five period interval** we would start with the first five pieces of data. This set of 3.2, 1.1, 3.6, 2.3, 3.6 would have a median of 3.2 still. The 2nd to 6th set of data 1.1, 3.6, 2.3, 3.6, 2.4 would have a median of 2.4. The first two results would be

Raw data 3.2, 1.1, 3.6, 2.3, 3.6, 2.4, 4.3, 2.5, 3.4,
Smoothed   3.2, 2.4

See Example 1.

Example 1

Use 3 point medians to smooth the data on the right
and graph both raw data and the moving median on
the same axes.

Time	Income
1	325
2	285
3	315
4	165
5	325
6	415
7	370

Solution

Examining the data values in sets of three, the first three pieces of data 325, 285, 315 have a median of 315,
which we plot in interval

Time	Income	Median 3 point
1	325	
2	285	315
3	315	
4	165	
5	325	
6	415	
7	370	

We continue to repeat this in sets of three points.

Time	Income	Median 3 point
1	325	
2	285	315
3	315	285
4	165	315
5	325	325
6	415	370
7	370	

Now we use the 2nd, 3rd and 4th pieces of data. The
median of 285, 315, 165 is 285 and we insert this in
interval 3.

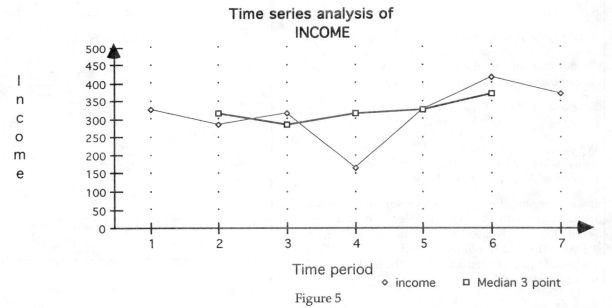

Figure 5

Note one data point is lost at the start and the end. It is characteristic of time series graphs that you will
lose points off either end.

**Extreme data values (eg. year 4, 165) have no effect on the medians. This is the main advantage of
using medians over moving means**

Problems

Use moving medians to smooth the following time series.

1.   Use three point medians to smooth the data for total net migration to New Zealand. Plot the raw and smoothed data on the grid provided.

Year	Net Migration	3 pt median	Year	Net Migration	3 pt median
1984	10557		1990	-1633	
1985	217		1991	14576	
1986	-18518		1992	2938	
1987	-4357		1993	8080	
1988	-957		1994	15793	
1989	-1829		1995	20401	

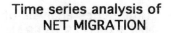

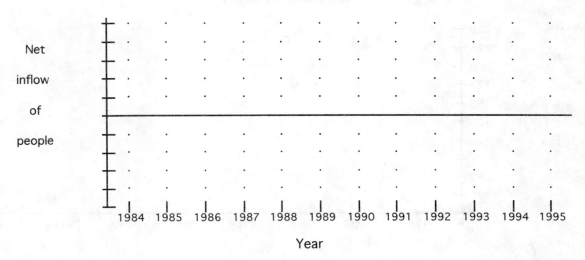

Problems continued

2. Use three point moving medians to smooth the following data of exports to France for the period 1979 to 1994. Plot the raw and smoothed data on the graph.

You may plot the median value in the empty column.

Year	Exports $m to France	3 pt median	Year	Exports $m to France	3 pt median
1979	94.5		1987	226.0	
1980	126.7		1988	188.7	
1981	94.7		1989	204.8	
1982	107.3		1990	176.9	
1983	143.0		1991	167.8	
1984	170.1		1992	217.3	
1985	214.2		1993	221.6	
1986	147.8		1994	211.6	

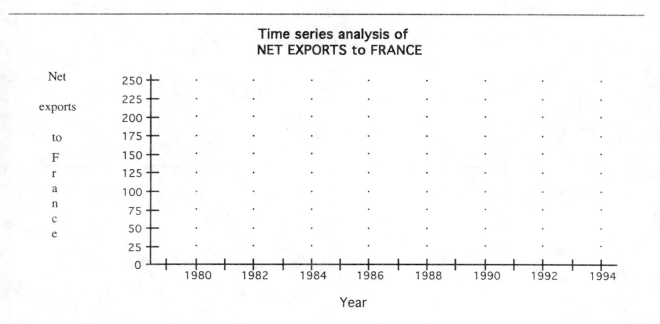

Time series analysis of
NET EXPORTS to FRANCE

Problems continued

3. Use three point medians to smooth the data for net total migration to New Zealand from the United Kingdom. Plot the raw and smoothed data on the grid provided.

You may plot the median value in the empty column.

Year	Net Migration UK	3 pt median	Year	Net Migration UK	3 pt median
1986	868		1991	-2618	
1987	1467		1992	-136	
1988	2566		1993	754	
1989	-12		1994	3551	
1990	-393		1995	2722	

_____

_____

_____

_____

_____

_____

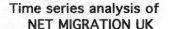

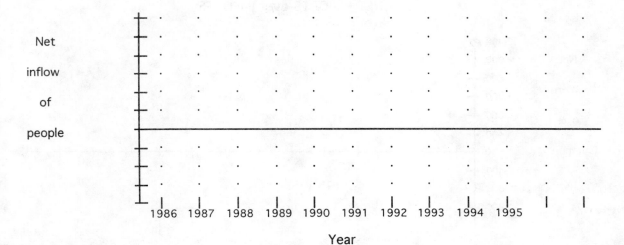

Time series analysis of
NET MIGRATION UK

Problems continued

4.   Use five point medians to smooth the data for net exports over imports of New Zealand. Plot the raw and smoothed data on the grid provided. Data in $ millions.

Year	Net Exports $m	5 pt median	Year	Net Exports $m	5 pt median
1981	42		1988	845	
1982	-660		1989	2413	
1983	339		1990	-606	
1984	-396		1991	443	
1985	-1156		1992	2357	
1986	-895		1993	1638	
1987	307		1994	1358	

_____

_____

_____

_____

_____

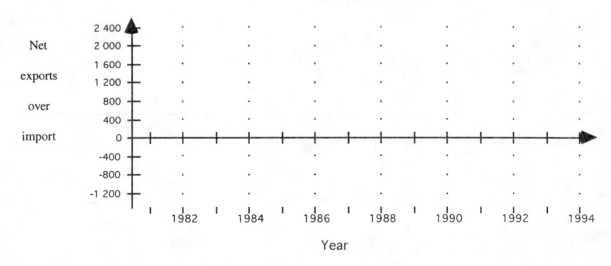

**Time series analysis of
NET EXPORTS over IMPORTS**

2.4 Smoothing Techniques - Moving Medians (even)

Prescription

Investigate a process which produces time series data

- graphing data and smoothing it using moving averages

Notes: Candidates should

- be able to smooth time series data using moving averages with an odd or an even number of terms.

Moving Medians - with an even number of cycles

In selecting how many points we wish to take our medians over, we may be attempting to smooth out any seasonal effects, while still maintaining any trends and long term cycles.

The most effective approach is to take the same number of intervals as the seasonal cycle. If our seasonal pattern is yearly then the number of points we wish to smooth over is even.

If we have an **even** number of pieces of data we have an additional complication. The median of four bits of data is between the 2nd and 3rd piece. It therefore does not correspond to the 2nd or 3rd time interval.

For example with the four pieces of data

Spring	$42 250
Summer	$63 600
Autumn	$38 450
Winter	$16 340

Has a median mid way between 38450 and 42250 ie. 40350, but it should not be plotted against the Summer or Autumn periods as it is between them.

We place this median between the Summer and Autumn seasons.

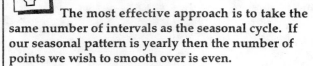

With an even numbers of intervals, we continue to place the medians between the original time intervals.

When we graph this time series we plot the medians mid-way between the original time intervals.

Example 2

Use four point medians to smooth the data below and graph both raw data and medians on the same axis.

Sam's Ice Cream Sales

Period	Sales		Period	Sales
Spring 93	825		Autumn 95	789
Summer 93	1143		Winter 95	479
Autumn 94	743		Spring 95	940
Winter 94	345		Summer 95	1321
Spring 94	843		Autumn 96	371
Summer 94	1203		Winter 96	213

Solution

Examining the data values in sets of four, the first four pieces of data 825, 1143, 743, 345 have a median of 785 which we plot between Summer 93 and Autumn 93.

Sam's Ice Cream Sales

Period	Sales	Smoothed
Spring 93	825	
Summer 93	1143	
		784
Autumn 93	743	
Winter 93	345	

Now we use the 2nd, 3rd, 4th and 5th pieces of data. The median of 1143, 743, 345 and 843 is 793 and we insert this between Autumn 93 and Winter 93. We continue to repeat this in sets of four points.

Sam's Ice Cream Sales

Period	Sales	Smoothed 4 point medians		Period	Sales	Smoothed 4 point medians
Spring 93	825			Autumn 95	789	
						865
Summer 93	1143			Winter 94	479	
		784				865
Autumn 94	743			Spring 95	940	
		793				710
Winter 94	345			Summer 95	1321	
		793				656
Spring 94	843			Autumn 96	371	
		816				
Summer 94	1203			Winter 96	213	
		816				

The graph of Example 2 is on the next page.

Example 2 continued.

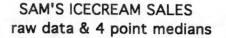

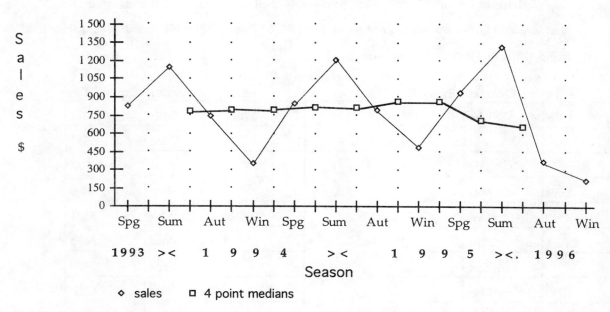

Effectively the smoothed value is the median of Spring and Autumn values (ie. the Summer and Winter values did not contribute to the smoothed values) except for the last two points.

Medians of medians

It is possible to plot the smoothed data of an even number of points directly against a value by plotting the average of two successive medians. This technique is needed when you are working with an even number of points and you are attempting to make predictions.

Period	Sales	Smoothed 4 point medians	Smoothed Median of medians	
Spring 93	825			
Summer 93	1143			
		784		
Autumn 94	743		789	(mid way between 784 and 793)
		793		
Winter 94	345		793	
		793		
Spring 94	843		805	
		816		
Summer 94	1203			
etc.				

Time Series

Problems

Use moving medians to smooth the following time series. Select the period of the seasonal cycle.

5.   New Zealand Gross Domestic Product (based 1982-83 Prices). Plot the raw data and smoothed data.

Expenditure on Private Consumption.

You may put your moving medians into the empty 4th column.

Year	Quarter	Exp on GDP		Year	Quarter	Exp on GDP	
1988	June	5496		1991	Mar	5211	
	Sept	5579			June	5542	
	Dec	5762			Sept	5537	
1989	Mar	5202			Dec	5899	
	June	5737		1992	Mar	5401	
	Sept	5453			June	5673	
	Dec	5723			Sept	5679	
1990	Mar	5117			Dec	6170	
	June	5602		1993	Mar	5523	
	Sept	5564			June	5627	
	Dec	5897			Sept	5702	

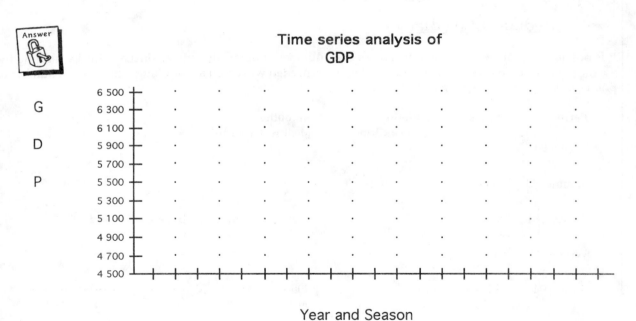

Time series analysis of
GDP

Year and Season

Problems continued

6. New Zealand expenditure on footwear in millions of dollars

Expenditure on Footwear $m.

You may put your moving medians into the empty 4th column

Year	Quarter	Shoes $m		Year	Quarter	Shoes $m	
1990	June	79.9		1993	Mar	61.7	
	Sept	62.1			June	71.5	
	Dec	69.1			Sept	56.4	
1991	Mar	62.5			Dec	67.8	
	June	72.6		1994	Mar	61.1	
	Sept	60.8			June	69.6	
	Dec	67.6			Sept	52.7	
1992	Mar	61.4			Dec	70.5	
	June	67.4		1995	Mar	60.2	
	Sept	56.4			June	67.4	
	Dec	68.3			Sept	54.6	

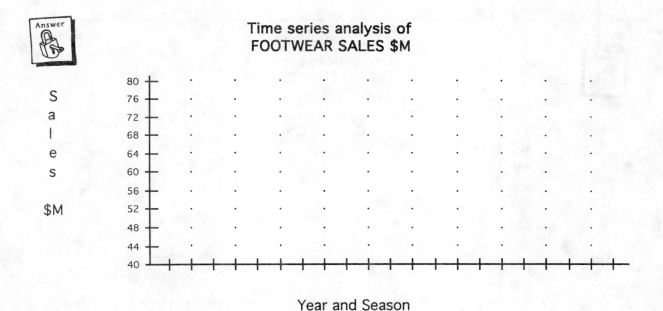

Time series analysis of
FOOTWEAR SALES $M

Year and Season

Problems continued

7. Building permits issued for residential dwellings over each two month period in $m.
   What would be an appropriate number of periods to smooth over?

Building Permits issued in $ m.

You may put your moving medians into the empty 4th column.

Year	Period	$m		Year	Period	$m	
1991	Mar - Apr	275			Jul - Aug	368	
	May - Jun	269			Sep - Oct	362	
	Jul - Aug	275			Nov - Dec	372	
	Sep - Oct	319		1994	Jan - Feb	341	
	Nov - Dec	296			Mar - Apr	419	
1992	Jan - Feb	264			May - Jun	457	
	Mar - Apr	297			Jul - Aug	493	
	May - Jun	286			Sep - Oct	505	
	Jul - Aug	300			Nov - Dec	532	
	Sep - Oct	317		1995	Jan - Feb	428	
	Nov - Dec	353			Mar - Apr	444	
1993	Jan - Feb	280			May - Jun	448	
	Mar - Apr	326			Jul - Aug	416	
	May - Jun	341			Sep - Oct	472	

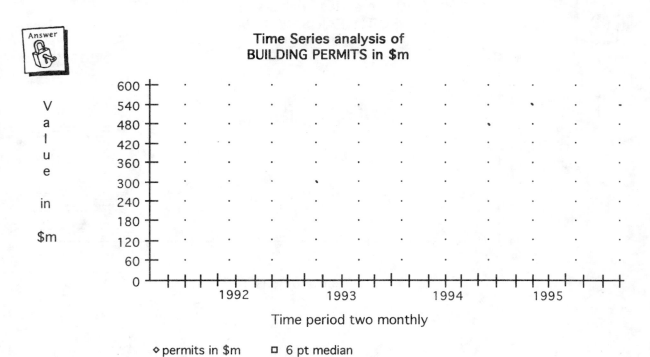

Time Series analysis of BUILDING PERMITS in $m

◇ permits in $m   ◻ 6 pt median

Problems

8.   The number of females employed in the NZ workforce (in thousands).

Females Employed in the NZ workforce.

You may put your moving medians into the empty 4th column

Year	Quarter	Employed		Year	Quarter	Employed	
1990	Marc	635		1993	Marc	646	
	June	646			June	650	
	Sept	638			Sept	663	
	Dec	643			Dec	671	
1991	Marc	638		1994	Marc	674	
	June	638			June	680	
	Sept	632			Sept	691	
	Dec	644			Dec	711	
1992	Marc	638		1995	Marc	707	
	June	648			June	715	
	Sept	643			Sept	724	
	Dec	655					

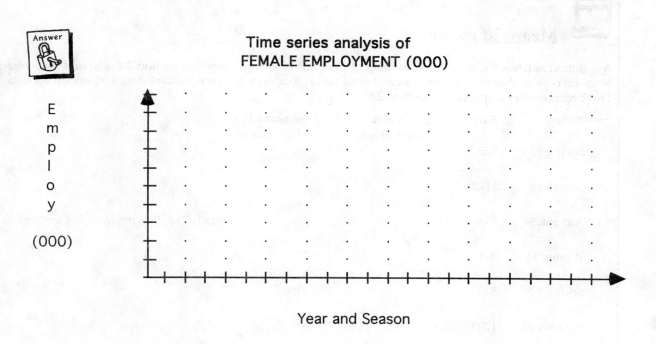

Time series analysis of
FEMALE EMPLOYMENT (000)

Employ (000)

Year and Season

2.5 Smoothing Techniques - Moving Means
Prescription

Investigate a process which produces time series data

- **graphing data and smoothing it using moving averages**

Moving Means

Using **Moving Means** incorporates the extreme values and spreads their effects.

This is an advantage when outliers (high or low values) are significant, such as regular high summer sales, but is a disadvantage when irregular outliers are not a significant part of the overall picture.

You determine the number of points over which you intend to average the result using the same approach as in Moving Medians.

The mean of this group of n data values is then found. The mean is plotted against the midpoint of the time interval included in the group. The process is repeated with the 2nd to $n+1$ values etc. until all possible means have been found.

Means of means

A common approach with an even number of intervals as was explained in section 2.4 is to find the average of an average so that you can have a one to one correspondence between the raw data and smoothed data. This becomes very important in section 2.8.

Period	Sales	Smoothed 4 point means	Smoothed Mean of means	
Spring 93	825			
Summer 93	1143			
		764		
Autumn 94	743		766	(actually 766.25 = mean of 764 and 768.5)
		768.5		
Winter 94	345		776	
		783.5		
Spring 94	843		789	
		795		
Summer 94	1203			
Autumn 95 etc.	789			

Example 3

Use three point moving means to smooth the following data of exports to France for the period 1979 to 1994. Plot the raw and smoothed data on the graph.

You may plot the mean value in the empty column.

Year	Exports $m	3 pt Mean	Year	Exports $m	3 pt Mean
1979	94.5	/////////	1987	226.0	
1980	126.7		1988	188.7	
1981	94.7		1989	204.8	
1982	107.3		1990	176.9	
1983	143.0		1991	167.8	
1984	170.1		1992	217.3	
1985	214.2		1993	221.6	
1986	147.8		1994	211.6	/////////

Solution

The first three data values (94.5, 126.7, 94.7) have a mean of $m 105.3. This is plotted against year 1980. Note: If we were still working with medians, the median would have been $m 94.7.
The mean for the next three (126.7, 94.7, 107.3) is $m 109.6. This is plotted against year 1981.

Year	Exports $m	3 pt Mean	Year	Exports $m	3 pt Mean
1979	94.5	/////////	1987	226.0	
1980	126.7	105.3	1988	188.7	
1981	94.7	109.6	1989	204.8	
1982	107.3		1990	176.9	
1983	143.0		1991	167.8	
1984	170.1		1992	217.3	
1985	214.2		1993	221.6	
1986	147.8		1994	211.6	/////////

We continue calculating the mean value until the year 1993.

Year	Exports $m	3 pt Mean	Year	Exports $m	3 pt Mean
1979	94.5	/////////	1987	226.0	187.5
1980	126.7	105.3	1988	188.7	206.5
1981	94.7	109.6	1989	204.8	190.1
1982	107.3	115.0	1990	176.9	183.2
1983	143.0	140.1	1991	167.8	187.3
1984	170.1	175.8	1992	217.3	202.2
1985	214.2	177.4	1993	221.6	216.8
1986	147.8	196.0	1994	211.6	/////////

The graph of Example 3 is on the next page.

Example 3 continued

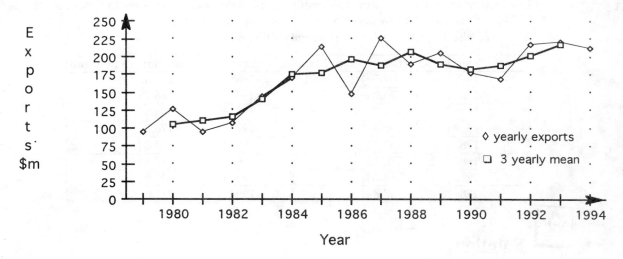

Time series of EXPORTS to FRANCE

The smoothed three point mean in Example 3 is still fluctuating.

We could smooth it further by averaging it over five points (ie. 5 years).

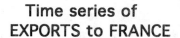

_____

_____

_____

_____

_____

_____

_____

_____

_____

_____

_____

Example 4

Use four point moving means to smooth the following data of appliance sales.

Year	Sales $m	4 pt Mean	Year	Sales $m	4 pt Mean
91 Dec	187.1		93 Dec	216.4	
92 Mar	166.3		94 Mar	181.5	
92 Jun	156.2		94 Jun	174.8	
92 Sep	156.9		94 Sep	182.1	
92 Dec	216.8		94 Dec	224.5	
93 Mar	187.5		95 Mar	186.8	
93 Jun	177.6		95 Jun	173.0	
93 Sep	165.5		95 Sep	161.6	

Solution

Year	Sales $m	4 pt Mean	Year	Sales $m	4 pt Mean
91 Dec	187.1		93 Dec	216.4	
					185
92 Mar	166.3		94 Mar	181.5	
		167			189
92 Jun	156.2		94 Jun	174.8	
		174			191
92 Sep	156.9		94 Sep	182.1	
		179			192
92 Dec	216.8		94 Dec	224.5	
		185			192
93 Mar	187.5		95 Mar	186.8	
		187			186
93 Jun	177.6		95 Jun	173.0	
		187			
93 Sep	165.5		95 Sep	161.6	
		185			

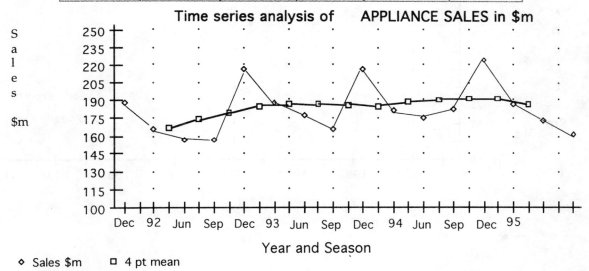

Note: We now lose two points at each end. The smoothed data now clearly shows the long term trend.

Problems

Calculate the moving means and plot a time series graph for the following problems.

9.   Use five point moving means to smooth the following data of exports to France for the period 1979 to 1994. Plot the raw and smoothed data on the graph.

You may plot the mean value in the empty column

Year	Exports $m	5 pt Mean	Year	Exports $m	5 pt Mean
1979	94.5	/////	1987	226.0	
1980	126.7	/////	1988	188.7	
1981	94.7		1989	204.8	
1982	107.3		1990	176.9	
1983	143.0		1991	167.8	
1984	170.1		1992	217.3	
1985	214.2		1993	221.6	/////
1986	147.8		1994	211.6	/////

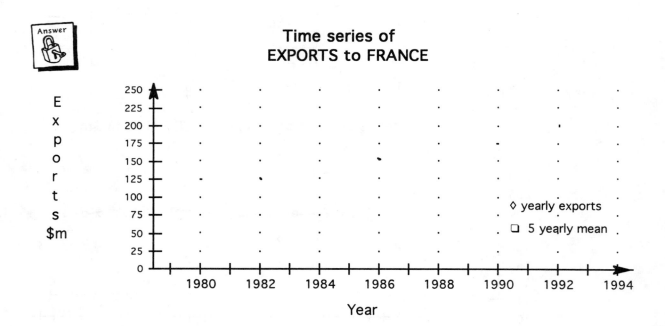

**Time series of
EXPORTS to FRANCE**

◇ yearly exports

❑ 5 yearly mean

Problems contined

10. Use an appropriate period to calculate the moving means to smooth the following data of absences from school in Form 6.

You may plot the mean value in the empty column.

Day	Absences	Means	Day	Absences	Means
Mon	17		Mon	14	
Tue	14		Tue	13	
Wed	11		Wed	2	
Thu	18		Thu	19	
Fri	23		Fri	29	
Mon	14		Mon	18	
Tue	16		Tue	7	
Wed	11		Wed	11	
Thu	19		Thu	15	
Fri	21		Fri	26	

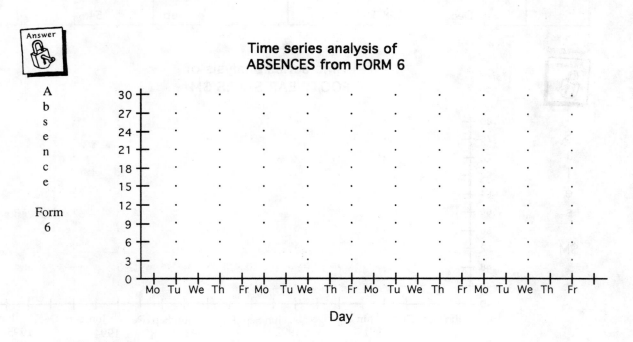

Time series analysis of
ABSENCES from FORM 6

Problems continued

11. New Zealand expenditure on footwear in millions of dollars is in the table below. Smooth the data using an appropriate period and plot your time series analysis on the axes provided.

Expenditure on Footwear $m.

You may put your moving means into the empty 4th column.

Year	Quarter	Shoes $m		Year	Quarter	Shoes $m	
1990	June	79.9		1993	Marc	61.7	
	Sept	62.1			June	71.5	
	Dec	69.1			Sept	56.4	
1991	Marc	62.5			Dec	67.8	
	June	72.6		1994	Marc	61.1	
	Sept	60.8			June	69.6	
	Dec	67.6			Sept	52.7	
1992	Marc	61.4			Dec	70.5	
	June	67.4		1995	Marc	60.2	
	Sept	56.4			June	67.4	
	Dec	68.3			Sept	54.6	

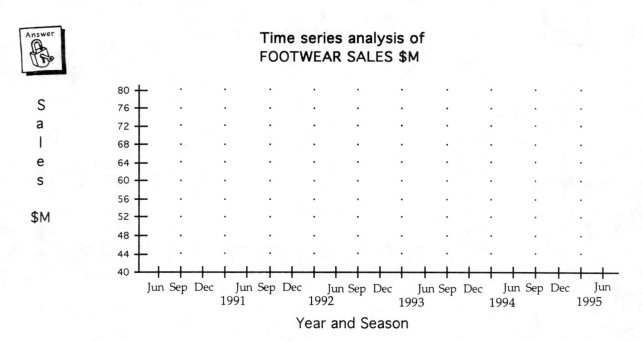

Time series analysis of
FOOTWEAR SALES $M

Year and Season

Problems continued

12. Use an appropriate interval to calculate moving means to smooth the following data of exports of crustaceans from NZ (shellfish) in $m. (Data is a three monthly total).

You may plot the mean value in the empty column

Year	Exports $m	4 pt Mean	Year	Exports $m	4 pt Mean
91 Sep	34.7		93 Dec	39,2	
91 Dec	41.8		94 Mar	19.9	
92 Mar	24.9		94 Jun	20.2	
92 Jun	16.6		94 Sep	48.5	
92 Sep	35.4		94 Dec	42.6	
92 Dec	36.3		95 Mar	17.4	
93 Mar	23.5		95 Jun	23.1	
93 Jun	19.4		95 Sep	52.4	
93 Sep	49.6		95 Dec	34.4	

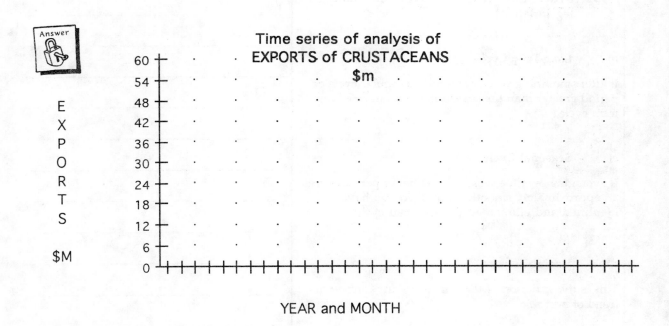

Time series of analysis of
EXPORTS of CRUSTACEANS
$m

EXPORTS $M

YEAR and MONTH

2.6 Identifying Patterns

Prescription

Investigate a process which produces time series data

- identifying patterns, including assignable and inherent variability
- commenting on the features

Identifying Patterns

a)   The Overall Trend.

After the process of smoothing the overall trend is given by the shape of the graph.

- If the smoothed graph is a horizontal line then there is no overall trend.

- If the smoothed graph is best approximated by a straight line then the trend is a constant addition (or subtraction) each complete cycle.

- If the smoothed graph is best approximated by a curve then the trend is a constant multiplier (eg inflation)

b)   Long Term Cycles.

If after smoothing you can identify a regular cycle of period greater than the season then you have a long term cycle.

c)   Seasonal Cycle.

If averaging over the seasonal number of periods gives an approximately smooth graph then you have identified and eliminated the seasonal cycle.

d)   Variability.

This is the variation of the data from any long term trend of best fit.

e)   Ramps or Steps.

A sudden displacement of the data appears as a slide or step.

Example 5

Use some of the terms Long Term trend, Seasonal Cycle, Long Term Cycle, Variability and Ramps to describe the patterns in the following time series graph.

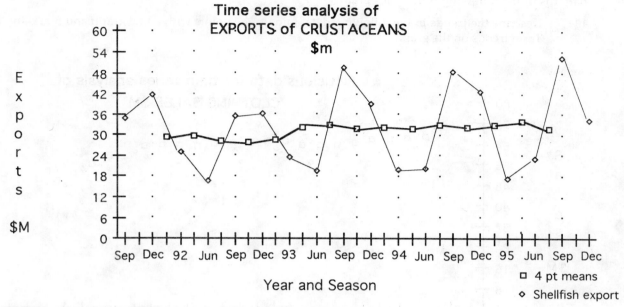

Solution

The smoothed graph has used the number of periods in a season to smooth out the Season Cycle. The Seasonal Cycle shows strong sales in spring and summer and heavily reduced sales in autumn and winter.

The line about which the smoothed graph varies shows the Long Term Trend. As this can be approximated by a straight line, it implies that export growth is increasing by about the same amount each year. The gradient of the straight line is approximately $m 1.1 per year so each year you would expect the corresponding season to increase by $m 1.1. There is no Ramps, or Long Term Cycles evident.

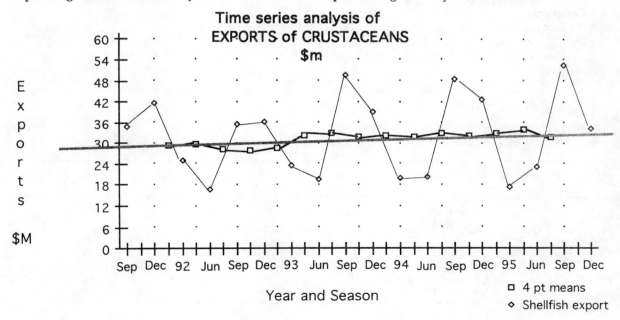

Problems

Use some of the terms *long term trend*, *seasonal cycle*, *long term cycle*, *variability* and *ramps* to describe the patterns in the following time series graphs.

13.   Describe the trends in the following data. Join up the points with a line graph and mark any Long Term trends on the graph.

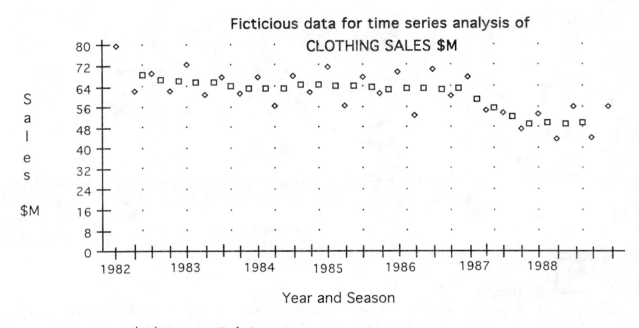

Year and Season

◇ sales/ season   □ 4 pt mean

Comments

_____

_____

_____

_____

_____

_____

_____

_____

Problems continued

14.   Describe the trends in the following data. Join up the points with a line graph and mark any long term trends on the graph.

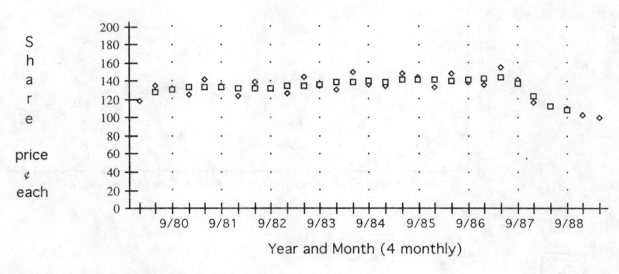

Share price with 3 point mean

◇ share price   □ 3 point mean

Comments

_____

_____

_____

_____

_____

_____

_____

_____

_____

Problems continued

15.   Describe the trends in the following data. Mark any long term trends on the graph.

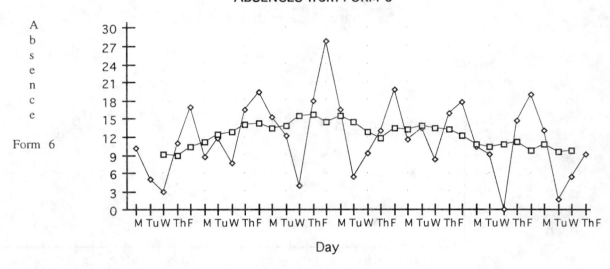

Time series analysis of
ABSENCES from FORM 6

◇ Raw data absence   ☐ 5 pt Mean

Comments

_____

_____

_____

_____

_____

_____

_____

_____

_____

2.7 Indexed Series

Prescription

Investigate a process which produces time series data

- commenting on the features

Notes: Candidates should

- note that specific knowledge of index series is not required.

Indexed Series

So that we can make comparisons with previous results and compare different series, time series are often indexed. You may wish to compare the trends in the export of wine and wool. If both start at the same base point, comparison is easier.

An example of an indexed series is the Consumer Price Index. An indexed series is created by dividing each data value by a **base value** or starting value and multiplying by a hundred (or a thousand).

The Consumer Price Index is based on the December quarter 1993 which is set at 1000.

The Index since Mar 1984 is

Year	Qtr	Index	Year	Qtr	Index
1984	Mar	505	1989	Mar	867
	Jun	516		Jun	877
	Sep	531		Sep	908
	Dec	548		Dec	919
1985	Mar	572	1990	Mar	928
	Jun	601		Jun	944
	Sep	618		Sep	954
	Dec	632		Dec	964
1986	Mar	647	1991	Mar	970
	Jun	664		Jun	971
	Sep	666		Sep	974
	Dec	747		Dec	973
1987	Mar	765	1992	Mar	978
	Jun	790		Jun	980
	Sep	802		Sep	984
	Dec	819		Dec	986
1988	Mar	834	1993	Mar	987
	Jun	840		Jun	993
	Sep	848		Sep	998
	Dec	858		Dec	1000
			1994	Mar	1000

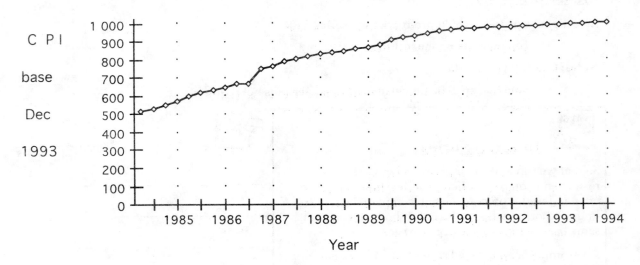

Time series analysis of the CONSUMERS PRICE INDEX

We can see from this indexed graph the increasing CPI around 1986, 1987 (high inflation) and the recent low rate of increase (low inflation period).

Problems

16. For each of the following time series calculate the index based on Mar 1992, plot all three on the one graph, and comment on your graph.

You may plot the index value in the empty columns.

Period	Food $m	Food Index	Hardware $m	Hardware Index	Dept stores $m	Dept store Index
Dec	1800		187		397	
92 Mar	1680	100	166	100	288	100
Jun	1650		156		337	
Sep	1710		157		308	
Dec	1855		217		429	
93 Mar	1700		187		311	
Jun	1690		178		359	
Sep	1792		166		380	
Dec	1949		216		560	
94 Mar	1810		182		368	
Jun	1817		175		430	
Sep	1892		182		404	
Dec	2081		224		609	
95 Mar	1966		187		392	
Jun	1928		173		437	
Sep	1899		162		395	

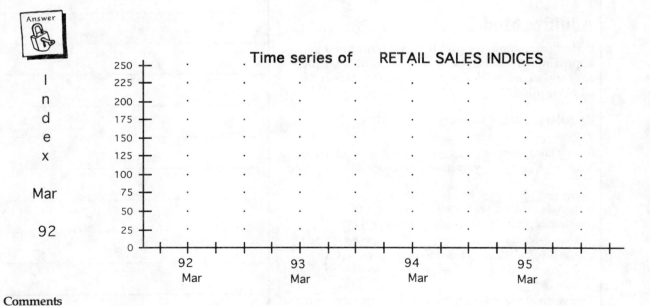

Time series of RETAIL SALES INDICES

Comments

Food Index _____

Hardware Index _____

Department Store Index _____

2.8 Making Predictions

Prescription

Investigate a process which produces time series data

-   **commenting on the features and making predictions**

Notes: Candidates should

-   know that time series data may include a trend component, a cyclic component, a seasonal component and a random error component and be able to describe the meaning of each of these components.

-   be able to apply an additive model to analyse time series data which contain a trend, a seasonal component and an error component and be aware of the limitations of this model for some data types. Candidates will not be expected to apply the multiplicative model in the examination but should be aware of its existence. This does not preclude candidates from using the multiplicative model in the internally assessed component of the course.

-   be able to estimate seasonal effects from data.

-   be able to seasonally adjust data in a time series and interpret results.

-   be able to predict (forecast) future values in a time series.

Seasonal Adjustment

We can adjust data to remove the effect of a seasonal fluctuation and the adjusted data will still contain the long term trend and long term cycle as well as the inherent variability.

Additive Model

If after smoothing, we find the long term trend is approximately linear (ie. it is a straight line) the appropriate model for representing the data is the additive model.

Each data value or result is composed of

$$\text{Raw data} = \text{Long term trend} + \text{Seasonal variation} + \text{Long term cycle} + \text{Variability or error}$$

If there is no long term cycle then the above relationship can be rearranged to give

$$\text{Variability or error} = \text{Raw data} - \left(\text{Long term trend} + \text{Seasonal variation} \right)$$

Therefore, if we subtract the trend component and the seasonal variations from the raw data we should be left with the random error.

Seasonal Adjustment cont...

Multiplicative Model

If the long term trend is NOT linear (ie. it is a curved line) the multiplicative model is more appropriate

Each data value or result would be composed of

$$\text{Raw data} = \text{Long term trend} \times \text{Seasonal variation} \times \text{Long term cycle} \times \text{Variability or error}$$

This can similarly be rearranged to find the error component.

Seasonally Adjusting Data

Using the additive model we have

$$\text{Variability or error} = \text{Raw data} - \left(\text{Long term trend} + \text{Seasonal variation} \right)$$

or

$$\text{Variability or error} + \text{Seasonal variation} = \text{Raw data} - \text{Long term trend}$$

Therefore, if we subtract the long term trend off the raw data you get the seasonal component and the random error.

By finding the mean of each season's

$$\text{Varibility or error} + \text{Seasonal variation}$$

and assuming the error component cancels itself out, each seasonal component can then be identified.

Making Predictions

We can use the long term trend identified by smoothing out a time series to predict results. By extending the trend (extrapolation) and by adding (or subtracting) the appropriate seasonal component we can predict particular values.

Example 6

The attendance figures at a particular High School for Form 7 show a strong seasonal pattern. Analyse the results and identify the seasonal component. Predict the attendance on the 5th Friday of the term.

week 1	absent	week 2	absent	week 3	absent	week 4	absent
Mon	21	Mon	20	Mon	22	Mon	21
Tue	18	Tue	17	Tue	20	Tue	18
Wed	13	Wed	16	Wed	19	Wed	17
Thu	17	Thu	20	Thu	18	Thu	22
Fri	23	Fri	26	Fri	25	Fri	27

Solution

We use 5 point moving means to smooth out the data (5 point as the natural period is one week)

day	absent	5 pt mean	difference
Mon	21	smoothed	error +
Tue	18		seasonal
Wed	13	18.4	-5.4
Thu	17	18.2	-1.2
Fri	23	18.0	5.0
Mon	20	18.6	1.4
Tue	17	19.2	-2.2
Wed	16	19.8	-3.8
Thu	20	20.2	-0.2
Fri	26	20.8	5.2
Mon	22	21.4	0.6
Tue	20	21.0	-1.0
Wed	19	20.8	-1.8
Thu	18	20.6	-2.6
Fri	25	20.2	4.8
Mon	21	19.8	1.2
Tue	18	20.6	-2.6
Wed	17	21.0	-4.0
Thu	22		
Fri	27		

To find the seasonal adjustments we find the mean of each component

$$\textbf{Monday} = (1.4 + 0.6 + 1.2) \div 3$$
$$= 1.1 \text{ students above the trend}$$

$$\textbf{Tuesday} = (^-2.2 + ^-1.0 + ^-2.6) \div 3$$
$$= ^-1.9 \text{ students below the trend}$$

$$\textbf{Wednesday} = (^-5.4 + ^-3.8 + ^-1.8 + ^-4.0) \div 4$$
$$= ^-3.8 \text{ students below the trend}$$

$$\textbf{Thursday} = (^-1.2 + ^-0.2 + ^-2.6) \div 3$$
$$= ^-1.3 \text{ students below the trend}$$

$$\textbf{Friday} = (5.0 + 5.2 + 4.8) \div 3$$
$$= 5.3 \text{ students above the trend}$$

The prediction for the 5th Friday is that the number of students absent will be 5.3 above the trend. The trend line drawn on the graph, passes through 24 on the 5th Friday giving the predicted value

$$\text{5th Friday} = \text{trend} + \text{seasonal variation}$$
$$= 24 + 5.3$$
$$= 29 \qquad \text{(0 dp)}$$

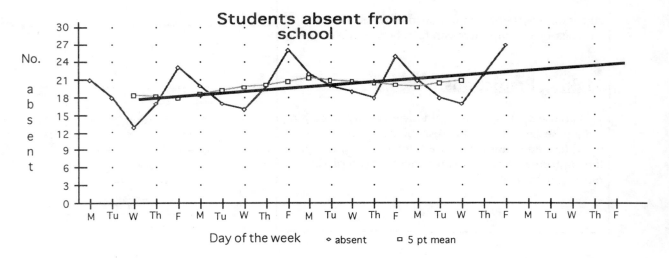

Example 7

The data on the right is for the crustacean exports from New Zealand. Analyse the results and identify the seasonal component. Make a prediction on the level of exports in December 1996.

Solution

Quarter /Year	Mar	Jun	Sep	Dec
90	20.2	8.3	22.8	36.4
91	19.6	8.7	34.7	41.8
92	24.9	16.6	35.4	36.3
93	23.5	19.4	49.6	39,2
94	19.9	20.2	48.5	42.6
95	17.4	23.1	52.4	34.4

Date	exports	4 pt mean	mean of mean	Difference (1 dp)
90 Mar	20.2			
Jun	8.3			
		21.9		
Sep	22.8		21.85	1.0
		21.8		
Dec	36.4		21.85	14.6
		21.9		
91 Mar	19.6		23.35	-3.8
		24.8		
Jun	8.7		25.5	-16.8
		26.2		
Sep	34.7		26.85	7.9
		27.5		
Dec	41.8		28.5	13.3
		29.5		
92 Mar	24.9		29.6	-4.7
		29.7		
Jun	16.6		29.0	-12.4
		28.3		
Sep	35.4		28.15	7.3
		28.0		
Dec	36.3		28.3	8.0
		28.6		
93 Mar	23.5		30.4	-6.9
		32.2		
Jun	19.4		32.55	-13.2
		32.9		
Sep	49.6		32.45	17.2
		32.0		
Dec	39.2		32.1	7.1
		32.2		
94 Mar	19.9		32.1	-12.2
		32.0		
Jun	20.2		32.4	-12.2
		32.8		
Sep	48.5		32.5	16.0
		32.2		
Dec	42.6		32.55	10.1
		32.9		
95 Mar	17.4		33.4	-16.0
		33.9		
Jun	23.1		32.85	-9.8
		31.8		
Sep	52.4			
Dec	34.4			

To find the seasonal adjustments we find the mean of each component

March

= ($^-$3.8 + $^-$4.7 + $^-$6.9 + $^-$12.2 + $^-$16.0) ÷ 5

= \$M $^-$8.7 below the trend

June

= ($^-$16.8 + $^-$12.4 + $^-$13.2 + $^-$12.2 + $^-$9.8) ÷ 5

= \$M $^-$12.9 below the trend

September

= (1.0 + 7.9 + 7.3 + 17.2 + 16.0) ÷ 5

= \$M 9.9 above the trend

December

= (14.6 + 13.3 + 8.0 + 7.1 + 10.1) ÷ 5

= \$M 10.6 above the trend

The graph of Example 7 is on the next page.

The raw data shows the strong seasonal cycle with high exports in September and December and lower exports in March and June. The moving average is best approximated by a straight line but there is a dip around September 1992.   The long term trend is for exports to increase at about 2.2 million dollars per year (the gradient of the straight line).

As the Long Term Trend passes through $m 36 in December 1995, in December 1996 the long term trend should be passing through 36 + 2.2 or about $m 38.2. The predicted exports then would be

Dec 1996   Prediction = 38.2 + seasonal difference

                                    = 38.2 + 10.6

                                    = $m 48.8

Problems

Analyse the following time series data and comment on any trends.

17.   For the Food Index (based on Mar 1992) calculate the smoothed index. Plot both the raw and
       smoothed data on the graph and comment on seasonal trends and any long term trends. What
       would you expect the index to be in March 1997. *You may use the empty columns for your working.*

Date	Food index	4 pt mean	mean of mean	Difference
De	107			
Ma 92	100			
Ju	98			
Se	102			
De	110			
Ma 93	101			
Ju	101			
Se	107			
De	116			
Ma 94	108			
Ju	108			
Se	113			
De	124			
Ma 95	117			
Ju	115			
Se	113			

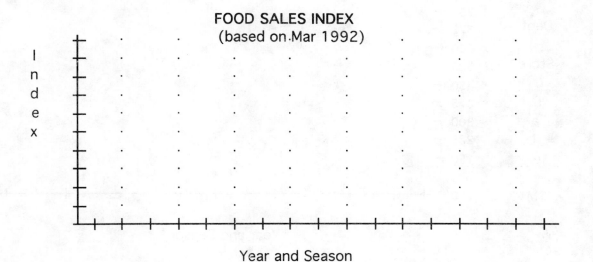

FOOD SALES INDEX
(based on Mar 1992)

Index

Year and Season

18.   For the Department Store sales calculate the smoothed data. Plot both raw and smoothed data on the graph and comment on seasonal trends and any long term trends. What would you expect the March 1996 sales to be? *You may use the empty columns for your working.*

Date	Dept sales $m	4 pt mean	mean of mean	Difference
De	397			
Ma 92	288			
Ju	337			
Se	308			
De	429			
Ma 93	311			
Ju	360			
Se	380			
De	559			
Ma 94	369			
Ju	429			
Se	403			
De	608			
Ma 95	392			
Ju	438			
Se	395			

Answer

Seasonally adjusted
DEPARTMENT STORE SALES

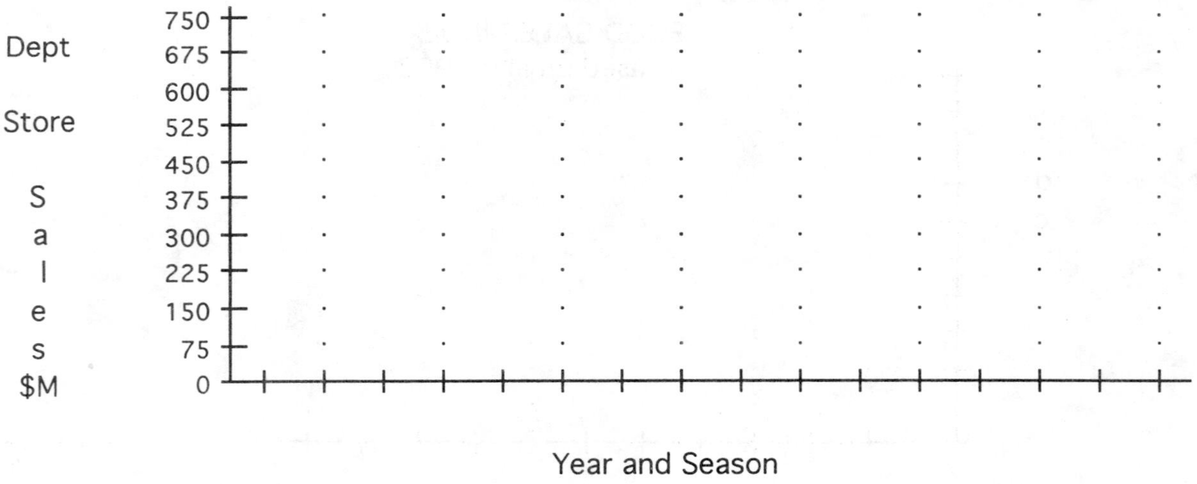

Dept Store Sales $M

750
675
600
525
450
375
300
225
150
75
0

Year and Season

19.   Complete a time series analysis for the hardware sales from a local shop. Plot both raw and smoothed data on the graph and comment on seasonal trends and any long term trends. What would you expect the sales to be in three Saturdays time. *You may use the empty columns for your working.*

Day	Sales	smoothed	Differences
Mo	86		
Tu	125		
We	115		
Th	150		
Fr	168		
Sa	291		
Su	102		
Mo	83		
Tu	118		
We	112		
Th	141		
Fr	171		
Sa	282		
Su	99		
Mo	82		
Tu	117		
We	108		
Th	155		
Fr	165		
Sa	271		
Su	88		
Mo	75		
Tu	127		
We	109		
Th	141		
Fr	155		
Sa	269		
Su	78		

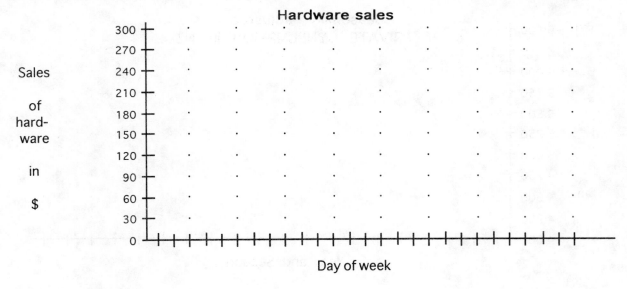

Hardware sales

Sales of hard-ware in $

Day of week

20.   Calculate the smoothed figures for the Private Consumption component of the GNP. Plot both the raw and smoothed data on the graph and comment on seasonal trends and any long term trends. What would you expect the December 1997 consumption to be to be?

Date	Pvte $m	4 pt mean	mean of mean	Differenc
De	5897			
Ma 91	5211			
Ju	5602			
Se	5600			
De	5999			
Ma 92	5401			
Ju	5673			
Se	5679			
De	6170			
Ma 93	5523			
Ju	5627			
Se	5702			
De	6174			
Ma 94	5445			
Ju	5898			
Se	5948			
De	6437			
Ma 95	5713			
Ju	6061			
Se	6220			

Answer

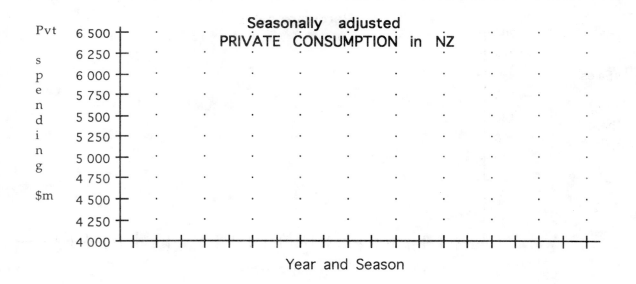

Seasonally adjusted
PRIVATE CONSUMPTION in NZ

Pvt
spending
$m

6 500
6 250
6 000
5 750
5 500
5 250
5 000
4 750
4 500
4 250
4 000

Year and Season

3.0 Probability

Introduction

In this chapter we look to introduce the concept of probability, and its definition. Our aim is to be able to solve a range of probability problems using both first principles and appropriate distribution models.

Prescription

Explain the basic terms and concepts of probability, and use them to solve problems
- **theoretical and experimental probability**
- **tree diagrams, Venn diagrams and formulae**
- **mutually exclusive and independent events**
- **conditional probability**

Calculate and interpret expected values for practical situations
- **discrete random variables**
- **probability distribution for a discrete random variable**
- **mean and variance of a random variable, including the derivation of the identity**
  $$E(X - \mu)^2 = E(X^2) - \mu^2$$
- **mean and variance of a linear function of a random variable**
- **mean and variance of the sum of independent random variables**

Choose the appropriate distribution to model a given situation, calculate probabilities and expected values, and make predictions using the model
- **binomial, Poisson and normal distributions**
- **approximating, in the appropriate circumstances, the binomial distribution by the Poisson or the normal distribution (including correction for continuity)**

3.1 Theoretical and Experimental Probability

Prescription

Explain the basic terms and concepts of probability, and use them to solve problems
- **theoretical and experimental probability**

Probability

Experience resulting from repeated experiments can be used to predict outcomes of future events. If we toss a fair coin we can predict with certainty that it will fall with head or tail uppermost. We say that the coin has a probability of $\frac{1}{2}$ of landing with head uppermost. We use the word **probability** to represent the **chance** of an event occurring, founded on certain evidence.

We begin by identifying some basic **probability** facts.

- all probabilities are assigned a numerical value between 0 and 1 inclusive.

- an impossible event has a probability of 0.

- an event which is a certainty has a probability of 1.

- we denote the probability of an event A occurring, by using the notation P(A).

Probability cont...

To calculate the probability of an event occurring we begin by considering an "experiment", namely tossing a die.

The possible outcomes (**sample space**) when tossing a die are {1, 2, 3, 4, 5, 6}, which we shall call E. The number of outcomes in E is 6, written n(E) = 6.

If we wish to calculate the probability of scoring a 3 or 4 when throwing a die (we refer to this event as event A) then A={3,4} and n(A) = 2.

Therefore $\quad P(A) = \dfrac{n(A)}{n(E)}$

$$= \frac{2}{6}$$

Formally, if E is the set of all possible outcomes of an experiment (all of which are assumed to be equally likely), then the probability of an event A occurring is

$$P(A) = \frac{n(A)}{n(E)}$$

we often restate this as

$$P(A) = \frac{\text{number of successful outcomes}}{\text{total number of possible outcomes}}$$

Theoretical Probability

Where we have prior knowledge of possible outcomes and the physical situation allows us to deduce or infer the relevant probabilities.

eg. P(drawing a heart from a pack of 52 cards)= $\dfrac{1}{4}$

Experimental Probability

Where we must use an experiment to find the probabilities.

eg. P(a particular brand of seed will germinate) is found by planting a number of seeds and using the results to give us the probability.

It may be necessary to conduct more than one experiment to gain an accurate estimate of the probability.

As we repeat an experiment a large number of times the probability approaches a consistent value. This is called **long run relative frequency**.

Complementary Events

In general, if A is an event, then we denote A' as the event that A does not happen. A' is commonly known as the **complementary** event. Therefore

$$P(A') = 1 - P(A)$$

or $\quad P(A) + P(A') = 1$

We can represent this in a Venn diagram. (see Fig 1)

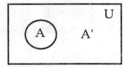

Fig 1

Addition Rule (Mutually Exclusive)

Two or more events in probability are deemed to be **mutually exclusive** if they have nothing in common with each other and cannot occur simultaneously.

eg. consider the three events of a set of traffic lights (red, amber and green) - these events would be mutually exclusive. If two or more events are mutually exclusive then we can sum their probabilities. We can write

$$P(A \text{ or } B) = P(A) + P(B)$$

or $\quad P(A \cup B) = P(A) + P(B)$

We can represent this in a Venn diagram. (see Fig 2)

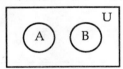

Fig 2

Addition Rule (Not Mutually Exclusive)

Two or more events in probability are NOT mutually exclusive if they can occur simultaneously.

eg. consider the events of obtaining a diamond or an ace from a pack of 52 playing cards. Obviously it is possible to meet both events simultaneously by drawing the ace of diamonds.

If two or more events are NOT mutually exclusive then we must remember to minus the probability that the events can occur simultaneously.

We now write

$$P(A \text{ or } B) = P(A) + P(B) - P(A \text{ and } B)$$

or

$$P(A \cup B) = P(A) + P(B) - P(A \cap B)$$

We can represent this in a Venn diagram. (see Fig 3)

Fig 3

Multiplication Rule (Independent Events)

Two or more events are independent if the probability of any one of them occurring is not influenced by any other occurring.

eg. consider the two events

A= {a person weighs more than 60 kg}

B= {a person passes Bursary Statistics}

are clearly independent for the first event should have no effect on the outcome of the second event.

eg. consider the two events

C= {I go to the movies on a Sunday}

D= {My wife goes to the movies on a Sunday}

These events are unlikely to be independent for one of the events is probably influenced by the other event.

If the probabilities of two or more independent events are $p_1, p_2, p_3, \ldots p_n$ then the probability that all of them will occur is found by the product (ie. $p_1 \cdot p_2 \cdot p_3 \cdots p_n$).

For two independent events A and B we write

$$P(A \text{ and } B) = P(A).(B)$$

or $\quad P(A \cap B) = P(A).(B)$

This formula is in your tables.
Make sure you can locate it when needed.

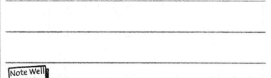

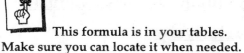

This formula is in your tables.
Make sure you can locate it when needed.

Example 1

David draws a card from a pack of 52 cards.

a) What is the probability that the card drawn is a king.

b) What is the probability that the card is an ace or red.

Solution

a) $P(\text{king}) = \dfrac{4}{52}$

$= \dfrac{1}{13}$

b) Not mutually exclusive

$P(\text{ace or red}) = P(\text{ace}) + P(\text{red}) - P(\text{ace and red})$

$= \dfrac{4}{52} + \dfrac{26}{52} - \dfrac{2}{52}$

$= \dfrac{28}{52}$

$= \dfrac{7}{13}$

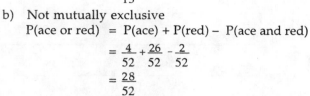

Example 2

The probability that a person wears a hearing aid is $\dfrac{2}{5}$ and the probability that a person wears a hair piece is $\dfrac{1}{3}$. Assuming the two events are independent, find the probability of a person chosen at random

a) wearing a hearing aid and a hair piece.

b) wearing a hair piece but not a hearing aid.

c) wearing a hearing aid or a hair piece.

Solution

$P(\text{wearing a hearing aid}) = \dfrac{2}{5}$

$P(\text{not wearing a hearing aid}) = \dfrac{3}{5}$

$P(\text{wearing a hair piece}) = \dfrac{1}{3}$

$P(\text{not wearing a hair piece}) = \dfrac{2}{3}$

a) $P(\text{wearing a hearing aid and a hair piece}) = P(\text{hearing aid}) \times P(\text{hair piece})$

$= \dfrac{2}{5} \times \dfrac{1}{3}$

$= \dfrac{2}{15}$

b) $P(\text{wearing a hair piece but not a hearing aid}) = P(\text{hair piece}) \times P(\text{not hearing aid})$

$= \dfrac{1}{3} \times \dfrac{3}{5}$

$= \dfrac{1}{5}$

c) $P(\text{wearing a hearing aid or a hair piece}) = P(\text{hearing aid}) + P(\text{hair piece}) - P(\text{both})$

$= \dfrac{2}{5} + \dfrac{1}{3} - \left(\dfrac{2}{5} \times \dfrac{1}{3}\right)$

$= \dfrac{3}{5}$

Example 3

Three archers are in a competition. Their probabilities (assuming independence) of getting a bullseye when they shoot is 0.7, 0.4 and 0.5 respectively. What is the probability that at least one of them gets a bullseye.

Solution

('at least one' implies one or more bullseyes)

Either $1 - $ P(all three miss)

    $=$ $1 - $ P(1st miss) x P(2nd miss) x P(3rd miss)

    $=$ $1 - (0.3 \times 0.6 \times 0.5)$

    $=$ $1 - .09$

    $=$ $.91$

Or   P(Hit, Miss, Miss) $= 0.7 \times 0.6 \times 0.5$

    $+$ P(Miss, Hit, Miss) $= 0.3 \times 0.4 \times 0.5$

    $+$ P(Miss, Miss, Hit) $= 0.3 \times 0.6 \times 0.5$

    $+$ P(Hit, Hit, Miss) $= 0.7 \times 0.4 \times 0.5$

    $+$ P(Miss, Hit, Hit) $= 0.3 \times 0.4 \times 0.5$

    $+$ P(Hit, Miss, Hit) $= 0.7 \times 0.6 \times 0.5$

    $+$ P(Hit, Hit, Hit) $= 0.7 \times 0.4 \times 0.5$

    $=$ 0.91

Example 4

In a bag containing 20 marbles there are 4 marbles each of 5 different colours, white, red, green, blue and yellow. Find the probability that 3 marbles drawn together at random from the bag are

a)   all white

b)   all of one colour

Solution

a)   P(all white)$= \dfrac{4}{20} \times \dfrac{3}{19} \times \dfrac{2}{18}$

    $= \dfrac{1}{285}$

b)   P(all one colour)$= \left(\dfrac{4}{20} \times \dfrac{3}{19} \times \dfrac{2}{18}\right) \times 5$

    $= \dfrac{1}{57}$

(multiplied by 5, since 5 different colours)

Problems

1. Peter and Susan take the bus to work each day. The probability of Peter missing the bus is 0.15 and the probability of Susan missing the bus is 0.20. Assuming the probabilities are independent find the probability that

    a) both Peter and Susan miss the bus.

    b) one of them is late.

    c) neither Peter nor Susan miss the bus.

a) _____

_____

_____

b) _____

_____

_____

c) _____

_____

_____

2. From a box containing 6 green balls and 4 red balls, 3 balls are drawn at random. Find the probability that 2 balls are green and 1 ball is red if

    a) each ball is returned before the next ball is drawn.

    b) the three balls are drawn one after another without replacement.

a) _____   b) _____

_____   _____

_____   _____

_____   _____

_____   _____

3. Three students are working independently on a statistics problem. The probabilities that they will solve the problem are 0.2, 0.25 and 0.4. What is the probability that the problem will be solved.

Answer

_____

_____

_____

_____

4. A box contains 10 computer chips, 4 of them are faulty. Find the probability that if 2 chips are removed from the box, they will both be faulty.

Answer

_____

_____

_____

_____

5. A shop has 3 lolly jars on a shelf. The first jar has 50 lollies inside it, 10 of which are green, the second lolly jar has 30 lollies in it, 10 of which are green, and the third lolly jar has 20 lollies in it, 10 of which are green. A child walks into the store and randomly chooses one of the jars and randomly selects a lolly from the jar. Find the probability that

a) a green lolly will be taken from the first jar.

b) a green lolly will be taken.

c) if a lolly is chosen at random from the 100 lollies in the jars, find the probability that the lolly will be green.

Answer

a) _____   b) _____

_____   _____

c) _____

_____

_____

6. Abe, Bernadette, and Colin toss a coin one after another. The first one to throw a head wins the game. What are the respective chances of Abe, Bernadette, and Colin winning the game.

Answer

_____

_____

_____

_____

3.2 Tree Diagrams

Prescription

- tree diagrams

Tree Diagrams

Some probability problems can be more easily solved by using **Tree Diagrams**. A tree diagram displays all the possible outcomes of a probability experiment. On each branch of the tree appropriate probabilities are assigned.

Tree diagrams can be drawn from left to right or top to bottom. In this text we have chosen to draw all probability trees from top to bottom.

The basic structure of a Tree Diagram is shown in Figure 4.

To find the final probabilities for an outcome we multiply together, from top to bottom, the probabilities on the branches for the required path.

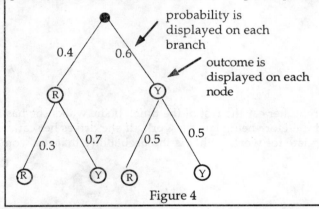

probability is displayed on each branch

outcome is displayed on each node

Figure 4

Example 5

A man plays a two game chess tournament. For the first game his probability of winning, losing and drawing are 0.6, 0.3, 0.1. If he wins the first game his probabilities change to 0.7, 0.2, 0.1. If he loses they change to 0.5, 0.2, 0.3. If he draws they remain the same. He scores 1 point for a win, $\frac{1}{2}$ a point for a draw and 0 points for a loss. What is the probability of scoring $1\frac{1}{2}$ or more points.

Solution

We begin by drawing a tree diagram to represent the two game tournament and all the possible outcomes (see Figure 5).
Note that all the respective probabilities have been assigned to each branch and that each group of win, loss and draw probabilities total to 1.
Underneath the tree diagram we have assigned the total number of points the man would have accumulated if he had obtained those results. We then calculate the probabilities for the required route(s) and add them.

Solution continued

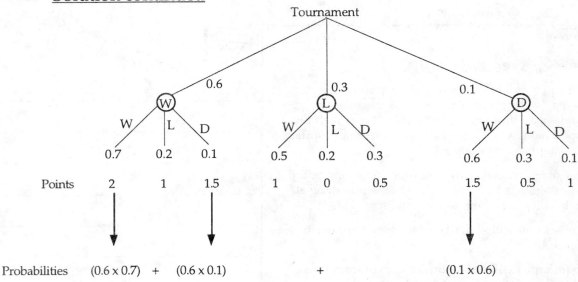

Figure 5

$$P(\text{scoring} \geq 1\tfrac{1}{2} \text{ points}) = 0.42 + 0.06 + 0.06$$
$$= 0.54$$

Example 6

A woman walks to work 30% of the time, and drives her car the rest of the time. If she walks she has a 40% chance of breaking the heel on her shoe and therefore being late for work. If she drives her car she has a 15% chance of getting a flat tyre and being late for work. What is the probability that the woman is on time for work.

Solution

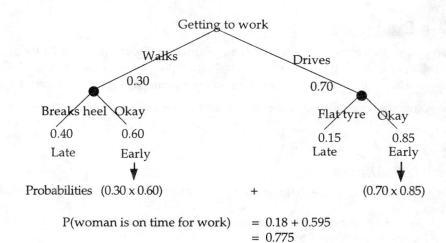

$$P(\text{woman is on time for work}) = 0.18 + 0.595$$
$$= 0.775$$

Problems

7. A bag contains 2 white marbles and 2 black marbles. One marble after another is drawn until 2 black marbles have been drawn. What is the probability that 3 draws are required. (The tree diagram has been drawn for you)

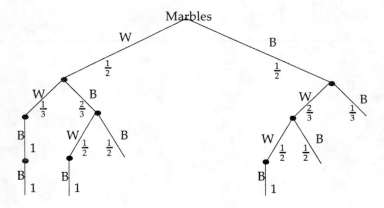

Probability (3 draws are required) = _____

8. A coin is tossed. If it lands head uppermost then a die is thrown. If it lands tail uppermost then the coin is tossed again. Complete the tree diagram for this sequence of events and find the probability that

a) the die is thrown and a 2 appears.

b) the coin is tossed twice.

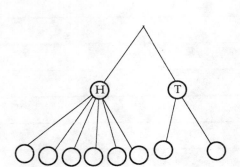

© Robert Lakeland & Carl Nugent

Problems continued

9.   A student sitting three university papers has a probability of 0.6 of passing her first paper. If she passes the paper her probability of passing the next one increases by 0.1. If, however, she fails the paper her probability of passing the next one drops by 0.1. Assuming this pattern continues for all three papers, find the probability that. (Draw a tree diagram)

a)   she passes all three papers.

b)   she passes only one paper.

Tree Diagram

a)

b)

Problems continued

10. Two identical boxes are put on a table. In the first box there are nine blocks, 3 of them red and the
     remaining 6 white. In the second box there are 8 blocks, 4 of them red and 4 of them white. A
     person randomly chooses one of the boxes and draws out a block. Draw a tree diagram to represent
     this situation and then calculate the probability that the block drawn out is red.

Tree Diagram

Answer

Problems continued

11.   Five cards are made with the numbers 1, 2, 3, 4, and 5 printed, one on each card. These cards are

        placed in a box and a person randomly draws out two cards, one after another, without

        replacement. Draw a tree diagram to represent this and find the probability that

        a)   the sum of the two numbers is less than 7

        b)   the sum of the two numbers is greater than or equal to 5

Tree Diagram

Answer

a)

b)

3.3 Conditional Probability

Prescription

- conditional probability

Conditional Probability

Often when dealing with probability problems we do not use all the sample space for the experiment, but only a restricted part of it.

Probability problems that use a restricted or reduced sample space are called **conditional probabilities.**

Consider - the probability that a person selected at random in New Zealand has green eyes, as opposed to the probability that a person randomly selected from brown hair people in New Zealand has green eyes.

In the first instance we are looking at the probability of all green eyed people in the entire population.

In the second instance the sample space is restricted to brown hair people in New Zealand, which is a subset of the original sample space, namely all New Zealanders.

To indicate conditional probability we introduce a new notation namely, $P(A \mid B)$ which is read the **"probability of A given B"** and is defined as

$$P(A \mid B) = \frac{P(A \cap B)}{P(B)}, \qquad P(B) \neq 0$$

This formula is in your tables.
Make sure you can locate it when needed.

Example 7

What is the probability that a family of 3 children with at least 2 boys is all boys.

Solution

The sample space for a family of three children is as follows:

BBB, BBG, BGB, BGG, GBB, GGG, GGB, GBG, where 'B' represents a boy and 'G' represents a girl.

As it is known that the family has at least two boys the reduced or restricted sample space is now:

BBB, BBG, BGB, GBB.

Therefore the probability that a family of 3 children with at least 2 boys is all boys is $\frac{1}{4}$.

Example 8

Two dice are tossed. One die is red, the other die is yellow.

a) Find the probability of obtaining a total greater than 9, given that the red die shows a 6.

b) Find the probability that the total is less than 7, given that the yellow die shows a 2.

Solution

The sample space for the throw of two dice is

RY	RY	RY	RY	RY	RY
(1,1)	(1,2)	(1,3)	(1,4)	(1,5)	(1,6)
(2,1)	(2,2)	(2,3)	(2,4)	(2,5)	(2,6)
(3,1)	(3,2)	(3,3)	(3,4)	(3,5)	(3,6)
(4,1)	(4,2)	(4,3)	(4,4)	(4,5)	(4,6)
(5,1)	(5,2)	(5,3)	(5,4)	(5,5)	(5,6)
(6,1)	(6,2)	(6,3)	(6,4)	(6,5)	(6,6)

'R' is the red dice and 'Y' is the yellow dice)

a)   Let   A = {total greater than 9} and
                 B = {red die shows a 6}

$$P(B) = \frac{6}{36} \quad \text{and} \quad P(A \cap B) = \frac{3}{36}$$

$$\therefore P(A \mid B) = \frac{P(A \cap B)}{P(B)}$$

$$\therefore P(A \mid B) = \frac{\frac{3}{36}}{\frac{6}{36}}$$

$$= \frac{1}{2}$$

b)   Let   A = {total is less than 7} and
                 B = {yellow die shows a 2}

$$P(B) = \frac{6}{36} \quad \text{and} \quad P(A \cap B) = \frac{4}{36}$$

$$\therefore P(A \mid B) = \frac{P(A \cap B)}{P(B)}$$

$$\therefore P(A \mid B) = \frac{\frac{4}{36}}{\frac{6}{36}}$$

$$= \frac{2}{3}$$

Problems

12.   In a recent exam 20% of the students failed Mathematics with Calculus and 15% failed Mathematics with Statistics. 8% of the students failed both Mathematics with Statistics and Mathematics with Calculus. A student is selected at random.

a)   Find the probability that he failed Mathematics with Statistics or Mathematics with Calculus.

b)   What is the probability that if the student failed Mathematics with Statistics, he also failed Mathematics with Calculus.

a) _____

_____

_____

_____

_____

_____

b) _____

_____

_____

_____

_____

_____

13.   An appliance store sells 7 Wonder TV's, 5 Allbright TV's and 8 Neverfail TV's. If the probability of the respective TV failing within one year is 0.6, 0.8 and 0.4. Find the probability

a)   that a TV chosen at random fails.

b)   that given that a TV fails within the first year it is an Allbright TV.

a) _____

_____

_____

_____

_____

_____

b) _____

_____

_____

_____

_____

_____

Problems continued

14. A survey was taken of 200 individuals to ascertain whether they undertook regular exercise. The following results were obtained.

	Exercises regularly	Does not exercise
Under 50 years of age	55	40
50 years of age and over	20	85

Find the probability

a) that an individual selected at random exercises regularly.

b) that given that a person does not exercise find the probability they are under 50 years of age.

a) _____

_____

_____

_____

_____

b) _____

_____

_____

_____

_____

15. Two dice are tossed. Find the probability that

a) the numbers are the same, given that one was a 3.

b) the product of the numbers is greater than 20, given that one number was a 5.

a) _____

_____

_____

_____

_____

b) _____

_____

_____

_____

_____

Problems continued

16.   A lolly jar contains x chocolate lollies and y caramel lollies. Random lollies are removed from the jar without replacement. Find in terms of x and y the probability that

a)   the first lolly removed is a chocolate one.

b)   the first two lollies removed are chocolate.

c)   the first lolly is chocolate and the second lolly is caramel.

d)   the second lolly removed is caramel, given that the first one was chocolate.

e)   if three lollies are removed most are caramel (2 or more).

f)   if three lollies are removed most are caramel given that the first one was chocolate.

a)

b)

c)

d)

Tree diagram for parts c) and d)

e)

Tree diagram for parts e) and f)

f)

3.4 Venn Diagrams

Prescription

- **Venn diagrams**

Venn Diagrams

When defining probability rules, or solving probability problems, we frequently use set notation. ie. $P(A \cap B)$, $P(A \cup B)$, $P(A')$ etc.

When representing sets pictorially we often use **Venn Diagrams**. These Venn diagrams can also be applied to probability problems as well.

Consider the following - the probability that a school softball team beats a local high school is 0.72, while the probability that it will beat a touring overseas team is 0.48. The probability it wins both games is 0.35. What is the probability the school softball team loses both games. We begin by drawing a Venn diagram to represent this problem.

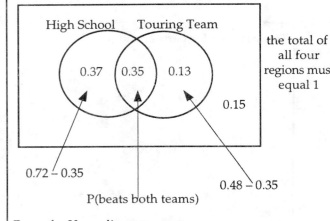

the total of all four regions must equal 1

0.72 − 0.35

P(beats both teams)

0.48 − 0.35

From the Venn diagram -

> P(softball team loses both games) = 0.15

Note: All the probabilities within the Venn diagram total 1.

The 0.15 outside the two circles represents the probability that the softball team loses both games.

The probabilities within each circle sum to give the total probability of the softball team beating that respective team.

The figure in the intersection of the two circles gives the probability of the softball team beating <u>both</u> teams.

Venn diagrams can also be drawn to represent probability problems with more than two situations or occurrences. (see Example 9 on the following page)

Example 9

At the end of a year 180 students were asked which of the three subjects English, Mathematics and Science they had studied. The results were

> 5 took all three subjects
>
> 20 took English and Mathematics
>
> 17 took Mathematics and Science
>
> 18 took Science and English
>
> 60 students studied Science
>
> 80 students studied Mathematics
>
> 83 students studied English

a) Represent the above using a Venn diagram, with three overlapping sets.

b) How many students did not take Mathematics, English or Science.

c) How many students studied two or more subjects.

Solution

a) We begin by drawing a Venn diagram to represent this situation

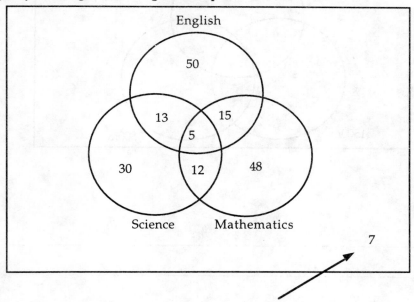

b) 7 students did not take English, Mathematics or Science.

c) 13 + 15 + 5 + 12 = 45 studied two or more subjects.

Problems

17. A group of 70 athletes were asked which of the events 400m, 800m, 1500m they intended to enter at the local sports competition.

   5 entered all 3 events

   6 entered the 400m and 1500m

   31 entered the 800m

   28 entered the 1500m

   8 entered the 400m and 800m

   9 entered the 800m and 1500m

   20 entered the 400m

   a) Represent the above situation, using the Venn diagram drawn below.

   b) How many athletes did not enter any of the three events.

   c) What is the probability of an athlete selected at random running in 2 or more events.

   d) What percentage of athletes competing run the 1500m.

Venn Diagram

a)

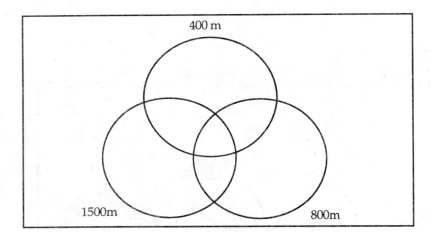

b) _____

_____

c) _____

_____

d) _____

_____

Problems

18. Of the 16 teachers in a particular High School who teach Calculus, Statistics and Physics, or some combination of these, 9 teach Calculus, 5 teach Statistics, 2 teach Calculus and Statistics, 6 teach Physics, 1 teaches Statistics and Physics, 2 teach Calculus and Physics and 1 teaches all three subjects.

   a) Represent the above situation, using the Venn diagram drawn below.

   b) What is the probability of a teacher selected at random teaching Calculus or Statistics, but not Physics.

   c) What is the probability of a teacher selected at random teaching more than one subject.

   d) What percentage of teachers teach only one subject.

   e) What is the probability that a teacher teaches another subject given that they teach Calculus.

Venn Diagram

a)

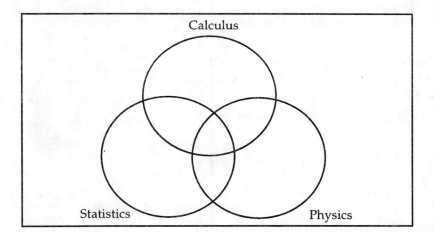

b) _____

_____

c) _____

_____

d) _____

_____

e) _____

_____

3.5 Discrete Random Variables

Prescription

Calculate and interpret expected values for practical situations
- discrete random variables
- probability distribution for a discrete random variable
- mean and variance of a random variable, including the derivation of the identity
  $E(X - \mu)^2 = E(X^2) - \mu^2$
- mean and variance of a linear function of a random variable
- mean and variance of the sum of independent random variables

Discrete Random Variables

A **Random Variable** is essentially one that cannot be predicted in advance, but relies upon information obtained by conducting an experiment.

There are two basic types of random variables - those which are discrete and those which are continuous. We are concerned in this section with discrete random variables.

Discrete random variables occur most commonly in *counting* situations and are characterised by having a finite sample space, eg. the number of cars past a certain point, the number of motorists killed on the road, etc.

We use uppercase letters to characterise a random variable, eg. 'X', and lowercase letters to represent the values they take on, eg. 'x'

We can represent a random variable by a formula or a table.

eg $P(X = x) = \dfrac{(x - 1)^2}{14}, \quad x = 2, 3, 4$

$= 0 \quad \text{otherwise}$

OR

x	2	3	4
P(X = x)	$\dfrac{1}{14}$	$\dfrac{4}{14}$	$\dfrac{9}{14}$

Note: By substituting 2, 3, and 4 into the formula, in the example above, we would get the same probabilities that are displayed in the table.

X is called the random variable and the set of probability values is called the probability distribution or probability function of X.

The probability values in a random variable table always add to give 1.

Expectation (Mean) of a Random Variable

Mathematical expectation or expected value is the term we use to denote an **average over a long run**. (ie. what you would expect to get if an experiment was conducted a large number of times).

For example consider, when a die is tossed a person receives the amount in dollars corresponding to the value on the die. What is a person's **expectation**?

After throwing the die 6 times you would expect

$$E(X) = 1 \times \frac{1}{6} + 2 \times \frac{1}{6} + 3 \times \frac{1}{6} + 4 \times \frac{1}{6} + 5 \times \frac{1}{6} + 6 \times \frac{1}{6}$$

$$= 3.5$$

Expectation $= \$3.50$

It is not possible to get 3.5 on a die but our expectation when we toss a die a large number of times is that it will average out to be 3.5. This expected value is an **estimate** only.

To calculate expectation we use the formula

$$E(X) = x_1 \cdot p(x_1) + x_2 \cdot p(x_2) + \ldots + x_n \cdot p(x_n)$$

$$= \sum_{i=1}^{n} x_i \cdot p(x_i)$$

which means we multiply each value of X by its probability and sum them.

Expectation can also be thought of as the mean of a population and hence we can write

$$\mu = E(X)$$

Example 10

Given in the table below is the probability distribution of X. Find E(X).

x	3	4	5	6
P(X = x)	0.2	0.4	0.3	0.1

Note - the probabilities add to 1

Solution

$$E(X) = 3(0.2) + 4(0.4) + 5(0.3) + 6(0.1)$$

$$= 4.3$$

using the formula $E(X) = \sum_{i=1}^{n} x_i \cdot p(x_i)$

Example 11

An urn has 8 balls in it, 4 are red, 3 white and 1 is black. A game is played whereby a person pays $2 and removes a ball from the urn. If it is red they receive $4. If it is white they lose their $2. If it is black they receive $5. What is a player's expected gain?

x	$-$2	$2	$3	These figures represent the amount won or lost, since each ball drawn costs $2
P(X = x)	$\frac{3}{8}$	$\frac{1}{2}$	$\frac{1}{8}$	These figures are the probability of obtaining the respective coloured ball (white, red, black)

Solution

$$E(X) = {}^-\$2(\tfrac{3}{8}) + \$2(\tfrac{1}{2}) + \$3(\tfrac{1}{8})$$
$$= .625$$
$$= \text{a gain of between 62 and 63 cents}$$

using the formula $E(X) = \sum\limits_{i=1}^{n} x_i \cdot p(x_i)$

Problems

19. a) Given in the table below is the probability distribution of X. Find E(X).

x	2	5	7	8
P(X=x)	0.21	0.34	0.17	0.28

b) Given in the table below is the probability distribution of X. Find E(X).

x	0	1	2	3
P(X=x)	$\frac{2}{11}$	$\frac{3}{11}$	$\frac{5}{11}$	$\frac{1}{11}$

a)

_____

_____

_____

_____

_____

_____

_____

b)

_____

_____

_____

_____

_____

_____

_____

20. The random variable X has a probability distribution defined by

$$P(X = x) = \frac{x^2 + 2x}{50}, \quad x = 1, 2, 3, 4$$

$$= 0, \text{ otherwise}$$

a) Find E(X)

b) Find P(X > 2)

a)

b)

21. Given in the table below is the probability distribution of X.

X	2	3	4	5	6	7
P(X = x)	$2k^2$	$4k^2$	k^2	$2k^2$	$3k^2$	k^2

a) Find the value of k

b) Find E(X)

c) Calculate P(X ≤ 3)

a)

b)

c)

22. A game is played whereby two dice are tossed. If the sum of the two dice is 12 the player wins $1, for a sum of 10 or 11 the player wins 50 cents, and for a sum of 7 the player wins 10 cents. The cost of each round is 5 cents. Give the probability distribution in table form and calculate the player's expected gain / loss.

23. You have in your pocket three $1 coins, two $2 coins and two 50 cent coins. You put your hand in your pocket and take out two coins at random. Complete the probability distribution table below and calculate the expected amount that you will take out of your pocket.

X	$1	$1.50	$2	$2.50	$3	$4
P(X = x)						

24. 90% of mail sent by fast post arrives the day after being posted, the other 10% takes one day longer. 15% of mail sent by standard post arrives the day after being posted, the rest one day longer. If 40% of mail goes by fast post, what is the expected delivery time for a letter.

Variance of a Random Variable

The Expectation or Mean of a random variable gives us information about what we can expect to happen over the long term, when an experiment is repeated over and over.

To complete the picture we need an indicator of the spread of results each time we conduct the experiment.

We know from Chapter 1 on Statistics that our best measure of spread is either the standard deviation or the variance. You should remember that the standard deviation is the square root of the variance.

If X is a random variable then we define the variance of X, written VAR(X) as

$$\text{VAR}(X) = E[(X - \mu)^2] \qquad (1)$$

$$= \sum (x_i - \mu)^2 \cdot p(x_i)$$

Effectively the variance is the average of the squared distances from the mean. The variance can also be written as

$$\text{VAR}(X) = E(X^2) - [E(X)]^2 \qquad (2)$$

In Bursary you are expected to be able to derive the following identity

$$\begin{aligned}
\text{VAR}(X) &= E[(X - \mu)^2] & (1) \\
&= E[X^2 - 2\mu X + \mu^2] \\
&= E(X^2) - E(2\mu X) + E(\mu^2) \\
&= E(X^2) - 2\mu E(X) + E(\mu^2) \\
&= E(X^2) - 2\mu\mu + \mu^2 \\
&= E(X^2) - 2\mu^2 + \mu^2 \\
&= E(X^2) - \mu^2 \\
&= E(X^2) - [E(X)]^2 & (2)
\end{aligned}$$

Of the two formulae for the VAR(X), it is easier to calculate the variance using formula (2), for you do not need to separately subtract the mean for each value of X. (see Example 12 on the next page)

When dealing with random variables and probability distributions we quite often use the notation E(X), VAR(X), SD(X) in preference to μ, σ^2 and σ.

This formula is in your tables. Make sure you can locate it when needed.

The expected value of a constant is the constant. ie. $E(\mu^2) = \mu^2$

If $\mu = E(X)$ then $\mu^2 = (E(X))^2$.

Example 12

Given in the table below is the probability distribution of X. Find the variance and standard deviation of the distribution.

x	1	2	3	4
P(X = x)	0.3	0.1	0.4	0.2

Note - the probabilities add to 1

Solution

$$E(X) = \sum_{i=1}^{n} x_i \cdot p(x_i)$$
$$= 1(0.3) + 2(0.1) + 3(0.4) + 4(0.2)$$
$$= 2.5$$

$$VAR(X) = E[(X - \mu)^2]$$
$$= E[(X - 2.5)^2]$$
$$= (1 - 2.5)^2 \times 0.3 + (2 - 2.5)^2 \times 0.1 + (3 - 2.5)^2 \times 0.4 + (4 - 2.5)^2 \times 0.2$$
$$= 2.25 \times 0.3 + 0.25 \times 0.1 + 0.25 \times 0.4 + 2.25 \times 0.2$$
$$= 1.25$$

or

$$VAR(X) = E(X^2) - \mu^2$$
$$= [1^2 \times 0.3 + 2^2 \times 0.1 + 3^2 \times 0.4 + 4^2 \times 0.2] - 2.5^2$$
$$= 7.5 - 6.25$$
$$= 1.25$$

The standard deviation is the square root of the variance

$$SD(X) = \sqrt{1.25}$$
$$= 1.118 \ (4sf)$$

Problems

25. a) Given in the table below is the probability distribution of X. Find VAR(X) and SD(X).

x	2	5	7	8
P(X=x)	0.21	0.34	0.17	0.28

b) Given in the table below is the probability distribution of X. Find VAR(X) and SD(X).

x	0	1	2	3
P(X=x)	$\frac{2}{11}$	$\frac{3}{11}$	$\frac{5}{11}$	$\frac{1}{11}$

a) _____

_____

_____

_____

b) _____

_____

_____

_____

26. The random variable X has a probability distribution defined by

$$P(X = x) = \frac{x+3}{30}, \quad x = 3, 4, 5, 6$$

$$= 0, \text{ otherwise}$$

a) Find E(X)

b) Find VAR(X)

c) Find SD(X)

d) Find P(X > 3)

a) _____

_____

c) _____

_____

_____

b) _____

_____

d) _____

_____

_____

27. A game is played whereby two dice are tossed. If the dice have the same number uppermost the player receives $10. If the numbers on the two dice total 3 the player receives $5. The cost of playing each round is $2.

a) Give the probability distribution in table form and calculate the player's expected gain / loss.

b) Calculate the variance of the distribution.

c) What should the cost of each round be, if the game is to be fair.

a) _____

_____

_____

_____

b) _____

_____

_____

_____

c) _____

_____

_____

_____

28. A woman has four keys on her key ring and only one fits her front door, but she does not know which one. Taking note of each key she tries, she tries until the door is open.

a) Draw up the probability distribution for the number of tries to open the door.

b) Calculate the woman's expected number of tries and the variance of the distribution.

a) _____

_____

_____

_____

_____

b) _____

_____

_____

_____

_____

29. At a certain intersection in town the probability of 0, 1, 2, or 3 accidents occurring during a week are 0.45, 0.27, 0.19 and 0.09.

a) Draw up the probability distribution for the number of accidents in a week.

b) Calculate the expected number of accidents in a week.

c) Calculate the variance and standard deviation for the number of accidents in a week.

a) _____

_____

_____

b) _____

_____

_____

c) _____

_____

_____

30. A gambler pays $50 to draw a card from a pack of 52. If he draws a diamond he receives $150. If he draws a king he receives $200. If he draws the king of diamonds he receives $1000.

a) Calculate the gambler's expected gain.

b) What is the standard deviation of the gambler's gain.

a) _____

_____

_____

_____

_____

b) _____

_____

_____

_____

_____

Mean of a Linear Function of a Random Variable

Sometimes the random variables we are dealing with may not be simply X, but a linear function instead, like 2X + 3.

Consider the numbers 1, 2, 3, 4, 5. The mean of these numbers is $\frac{15}{5} = 3$. If we now take these numbers and multiply them by 2 and add 3, we obtain the new values 5, 7, 9, 11, 13. Calculating the mean for these values we obtain $\frac{45}{5} = 9$. However taking the original mean and multiplying it by 2 and adding 3 would have achieved the same result.

Therefore consider the general linear function f(x) = aX + b, where 'a' and 'b' are constants. We can define

$$E[f(x)] = E[aX + b]$$

$$= aE(X) + b$$

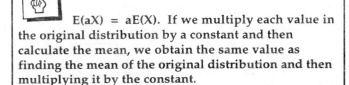

E(aX) = aE(X). If we multiply each value in the original distribution by a constant and then calculate the mean, we obtain the same value as finding the mean of the original distribution and then multiplying it by the constant.

E(b) = b. The mean of a constant term is the term itself, ie. the mean of 3 is 3.

Variance of a Linear Function of a Random Variable

Just as E(aX + b) = aE(X) + b for the mean, we have an equivalent result for the variance.

If we again consider the numbers 1, 2, 3, 4, 5 the variance of these numbers is 2. If we now take these numbers and multiply them by 2 and add 3, we obtain the new values 5, 7, 9, 11, 13. Calculating the variance for these values we obtain 8.

Consider the general linear function f(x) = aX + b, where 'a' and 'b' are constants. We define

$$VAR[f(x)] = VAR[aX + b]$$

$$= a^2 VAR(X)$$

VAR(aX) = a^2VAR(X). If we multiply each value in the original distribution by a constant and calculate the variance, we obtain the same value as finding the variance of the original distribution and multiplying it by the constant squared.

Variance of a Linear Function of a Random Variable cont...

This proof is implied by the syllabus

$$VAR(X) = E(X^2) - [E(X)]^2$$

$$VAR(aX + b) = E[(aX + b)^2] - E[(aX + b)]^2$$

$$= E(a^2X^2 + 2abX + b^2) - [aE(X) + b]^2$$

$$= E(a^2X^2) + 2abE(X) + E(b^2)$$
$$- a^2[E(X)]^2 - 2abE(X) - b^2$$

$$= a^2E(X^2) + 2abE(X) + b^2$$
$$- a^2\mu^2 - 2ab\mu - b^2$$

$$= a^2E(X^2) + 2ab\mu + b^2 - a^2\mu^2 - 2ab\mu - b^2$$

$$= a^2E(X^2) - a^2\mu^2$$

$$= a^2[E(X^2) - \mu^2]$$

$$= a^2\,VAR(X)$$

Carefully read the following points and accent mark new points.

- **SD(aX) = aSD(X).** If we multiply each value in the original distribution by a constant and calculate the standard deviation, we obtain the same value as finding the standard deviation of the original distribution and multiplying it by the constant.

- **VAR(b) = 0.** The variance of a constant term is 0. **SD(b) = 0.** The standard deviation of a constant is 0.

- We affect the variance and standard deviation of a distribution by multiplying or dividing by a constant value.

- We **CANNOT** affect the variance or standard deviation of a distribution by adding or subtracting a constant value.

Example 13

Given in the table below is the probability distribution for X.

x	1	2	3	4
P(X = x)	0.2	0.4	0.3	0.1

a) Calculate E(X)

b) Draw up a table that represents the probability distribution for 3X + 1

c) Calculate E(3X + 1)

d) Calculate VAR(X)

e) Calculate SD(X)

f) Calculate VAR(3X + 1)

g) Calculate SD(3X + 1)

Solution

a) $E(X) = \sum_{i=1}^{n} x_i \cdot p(x_i)$

$= 1(0.2) + 2(0.4) + 3(0.3) + 4(0.1)$

$= 2.3$

b) Letting Y = 3X + 1

y	4	7	10	13
P(Y = y)	0.2	0.4	0.3	0.1

c) $E(3X + 1) = 4(0.2) + 7(0.4) + 10(0.3) + 13(0.1)$

$= 7.9$

Note $7.9 = 3 \times 2.3 + 1$

$= 3E(X) + 1$

d) $VAR(X) = E(X^2) - \mu^2$

$= [\, 1^2 \times 0.2 + 2^2 \times 0.4 + 3^2 \times 0.3$
$+ 4^2 \times 0.1 \,] - 2.3^2$

$= 6.1 - 2.3^2$

$= 0.81$

e) $SD(X) = \sqrt{.81}$

$= 0.9$

f) $VAR(3X + 1) = [\, 4^2 \times 0.2 + 7^2 \times 0.4$
$+ 10^2 \times 0.3 + 13^2 \times 0.1 \,] - 7.9^2$

$= 7.29$

Note $3^2 \times 0.81 = 7.29$

$\therefore 9VAR(X) = VAR(3X + 1)$

g) $SD(3X + 1) = \sqrt{7.29}$

$= 2.7$

Note $3 \times 0.9 = 2.7$

$\therefore 3SD(X) = SD(3X + 1)$

Problems

31. If the random variable Y has a mean of 18 and standard deviation of 4. Find the mean and standard deviation of the random variables.

a) $Y + 4$ b) $Y - 2$

c) $5 - Y$ d) $3Y$

e) $4Y + 2$ f) $-2Y - 1$

a) _____

    _____

c) _____

e) _____

b) _____

d) _____

f) _____

32. Given in the table below is the probability distribution for W.

w	1	3	5	7
$P(W = w)$	$\frac{3}{7}$	$\frac{1}{7}$	$\frac{2}{7}$	$\frac{1}{7}$

Find

a) $E(W)$ b) $E(W^2)$

c) $VAR(W)$ d) $E(3W - 1)$

e) $E[(3W - 1)^2]$ f) $VAR(3W - 1)$

a) _____

c) _____

e) _____

b) _____

d) _____

f) _____

33.   A coin is tossed three times. Let X be the random variable representing the number of heads in three tosses.

a)   Complete the table below for the probability distribution of X.

x	0	1	2	3
P(X = x)				

b)   Find $P(X < 2)$.

c)   What is the expected number of heads from three tosses of a coin.

d)   Find the variance and standard deviation of the probability distribution X.

a) _____

_____

_____

b) _____

_____

_____

c) _____

_____

_____

d) _____

_____

_____

34.   10 cards with the numbers 0 through to 9 are placed in a hat. Let N represent the variable 'randomly chosen number'.

a)   Draw up a table to represent the probability distribution for N.

b)   Calculate the mean, variance and standard deviation of N.

c)   Find $P(N^2 < 25)$.

a) _____

_____

_____

b) _____

_____

_____

c) _____

_____

_____

_____

Mean and Variance of the Sum of Independent Random Variables

If A and B are two independent random variables and we define a third random variable as C = A + B.

Then we use the following results to calculate the mean and variance of the sum of these independent random variables.

$$E(C) = E(A) + E(B) \qquad (1)$$

$$VAR(C) = VAR(A) + VAR(B) \qquad (2)$$

If we define a random variable as C = A − B then we use the following results.

$$E(C) = E(A) − E(B) \qquad (3)$$

$$VAR(C) = VAR(A) + VAR(B) \qquad (4)$$

This proof is implied by the syllabus.

$$VAR(A − B) = VAR(A + -B)$$
$$= VAR(A) + VAR(-B)$$
$$= VAR(A) + (-1)^2 VAR(B)$$
$$= VAR(A) + VAR(B)$$

If we now define X and Y as independent random variables and let Z = aX + bY then we obtain the following results.

$$E(Z) = E(aX) + E(bY)$$
$$= aE(X) + bE(Y) \qquad (5)$$

$$VAR(Z) = VAR(aX) + VAR(bY)$$
$$= a^2 VAR(X) + b^2 VAR(Y) \qquad (6)$$

When we sum independent random variables we sum the means and the variances. When we subtract independent random variables we subtract the means but <u>add</u> the variances.

When we are asked to calculate the standard deviation of the sum of two independent random variables, find the sum of their variances first, then square root to find the standard deviation.

VAR(A + B) = VAR(A) + VAR(B)

Example 14

Four members of a 4 x 400m relay team have the following statistics for their individual lap times.

Albert   mean = 52 secs   std dev. = 2 secs

Brian   mean = 53 secs   std dev. = 1.5 secs

Cliff   mean = 53 secs   std dev. = 3 secs

Doug   mean = 51 secs   std dev. = 0.5 secs

Assuming each lap is independent of the previous.

Find the mean and standard deviation of the time taken for the members to complete the 4 x 400m relay.

Solution

Let A be the random variable representing 1 lap run by Albert

Let B be the random variable representing 1 lap run by Brian

Let C be the random variable representing 1 lap run by Cliff

Let D be the random variable representing 1 lap run by Doug

Let Z = A + B + C + D, the time to complete the 4 x 400m relay.

$$E(Z) = E(A) + E(B) + E(C) + E(D)$$

$$= 52 + 53 + 53 + 51$$

$$= 209 \text{ secs}$$

$$VAR(Z) = VAR(A) + VAR(B) + VAR(C) + VAR(D)$$

$$= 2^2 + 1.5^2 + 3^2 + 0.5^2$$

$$= 4 + 2.25 + 9 + 0.25$$

$$= 15.5 \text{ secs}$$

$$SD(Z) = \sqrt{15.5}$$

$$= 3.937 \text{ secs (4 sf)}$$

Example 15

A students final Calculus mark for the year, is obtained by adding their mid-year and end-of-year exam results together in the weighting 2 : 3. The mean of the mid-year exam was 46 with standard deviation 13. The mean of the end-of-year exam was 51 with standard deviation 9.

Assuming the exams are independent of one another find the mean and standard deviation of the students final Calculus mark.

Solution

Let M be the random variable representing the mid-year exam.

Let F be the random variable representing the end-of-year exam.

The students final mark is represented by the random variable $T = 2M + 3F$

$$E(T) = E(2M) + E(3F)$$
$$= 2E(M) + 3E(F)$$
$$= 2(46) + 3(51)$$
$$= 92 + 153$$
$$= 245$$

OR $= (49\%$ assuming percentages$)$

$$VAR(T) = VAR(2M) + VAR(3F)$$
$$= 2^2 VAR(M) + 3^2 VAR(F)$$
$$= 4 VAR(M) + 9 VAR(F)$$
$$= 4(169) + 9(81)$$
$$= 1405$$

$$SD(T) = \sqrt{1405}$$
$$= 37.48 \ (4sf)$$

OR $= (7.50\%$ assuming percentages$)$

Problems

35.   Complete the table for the random variables A and B. Assume they are independent.

	E(A)	E(B)	E(A+B)	VAR(A)	VAR(B)	VAR(A + B)	SD(A + B)
a)	9	5		2	1		
b)	4.7	8.9		3.6	2.5		
c)	53	49		16	12		

36. A manufacturing process produces cylindrical rods (R) with a mean diameter of 5.01 mm and a standard deviation of 0.03 mm, and round sockets (S) (which the rods go into) with a mean diameter of 5.11 mm and standard deviation 0.04 mm. Assume the two processes are independent. Z represents the total gap between the socket and the inserted rod.

   a) Obtain an equation linking Z, S and R.

   b) Use this to find the mean and standard deviation of Z.

a)

b)

37. A recycling firm sells second hand boilers to a scrap metal dealer. For each boiler the recycling firm sells, it gets $15 per kg for the scrap metal and $35 per kg for the copper components. The quantity of scrap metal and copper components that are recovered from a boiler have a standard deviation of 4 kg and 10 kg respectively. Let M be the random variable for the content of scrap metal and C be the random variable for the content of copper.

   a) Using T (for the total received for each boiler) formulate an equation linking the scrap metal and the copper components.

   b) What is the standard deviation of the amount received for each second hand boiler.

a)

b)

38. A manufacturing procedure is made up of two separate processes. The time to complete process A has mean of 30 secs and standard deviation of 3 secs. The time to complete process B has mean of 25 secs and standard deviation of 6 secs. To produce a required component (P) the manufacturer must undertake process A twice and process B three times. Assume process A is independent of process B.

    a) Formulate an equation linking A, B and P.

    b) Find the mean and standard deviation of P.

a)

b)

39. Two independent random variables are represented in the tables below, with associated probabilities.

x	1	2	3
P(X = x)	0.3	0.5	0.2

y	4	5	6
P(Y = y)	0.6	0.1	0.3

    a) Find $E(X + Y)$ b) Find $VAR(X + Y)$

    c) Find $E(X - Y)$ d) Find $VAR(X - Y)$

    e) Find $SD(X + Y)$ f) Find $SD(X - Y)$

a)

b)

c)

d)

e)

f)

3.6 The Binomial Distribution

Introduction

Up to this point we have solved all probability problems by first principles. We now attempt, if possible, to classify our probability problems into one of three types, Binomial, Normal or Poisson and then use an appropriate formula or tables to solve. The first distribution that we look at is the Binomial distribution.

Prescription

Choose the appropriate distribution to model a given situation, calculate probabilities and expected values, and make predictions using the model
- **binomial distribution**

The Binomial Distribution

In order to use the Binomial distribution to solve a probability problem it must meet the following conditions.

- the number of trials must be fixed.

- each trial must result in either success or failure.

- each trial must be independent of the other.

- he probability of success at each trial must be the same.

We use the parameters **n, x** and **π**, when dealing with the Binomial distribution.

- 'n' represents the number of trials conducted.

- 'x' represents the total number of successes in 'n' trials.

- 'π' is the probability of success for each trial.

- **(1 − π)** represents the probability of failure.

If all conditions are met then the Binomial distribution can be used to model the situation. We define the Binomial random variable X by the formula

$$P(X = x) = \binom{n}{x} \pi^x (1 - \pi)^{n-x}, 0 \le x \le n, x \in W$$

Rather than having to substitute appropriate values into the formula we can use the tables of the Binomial distribution.

They are restricted however to values of 'n' between 4 and 10 inclusive and selected 'π' values from 0.05 to 0.5.

Locate the Binomial distribution tables now, and make yourself familiar with them.

A trial is where there are two possible outcomes eg. the toss of a coin.

This formula is located in your tables

Example 16

A duck shooter has a probability of 0.4 of hitting any duck that he shoots at during a morning. In a morning where he fires 10 shots find the probability that he

a)   shoots exactly 10 ducks.

b)   shoots exactly 6 ducks.

c)   shoots more ducks than he misses.

Solution

We can use the Binomial distribution to solve this probability problem, because there are 'n' (10) shots. Each shot is independent of the other. The probability of hitting a duck, 'π', remains constant (0.4) and each shot results in a hit or a miss.

a)   Using $P(X = x) = \binom{n}{x} \pi^x (1 - \pi)^{n-x}$ or   Using tables with n = 10, x = 10 and π = 0.4

Substituting $P(X = 10) = \binom{10}{10} 0.4^{10} (0.6)^0$ $\therefore P(X = 10) = 0.0001$

$= 1 \times 0.0001 \times 1$

$= 0.0001 \ (4dp)$

b)   Using $P(X = x) = \binom{n}{x} \pi^x (1 - \pi)^{n-x}$ or   Using tables with n = 10, x = 6 and π = 0.4

Substituting $P(X = 6) = \binom{10}{6} 0.4^6 (0.6)^4$ $\therefore P(X = 10) = 0.1115$

$= 210 \times 0.004096 \times 0.1296$

$= 0.1115 \ (4dp)$

c)   To shoot more than he misses, we find the $P(X > 5)$

Using tables

$P(X > 5) = P(X = 6) + P(X = 7) + P(X = 8) + P(X = 9) + P(X = 10)$

$= 0.1115 + 0.0425 + 0.0106 + 0.0016 + 0.0001$

$= 0.1663$

When given a problem involving the Binomial distribution, where $\pi > 0.5$ and you wish to use the tables it is necessary to look at the problem in terms of 'failures' rather than 'successes'.

(see Example 17 below)

Example 17

In an examination where 75% of students are known to pass, 10 students scripts are selected at random and marked. Find the probability that

a)   only 3 pass.

b)   no more than 6 pass.

Solution

In this problem $\pi = 0.75$, and $n = 10$.

a)   Using $P(X = x) = \binom{n}{x} \pi^x (1 - \pi)^{n-x}$ or   Using tables, but rewriting the problem

  Substituting $P(X = 3) = \binom{10}{3} 0.75^3 (0.25)^7$ in terms of 'failure', since $\pi > 0.5$.

$= 120 \times 0.421875 \times 0.00006$ Therefore $n = 10$, $\pi = 0.25$ and $x = 7$ should

$= 0.0031$ (4dp)   give us the same result.

$\therefore P(X = 3) = 0.0031$

b)   No more than 6 passes implies $P(X \leq 6)$

  Using tables however and writing the problem in terms of 'failure' with, $n = 10$, $\pi = 0.25$ and $P(X \geq 4)$ should give us the same result.

$P(X \geq 4) = P(X = 4) + P(X = 5) + P(X = 6) + P(X = 7) + P(X = 8) + P(X = 9) + P(X = 10)$

$= 0.1460 + 0.0584 + 0.0162 + 0.0031 + 0.0004 + 0 + 0$

$= 0.2241$

Problems

40.   A test conducted at a garage shows 30% of all cars have some form of oil leak. If 8 cars are selected at random. Find the probability that

a)   none of the cars have an oil leak.

b)   exactly 4 cars have an oil leak.

c)   no more than 3 cars have an oil leak.

d)   at least 6 cars have an oil leak.

a) $n = 8, \pi = 0.3$ b) $n = 8, \pi = 0.3$

             $P(X = 0) =$ $P(X = 4) =$

c) $n = 8, \pi = 0.3$ d) $n = 8, \pi = 0.3$

             $P(X \leq 3) =$ $P(X \geq 6) =$

41.   15% of all computer chips manufactured are faulty. If a consignment of 5 computer chips are selected at random. Find the probability that

a)   all of the chips are faulty.

b)   none of the chips are faulty.

c)   more than 3 chips are faulty.

d)   less than 2 chips are faulty.

a)   b)

c)   d)

Problems continued

42. In a school it is noted that 32% of all the students are left handed. In a class of 8 students what is the probability that
(use the formula directly for this problem since 'π' is not in the tables).

   a) exactly 5 of them are left handed.

   b) more than half the students are left handed.

   c) only one student is left handed.

   d) no more than 4 students are left handed.

a)

b)

c)

d)

43. 85% of all tulip bulbs germinate and produce flowers. A customer buys 12 tulip bulbs from her local garden centre. Find the probability that
(use the formula directly for this problem since 'n' is greater than 10).

   a) all of the bulbs germinate and produce flowers.

   b) only half the bulbs germinate and produce flowers.

   c) more than 10 bulbs germinate and produce flowers.

   d) 25% of the bulbs fail to germinate and produce flowers.

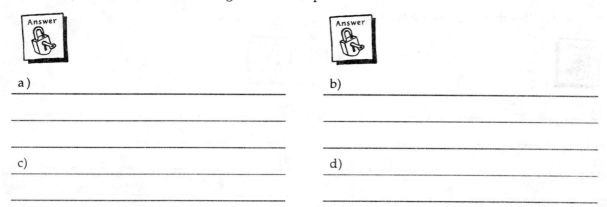

a)

b)

c)

d)

Problems continued

44. A mail order company knows that 80% of all customers use a credit card to purchase their goods. Out of the next 9 customers find the probability that

(Use tables with $\pi = 0.2$ and look at the problem in terms of 'failures')

a) exactly 6 of them use their credit card.

b) less than 5 use their credit card.

c) between 3 and 7 inclusive use their credit card.

d) all of them use their credit card.

a)

_____

_____

c)

_____

_____

b)

_____

_____

d)

_____

_____

45. 55% of all screws manufactured are rejected because they do not satisfy pre-defined tolerances. In a batch of 10 screws find the probability that

(Use tables with $\pi = 0.45$ and look at the problem in terms of 'failures')

a) exactly 2 screws are rejected.

b) less than half the screws are rejected.

c) none of the screws are rejected.

d) 80% of them are rejected.

a)

_____

_____

c)

_____

_____

b)

_____

_____

d)

_____

_____

3.7 The Poisson Distribution

Prescription

Choose the appropriate distribution to model a given situation, calculate probabilities and expected values, and make predictions using the model
- Poisson distribution

The Poisson Distribution

The Poisson distribution deals with discrete events or happenings which occur over a finite but continuous time interval, eg. breakdowns in an electric power supply over a one week period.

The Poisson distribution is sometimes referred to as the distribution of rare events.

Just like the Binomial distribution, if we wish to use the Poisson distribution to solve a probability problem certain conditions need to be met

- events or happenings must occur at random.

- each event or happening must be independent of any others.

- the probability of events occurring simultaneously should be negligible.

- the smaller the time interval the smaller the probability of the event occurring and conversely the larger the time interval the greater the probability of the event occurring.

We use the parameters x and λ, when dealing with the Poisson distribution.

- 'x' represents the total number of successes or occurrences of the event.

- 'λ' is the mean number of occurrences of the event over the given time interval.

If all conditions are met then the Poisson distribution can be used to model the situation. We define the Poisson random variable X by the formula

$$P(X = x) = \frac{e^{-\lambda} \lambda^x}{x!}, \text{ where } x = 0, 1, 2, \dots$$

Rather than having to substitute appropriate values into the formula we can use the tables of the Poisson distribution.

Locate the Poisson distribution tables now, and make yourself familiar with them and the formula.

© Robert Lakeland & Carl Nugent

Example 18

A local newspaper has an average of three misprints per page. Find the probability that

a)   there are no misprints on a single sporting page.

b)   there are exactly 6 misprints on the business page.

c)   there are more than 3 misprints on an entertainment page.

Solution

In this problem $\lambda = 3$

<u>Using the formula</u>

a) Using $P(X = x) = \dfrac{e^{-\lambda} \lambda^x}{x!}$

Sub $P(X = 0) = \dfrac{e^{-3} 3^0}{0!}$

$= 0.0498 \ (4dp)$

b) $P(X = 6) = \dfrac{e^{-3} 3^6}{6!}$

$= \dfrac{0.0498 \times 729}{720}$

$= 0.0504 \ (4dp)$

c) $P(X > 3) = 1 - P(X \le 3)$

$= 1 - P(X = 0) + P(X = 1) +$
$\quad P(X = 2) + P(X = 3)$

$= 1 - \dfrac{e^{-3} 3^0}{0!} + \dfrac{e^{-3} 3^1}{1!} + \dfrac{e^{-3} 3^2}{2!}$
$\quad + \dfrac{e^{-3} 3^3}{3!}$

$= 1 - 0.0498 + 0.1494 +$
$\quad 0.2240 + 0.2240$

$= 1 - 0.6472$

$= 0.3528 \ (4dp)$

<u>Using the Poisson distribution tables</u>

Using tables with $\lambda = 3$, $x = 0$

$\therefore P(X = 0) = 0.0498$

Using tables with $\lambda = 3$, $x = 6$

$\therefore P(X = 6) = 0.0504$

$P(X > 3) = 0.1680 + 0.1008 + 0.0504 + 0.0216 + 0.0081$
$\qquad\qquad + 0.0027 + 0.0008 + 0.0002 + 0.0001$

$= 0.3527$

or

$P(X > 3) = 1 - P(X \le 3)$

$= 1 - 0.0498 + 0.1494 + 0.2240 + 0.2240$

$= 0.3528$

When given a problem involving the Poisson distribution, where λ is not in the tables, it is necessary to use the formula. (see Example 19 below)

Example 19

At a busy intersection in a city centre there are, on average, 12 accidents per week. Find the probability that

a)   there are no accidents on a day chosen at random.

b)   at least two accidents occur on a day chosen at random

Solution

In this problem, although the initial time period stated is a week, the questions ask us to work out the probability per day.

Therefore we calculate $\lambda = 12/7 = 1.714$

a)   Using $P(X = x) = \dfrac{e^{-\lambda} \lambda^{x}}{x!}$

Sub $P(X = 0) = \dfrac{e^{-1.714} \, 1.714^{0}}{0!}$

$= 0.1801$ (4dp)

b)   At least two accidents implies 2 or more ie. $P(X \geq 2)$

$\therefore P(X \geq 2) = 1 - P(X < 2)$

$= 1 - P(X = 0) + P(X = 1)$

$= 1 - \dfrac{e^{-1.714} \, 1.714^{0}}{0!} + \dfrac{e^{-1.714} \, 1.714^{1}}{1!}$

$= 1 - 0.1801 + 0.3088$

$= 1 - 0.4889$

$= 0.5111$ (4dp)

Problems

46. The number of people using a particular telephone box in a suburb of a town is, on average, 4 per hour. What is the probability in a randomly chosen hour that

    a) no one uses the phone.

    b) exactly 2 people use the phone.

    c) more than 3 people use the phone.

    d) between 4 and 6 people, use the phone, inclusive.

a) $\lambda = 4$

   $P(X = 0) =$

b) $\lambda = 4$

   $P(X = 2) =$

c) $\lambda = 4$

   $P(X > 3) = 1 - P(X \leq 3)$

d) $\lambda = 4$

   $P(4 \leq X \leq 6) = P(X = 4) + P(X = 5) + P(X = 6)$

47. In a consignment of farm eggs that a supermarket receives each day there are, on average, 8 broken eggs. Find the probability that on a randomly chosen day there are

    a) 2 broken eggs only.

    b) more than 3 broken eggs.

    c) between 4 and 7 broken eggs, inclusive.

    d) no less than 6 broken eggs.

a)

b)

c)

d)

Problems continued

48.   Outside a school 408 cars go past the gate in a two hour period. Find the probability that in a randomly chosen minute

   a)   no cars go past.

   b)   more than 4 cars go past.

   c)   between 2 and 5 cars go past, inclusive.

a) _____

_____

_____

c) _____

_____

_____

b) _____

_____

49.   The number of electrical faults in a particular factory average 1.2 per day. Find the probability that

   a)   on a randomly chosen day 3 electrical faults occur.

   b)   on a randomly chosen day no electrical faults occur.

   c)   this factory has a single electrical fault on two consecutive days.

a) _____

_____

c) _____

_____

_____

_____

b) _____

_____

Problems continued

50. A shop sells on average 36 bottles of milk an hour. Find the probability that

    a) 3 bottles of milk are sold in a ten minute period.

    b) Find the probability that 4 bottles of milk are sold in 2 consecutive ten minute periods.

a) _____

_____

_____

_____

b) _____

_____

_____

_____

51. Accidents occur on a building site at the rate of 3 every 4 months. Find the probability

    a) that on a randomly chosen month no accident occurs.

    b) that on a randomly chosen month no more than 2 accidents occur.

    c) of having two consecutive months with no accidents.

a) _____   b) _____

_____   _____

c) _____

_____

_____

_____

_____

3.8 The Normal Distribution

Prescription

Choose the appropriate distribution to model a given situation, calculate probabilities and expected values, and make predictions using the model

- **normal distribution**

The Normal Distribution

The Normal distribution is undoubtedly the most important distribution in Statistics. The basis of the Normal distribution is the normal curve which is the familiar bell shaped curve that appears in statistical analysis, nature, industry and business. (see figure below)

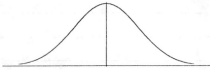

Unlike the Binomial or Poisson distributions, which are discrete distributions, the Normal distribution is a continuous distribution.

Instead of relating probability to a specific value as we do in a discrete distribution we now have to relate probability to an interval and find the probability by evaluating the area under the normal curve between the interval.

The normal or bell shaped curve has the formula

$$f(x) = \frac{1}{\sqrt{2\pi}\sigma} \cdot e^{\frac{-(x-\mu)^2}{2\sigma}}$$

where μ is the mean and σ the standard deviation.

Obviously as μ and σ vary in this formula so would the maximum value and spread along the x-axis, giving us an infinite number of possible normal curves.

To simplify the situation we concentrate on just one normal curve, known as the **standard normal curve**, which has mean zero ($\mu = 0$) and standard deviation one ($\sigma = 1$).

The properties of the standard normal curve are

- it is symmetrical about the y axis (μ=0).
- the area under the curve is one.
- the curve approaches the x-axis asymptotically (ie. never actually touches it).
- the curve theoretically extends to infinity in both directions.
- it has as its highest point $(0, \frac{1}{\sqrt{2\pi}})$

The Normal Distribution cont...

The figure below shows the standard normal curve which has the simplified equation

$$f(x) = \frac{1}{\sqrt{2\pi}} \cdot e^{\frac{-x^2}{2}}, \qquad \text{since } \mu = 0 \text{ and } \sigma = 1.$$

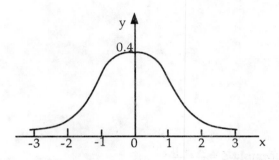

When dealing with problems that are modelled by the normal distribution it is unlikely they will all have a mean of zero and a standard deviation of 1.

Any normal curve that has different parameters is first transformed to a curve with a mean of 0 and standard deviation of 1 by standardising. To standardise we use the formula

$$Z = \frac{X - \mu}{\sigma}$$

By applying this transformation we are able to use the normal distribution tables to calculate the area under the normal curve and hence find the required probability.

Note Well

   Z indicates that we are dealing with the standardised normal curve whereas X indicates the curve is NOT standardised.

Note Well

   Locate the Normal distribution tables now, and make yourself familiar with them.

Example 20

Tests conducted on the manufacture of a new light-weight rope show that the breaking strain can be assumed to be normally distributed with a mean of 240kg and a standard deviation of 42kg. Find the probability that the new rope will break when subjected to a weight of

a)   more than 300 kg.

b)   between 190kg and 270kg.

Solution

To standardise the normal curve we use the formula $Z = \dfrac{X - \mu}{\sigma}$

a)   To find $P(X > 300)$

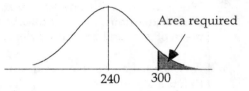

Standardising $= P(Z > \dfrac{300 - 240}{42})$

Simplifying $= P(Z > 1.429)$

Using tables $= 0.5 - 0.4235$

                     $= 0.0765$

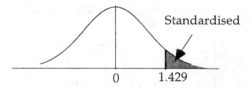

b)   To find $P(190 < X < 270)$

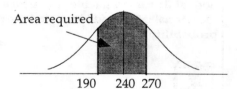

Standardising $= P(\dfrac{190 - 240}{42} < Z < \dfrac{270 - 240}{42})$

Simplifying $= P(-1.190 < Z < 0.7143)$

Using tables $= 0.3830 + 0.2624$

                     $= 0.6454$

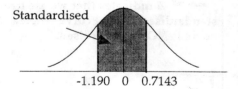

When asked to calculate a probability using the normal distribution begin by drawing a diagram to identify the required area. When you have standardised the curve draw another diagram to help you identify the area you need to calculate from the tables. (see above)

...

Example 21

A company manufacturing light bulbs has found that they have a mean life of 300 hours with a standard deviation of 60 hours. Assuming that the life in hours of light bulbs is normally distributed find the probability that a light bulb selected at random will last

a) less than 310 hours.

b) between 220 hours and 270 hours.

Solution

To standardise the normal curve we use the formula $Z = \dfrac{X - \mu}{\sigma}$

a) To find $P(X < 310)$

Standardising $= P(Z < \dfrac{310 - 300}{60})$

Simplifying $= P(Z < 0.1667)$

Using tables $= 0.5 + 0.0664$

               $= 0.5664$

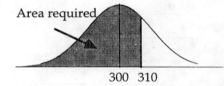

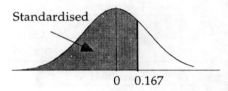

b) To find $P(220 < X < 270)$

Standardising $= P(\dfrac{220 - 300}{60} < Z < \dfrac{270 - 300}{60}$

Simplifying $= P(-1.333 < Z < -0.5)$

Using tables $= 0.4087 - 0.1915$

               $= 0.2172$

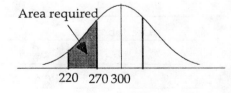

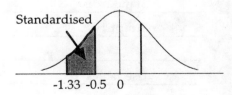

Problems

52. Chippie packets are filled by machine. The weights of the packets are found to be normally distributed with mean 100g and standard deviation 5g. A packet of chippies is randomly selected from the production line.

   a) Find the probability that

   (i)   it weighs more than 108g.

   (ii)   it weighs less than 95g.

   (iii)   it weighs between 98g and 107g.

   b) Packets that weigh less than 95g are rejected. How many packets out of 1000 would be rejected.

a) (i) P(X > 108)	Normal curves
Standardise	
Simplify	
Use tables	
(ii) P(X < 95)	
Standardise	
Simplify	
Use tables	
(iii) P(98 < X < 107)	
Standardise	
Simplify	
Use tables	
b) Multiply your answer in (ii) by 1000	

53. A business woman takes her car to work each morning. The time it takes her to travel to work is normally distributed with mean 28 minutes and standard deviation 3 minutes. The woman leaves for work at 8.00 am each morning.

a) Find the probability that

    (i)   she takes less than 24 minutes to travel to work.

    (ii)   she arrives at work after 8.20 am.

    (ii)   she arrives at work between 8.25 am and 8.30 am.

b) If she starts work at 8.30 am and works, on average, 240 days a year, how many days would you expect her to be late for work in the year.

a)   (i)

Normal curves

(ii)

(iii)

b)

54.   The average seasonal rainfall in a town is 500mm with a standard deviation of 150mm. Assuming that the seasonal rainfall for the town is normally distributed, in how many years in the next 50 would you expect the seasonal rainfall to be

   a)   greater than 750mm.

   b)   less than 100mm.

   c)   between 550mm and 840mm.

   d)   between 370mm and 480mm.

a)

	Normal curves
b)	
c)	
d)	

55. A manufacturer of televisions knows from records that the life of television tubes is normally distributed with a mean of 8 years and a standard deviation of 2.3 years. Find the probability that the tube from a television will last

a) more than 10 years.

b) less than 5 years.

c) between 12 and 15 years.

d) The manufacturer offers a three year guarantee on the tube of each TV he sells and he sells 460 TV's in a year. How many TV's will he have to replace under the guarantee.

a)

	Normal curves

b)

c)

d)

'Inverse' Normal

Frequently we are given problems where we know the probability and are required to find the random variable or the mean or standard deviation.

In these situations we use the normal tables in 'reverse' by looking in the body of the tables for the given probability and then reading off the associated standard normal value.

It is important when dealing with 'inverse' normal problems to correctly identify the area under the normal curve you are dealing with.

The importance of using a diagram in these situations cannot be over stressed.

Example 22

A company manufacturing light bulbs has found that they have a mean life of 300 hours with a standard deviation of 60 hours (assume normally distributed). The manufacturer wishes to guarantee his light bulbs for 'x' hours or more and wants the claim to be correct for 85% of the light bulbs produced. Find the value of x.

Solution

		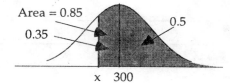
To find x	$P(X > x) = 0.85$	
Standardising	$\therefore P(Z > \dfrac{z - 300}{60}) = 0.85$	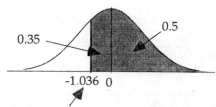
Using tables	$\therefore \dfrac{z - 300}{60} = -1.036$	
Simplifying	$\therefore z - 300 = 60 \times -1.036$	
	$\therefore z = 237.84$	look up 0.35 in the body of the tables to get -1.036
Rounding appropriately	$\therefore z = 237$	

When dealing with 'inverse' normal problems, draw a diagram to identify the required area correctly . Ensure you have the correct sign for the 'z' value.

Example 23

Records indicate that the expected life of a species of small turtle has standard a deviation of 2 years. The probability that a random turtles life exceeds 28 years is 0.03. Assuming turtles' lives are normally distributed find

a) the mean of the distribution.

b) the expected values between which 90% of all turtles can be expected to live to.

Solution

a)   Given $P(X > 28) = 0.03$

      Standardising $\therefore P\left(Z > \dfrac{28 - \mu}{2}\right) = 0.03$

      Using tables $\therefore \dfrac{28 - \mu}{2} = 1.881$

      Simplifying $\therefore 28 - \mu = 2 \times 1.881$

                               $\therefore \mu = 24.238$

      Rounding $\therefore \mu = 24$ years

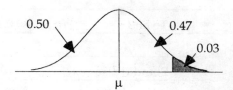

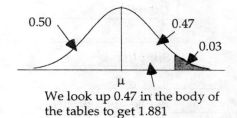

We look up 0.47 in the body of the tables to get 1.881

b)   To find x $P(x_1 < X < x_2) = 0.90$

                  $\therefore P\left(\dfrac{z_1 - 24.24}{2} < Z < \dfrac{z_2 - 24.24}{2}\right) = 0.90$

      Using tables $\therefore \dfrac{z_1 - 24.24}{2} = -1.645$

      and $\dfrac{z_2 - 24.24}{2} = 1.645$

      Simplifying $\therefore z_1 - 24.24 = 2 \times -1.645$

                             $\therefore z_1 = 20.95$ years

      and $z_2 - 24.24 = 2 \times 1.645$

                             $\therefore z_2 = 27.53$ years

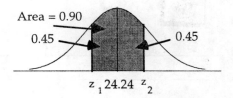

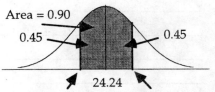

Look up 0.45 in the body of the tables to get -1.645 and 1.645

Problems

56. A Physical Education teacher tells her class that she will award an A grade to 15% of her class in the cricket ball throwing practical test. Experience has shown that the distance thrown is normally distributed with a mean of 65m and a standard deviation of 8m. How far does a student have to throw the cricket ball to obtain an A grade.

	Normal curves
To find x $P(X > x) = 0.15$	
Standardise	
Use tables	
Simplify	
Round appropriately	

57. The diameters of steel rods are normally distributed with a standard deviation of 3mm. It is known that 7% of the steel rods have a diameter less than 13mm. What is the mean of this distribution.

	Normal curves

58.   In a national mathematics competition the results are normally distributed with a mean of 45% and a standard deviation of 14%. Students who are in the top 10% gain a distinction award, while 15% immediately below the distinction award, gain a merit award. Calculate the marks a student would have to obtain to get either a distinction or a merit.

	Normal curves

59.   In grading "Zespri" kiwifruit for export their weights are found to be normally distributed with a mean of 110 g and a standard deviation of 17g. 10% are graded very large, 25% large, 35% medium and 30% small. Only kiwifruits that are graded large are suitable for export. What would the lower and upper bounds be for the large graded kiwifruit.

	Normal curves

3.9 Continuity Correction

Prescription

- normal distribution (including correction for continuity)

 ## Continuity Correction

We have now looked at three distributions in some detail, namely Normal, Binomial and Poisson. One essential difference between the distributions is that the binomial and Poisson are discrete, while the normal is a continuous distribution.

Sometimes it is advantageous to use the normal distribution when data is discrete. When we do this we need to make an 'allowance' for the fact that the data is not continuous. This allowance is called a **continuity correction**.

We need to make a continuity correction if

- the data is discrete eg. test scores etc.

- the data is being measured to the 'nearest' unit, eg. weight of boys to the nearest kg.

- if we are using the normal distribution to approximate either the binomial or Poisson distribution.

When using a continuity correction we focus on the end points of the required interval and change them to take into account the rules for rounding of continuous data.

 ## Example 24

The mean weight of fourth form boys to the nearest kg is normally distributed with a mean of 55kg and a standard deviation of 6kg. What is the probability that a fourth form boy selected at random weighs between 52kg and 60kg exclusive.

In the example above to be less than 60kg rounded to the nearest kg, it must be less than 59.5 (since 59.5 rounds to 60). Similarly if it is greater than 52kg rounded to the nearest kg it must be greater than or equal to 52.5 (since 52.5 rounds to 53). Hence, instead of finding the $P(52 < X < 60)$ we will find $P(52.5 \leq X < 59.5)$.

Solution

To find	$P(52 < X < 60)$
Continuity correction =	$P(52.5 \leq X < 59.5)$
Standardising	$= P\left(\dfrac{52.5 - 55}{6} \leq Z < \dfrac{59.5 - 55}{6}\right)$
Simplifying	$= P(-0.417 \leq Z < 0.75)$
Using tables	$= 0.1616 + 0.2734$
	$= 0.4350$

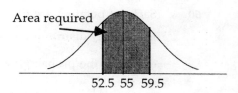

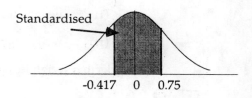

Example 25

A digital watch lasts on average 2 years before developing a fault. This time (to the nearest month) is normally distributed with a standard deviation of 5 months. Find the probability that a watch selected at random develops a fault within the guarantee period of 12 months.

Solution

To find	$P(X < 12)$
Continuity correction =	$P(X < 11.5)$
Standardising	$= P\left(Z < \dfrac{11.5 - 24}{5}\right)$
Simplifying	$= P(Z < -2.5)$
Using tables	$= 0.5 - 0.4938$
	$= 0.0062$

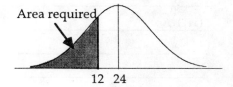

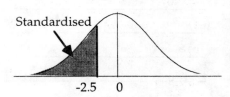

In the example above all units have been expressed in months.

Problems

60. Sacks of potatoes are filled by a machine. The weight of potatoes in each sack (to the nearest kg) is normally distributed with a mean of 60kg and a standard deviation of 4kg.

   a) Find the probability that a sack selected at random

      (i)   weighs more than 65kg.

      (ii)   weighs less than 58kg.

      (iii)   weighs between 57kg and 62kg.

   b) Sacks that weigh less than 55kg are rejected. How many sacks out of 500 would be rejected.

a)   (i)

	Normal curves
(ii)	
(iii)	
b)	

61. The Bursary Calculus examination marks for a local high school were normally distributed with a mean of 48% and a standard deviation of 12%.

a)   Find the probability that a Bursary Calculus candidate selected at random

   (i)   scored a mark of 50%.

   (ii)   gained a B pass by scoring a mark greater than 65%

   (iii)   scored between 40% and 60%.

b)   Calculate the upper and lower quartiles for the Bursary Calculus examination.

a)   (i)

	Normal curves
(ii)	
(iii)	
b)	

3.10 Approximations

Prescription

- approximating, in the appropriate circumstances, the binomial distribution by the Poisson or the normal distribution (including correction for continuity)

Approximations

We can in appropriate circumstances use one distribution to approximate another. This is useful when parameters exceed the limits of tables or become large and difficult to deal with.

Normal Approximation to the Binomial Distribution

We can use the normal distribution to approximate the binomial distribution when

$$n\pi \geq 5$$

and $$n(1 - \pi) \geq 5.$$

To use the normal distribution to approximate the binomial distribution we need to know the mean and the standard deviation. Therefore

$$\mu = n\pi \text{ and } \sigma = \sqrt{n.\pi.(1 - \pi)}$$

Normal Approximation to the Poisson Distribution

We can use the normal distribution to approximate the Poisson distribution when

$$\lambda > 15.$$

To use the normal distribution to approximate the Poisson distribution we need to know the mean and the standard deviation. Therefore

$$\mu = \lambda \text{ and } \sigma = \sqrt{\lambda}$$

Poisson Approximation to the Binomial Distribution

We can use the Poisson distribution to approximate the binomial distribution when

n is large

and π is close to 0.

To use the Poisson distribution to approximate the binomial distribution we need to know the mean. Therefore

$$\lambda = n\pi$$

Extra Notes

Note Well

These conditions are often asked for in justification for an approximation, learn them.

Note Well

When using the normal distribution to approximate either the binomial or Poisson distributions you must make a continuity correction.

Example 26

An electronics company producing motherboards for computers knows from experience that only 85% of them are operative when tested. In a batch of 700 motherboards what is the probability that more than 600 are operative. (Approximate using the normal distribution).

Solution

To find $P(X > 600)$

Continuity correction = $P(X \geq 600.5)$

Standardising $= P\left(Z \geq \dfrac{600.5 - 595}{9.447}\right)$

Simplifying $= P(Z \geq 0.582)$

Using tables $= 0.5 - 0.2197$

                          $= 0.2803$

Note Well

Since we are using the normal distribution to approximate the binomial distribution we have to use a continuity correction. To find $P(X > 600)$ we calculate $P(X \geq 600.5)$

$n = 700$, $\pi = 0.85$, $\mu = 700(0.85) = 595$,
$\sigma = \sqrt{700(0.85)(0.15)} = 9.447$

Example 27

The number of mechanical breakdowns in a one month period in a factory follows a Poisson distribution with mean 20. Find the probability that in any one month selected at random there are between 16 and 24 breakdowns. (Approximate using the normal distribution).

Solution

To find $P(16 < X < 24)$

Continuity correction = $P(16.5 \leq X < 23.5)$

Standardising $= P(\dfrac{16.5 - 20}{4.472} \leq Z$

                          $< \dfrac{23.5 - 20}{4.472})$

Simplifying $= P(-0.783 \leq Z < 0.783)$

Using tables $= 0.2832 + 0.2832$

                          $= 0.5664$

Note Well

Since we are using the normal distribution to approximate the Poisson distribution we have to use a continuity correction. To find $P(16 < X < 24)$, we calculate the $P(16.5 \leq X < 23.5)$

$\lambda = 20$, $\sigma = \sqrt{20} = 4.472$

Example 28

In a packet of 560 seeds, 1% of them fail to germinate. Find the probability that less than 10 seeds from a randomly selected packet fail to germinate. (Approximate using the Poisson distribution)

 Solution

To find $\qquad\qquad$ P(X < 10)

Tables $\qquad$ P(X < 10) = 0.0037 + 0.0207 + 0.0580

$\qquad\qquad\qquad\qquad$ + 0.1082 + 0.1515

$\qquad\qquad\qquad\qquad$ + 0.1697 + 0.1584

$\qquad\qquad\qquad\qquad$ + 0.1267 + 0.0887

$\qquad\qquad\qquad\qquad$ + 0.0552

We are using the Poisson distribution to approximate the Binomial distribution, since n is large and π is small.

$\lambda = n\pi = (560).01 = 5.6$

Simplifying $\qquad$ = 0.9408

 Problems

62. A fireworks manufacturing company knows from previous experience that its fireworks function effectively 97% of the time. In a box containing 2000 fireworks, what is the probability that more than 1950 function. (Approximate using the normal distribution).

63. The number of customers that a waiter serves in a one hour period follows a Poisson distribution with a mean of 27. Using the normal distribution find the probability that in a one hour period the waiter serves

   a)   less than 25 customers.

   b)   more than 40 customers.

   c)   between 20 and 30 customers inclusive.

a) _____

_____

_____

b) _____

_____

_____

c) _____

_____

_____

64. In a carton of 880 light bulbs 0.5% of them can be expected to be faulty. Find the probability using the Poisson distribution that

   a)   less than 5 are faulty.

   b)   more than 10 are faulty.

   c)   between 4 and 8, inclusive, are faulty.

a) _____

_____

_____

b) _____

_____

_____

c) _____

_____

_____

4.0 Combinations and the Binomial Theorem

Introduction

The number of ways a group can be selected from a larger group depends upon whether the order of selection is important. The mathematical approach to these problems can be extended to the expansion of $(ax + b)^n$.

Prescription

Exploring equations and expressions

Find numbers of distinct arrangements or selections from a given number of objects (permutations and combinations)

- **straightforward applications such as choosing a sample of 3 girls and 4 boys from a class of 16 girls and 12 boys**

- **cases where repetition is permissible such as selecting the two letters for New Zealand vehicle number plates**

Expand binomial expressions for positive integral exponents

- **Pascal's triangle and the notation ^nC_r or $\binom{n}{r}$**

4.1 Multiple Selections

Selection from Different Groups

One method of finding the number of possible arrangements of clothes that a person could select to wear if they were selecting from 2 different pairs of jeans, 3 tops and 2 pairs of shoes

would be to show all possibilities on a tree diagram

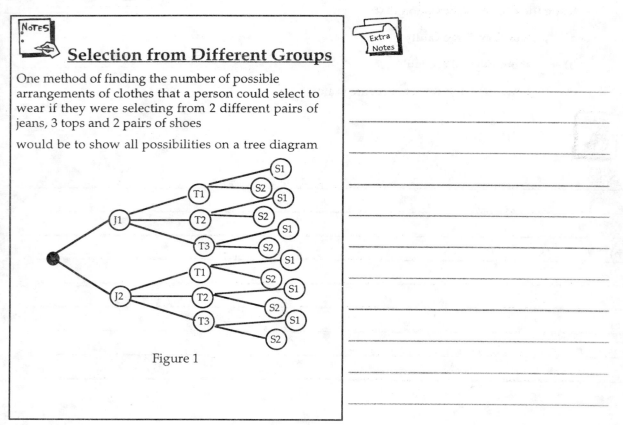

Figure 1

Selection from Different Groups cont...

The number of possible arrangements of different outfits is given by

Number jeans x number of tops x number of pairs of shoes

$$= 2 \times 3 \times 2$$

$$= 12 \text{ outfits}$$

This **Multiplication Principle** shows the number of possible arrangements of combining 2 items with 3 items with 2 items.

In general terms. The number of arrangements of combining N_1 items with N_2 items with N_3 items with N_4 and so on is given by

Arrangements $= N_1 \times N_2 \times N_3 \times N_4$

Care needs to be taken to check if the selection of the first item has an effect on the number of items available for selection in subsequent selections.

Example 1

A children's book has the pages cut so you can overlay the pages to make animals with different heads bodies and legs. If there are 5 heads, 7 bodies and 4 sets of legs how many arrangements are possible.

Solution

The number of arrangements is given by

Arrangements $= N_1 \times N_2 \times N_3$

$$= 5 \times 7 \times 4$$

$$= 140 \text{ different arrangements}$$

Example 2

How many different number plates are possible if each plate consists of 2 letters followed by exactly 4 digits.

Solution

Car number plates in New Zealand are made of two letters and up to four digits. How many possible number plates are there if all four digits are used

Number plates $= 26 \times 26 \times 9 \times 10 \times 10 \times 10$

$$= 6084000 \text{ different plates}$$

Note, the first digit of the number plate cannot be zero so only 9 choices are available for that digit.

Problems

1. In selecting dessert you are offered
    a choice of 4 different ice creams,
    3 different types of fruits and 4
    different sweet sauces. How many
    different desserts are possible?

2. In selecting clothes for a *Bad Taste
    Dance* you have 5 different coloured
    tops and the same 5 different colours
    of pants and caps.
    How many different arrangements
    are possible of the 3 items if

    a) you will wear any arrangement.

    b) you will not wear any two items
         the same colour.

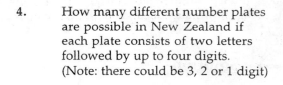

a)

_____

b)

3. A shop has a limited range of
    different numerals. Find the number
    of three digit house numbers that
    could be formed if the shop has

    a) only the numerals 2, 4, 6 and 8.

    b) only the numerals 0, 2, 4, 8.

    (repeats of any numeral are allowed)

4. How many different number plates
    are possible in New Zealand if
    each plate consists of two letters
    followed by up to four digits.
    (Note: there could be 3, 2 or 1 digit)

a)

_____

b)

4.2 Factorial Notation

Prescription

Exploring equations and expressions

Find numbers of distinct arrangements or selections from a given number of objects (permutations and combinations)

Factorial Notation

In finding the number of different arrangements possible, products similar to $6 \times 5 \times 4 \times 3 \times 2 \times 1$ are often used.

This product of consecutive terms is written with a special notation called **factorial**. The symbol for a factorial is the exclamation mark !.

The factorial of any natural number n is defined as

$$n! = n \times (n-1) \times (n-2) \times (n-3)..2 \times 1$$

An examples is

$$6! = 6 \times 5 \times 4 \times 3 \times 2 \times 1$$
$$= 720$$

Manipulation of Factorials

We note that any factorial can be written as a combination of the product of consecutive numbers with the remaining factors expressed as a factorial.

$$9! = 9 \times 8 \times 7 \times 6!$$

This property is the basis of all the manipulation.

An example of subtraction of factorials would be

$$8! - 4! = 8 \times 7 \times 6 \times 5 \times 4! - 4!$$

Taking out the common factor gives

$$8! - 4! = 4!(8 \times 7 \times 6 \times 5 \times 1 - 1)$$
$$= 1679 \times 4!$$

An example of division of factorials would be

$$\frac{7!}{5!} = \frac{7 \times 6 \times 5!}{5!}$$
$$= 42$$

Definition of zero factorial

By definition zero factorial is one

$$0! = 1$$

Factorials are usually found on the calculator. You should investigate this now and check you can show that $6! = 720$.

In attempting to simplify any factorial expression, always start expressing the larger factorial as a product of consecutive numbers as far as any other factorial present. In the problem above 7! was written as consecutive numbers as far as 5! and this enabled us to find the common factor.

Example 3

Simplify as far as possible $(n + 2)! - n!$

Solution

$$(n + 2)! - n! = (n + 2)(n + 1)n! - n!$$
$$= n![(n + 2)(n + 1) - 1]$$
$$= (n^2 + 3n + 1)n!$$

Example 4

Simplify $\frac{61!}{58!}$

Solution

$$\frac{61!}{58!} = \frac{61 \times 60 \times 59 \times 58!}{58!}$$
$$= 61 \times 60 \times 59$$
$$= 215\,940$$

Problems

Simplify the following factorial problems leaving your answer in factorial form if appropriate.

5.   Simplify $\frac{(m + 1)!}{(m - 1)!}$

6.   Simplify $61! + 62! + 63!$

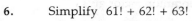

Problems continued

7. Simplify $\dfrac{17!}{3! \cdot 14!}$

8. Simplify $10! + (6!)^2$

9. Simplify $\dfrac{(m+4)!}{m(m+3)!}$

10. Evaluate $\dfrac{70!}{3! \cdot 5! \cdot 65!}$

4.3 Permutations

Prescription

Find numbers of distinct arrangements or selections from a given number of objects (permutations and combinations)

Arrangements of a set number of objects

If you have a set number of *n* objects being arranged in order then the possible arrangements would be given by

n	possibilities for the first position
n − 1	possibilities for the second position (as one has already been selected)
n − 2	possibilities for the third position (as two have already been selected)
n − 3	possibilities for the fourth position

and so on. Using the multiplication principle from section 4.1 the total number of arrangements becomes

$$\text{Arrangements} = n \times (n-1) \times (n-2) \times (n-3) \ldots 3 \times 2 \times 1$$
$$= n!$$

If n objects are arranged in order then the number of possible arrangements is n!

The exception - *n* objects around a circle

The only variation to this is if the *n* objects are arranged around a circle.

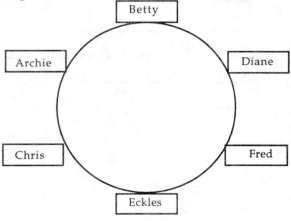

Figure 2

With a circle, there is no starting point, so the arrangements are relative to any one object. (eg. compared to Diane there are now five objects to place).

Therefore with *n* objects arranged in a circle there are $(n-1)$ objects to place giving $(n-1)!$ possible arrangements.

Example 5

A softball team has nine players. How many different ways can the batting line up be arranged?

Solution

The nine players have to be arranged in order so the possibilities are   = 9!

$$= 362\,880$$

Example 6

King Arthur and his 12 knights are to be seated at the round table. How many ways can the table be set?

Solution

The reference point is King Arthur so we are just arranging the 12 knights relative to him so the answer is   = 12!

$$= 479\,001\,600$$

Example 7

When King Arthur is away so just his 12 knights are to be seated at the round table. How many ways can the table be set?

Solution

There is no unique reference point so we are just arranging the 12 knights relative to any one of them so the answer is   = 11!

$$= 39\,916\,800$$

Problems

Find the number of possible arrangements for each of the following problems.

11. Six children run in a race. How many different ways can all six children cross the finish line (no dead heats).

12. Using the eight different digits 1 to 8, how many different 8 digit numbers can be formed if no digit can be used more than once.

13. A school has 12 students on the school council. A chairperson and 11 members. How many different ways can they sit around a circular table if

    a) they sit randomly and no seat has special significance.

    b) the chairperson always sits at the top of the table.

    c) there is a special chairperson's seat but they sit randomly as they have not appointed a chairperson.

a)

b)

c)

14. Using all the letters from each of the following words how many different arrangements of letters can be formed

    a) using the word NULAKE.

    b) using the word ZEALAND. (Note the repeat of the letter A)

    c) using the word MATHEMATICS which has three letters repeated.

a)

b)

c)

Permutations

If you are selecting a group in order, from a larger group then the approach is similar. For a group size r from a larger group size n we have

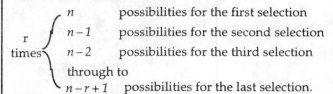

r times $\begin{cases} n & \text{possibilities for the first selection} \\ n-1 & \text{possibilities for the second selection} \\ n-2 & \text{possibilities for the third selection} \\ \text{through to} \\ n-r+1 & \text{possibilities for the last selection.} \end{cases}$

Using the multiplication principle this becomes

Arrangements $= n_\times(n-1)_\times(n-2)_\times(n-3) \ldots {}_\times(n-r+1)$

Using factorial notation this simplifies to the formula

Arrangements $= \dfrac{n!}{(n-r)!}$

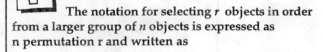

The notation for selecting r objects in order from a larger group of n objects is expressed as n permutation r and written as

$$^nP_r = \frac{n!}{(n-r)!}$$

Permutation on a Calculator

Some calculators have permutations built in. If you are lucky enough to have permutations on your calculator then check it out now.

Otherwise you will need to use the factorial button.

Example 8

The chairperson, secretary, and treasurer are to be selected from a group of 20 members. How many different ways can the posts be filled.

Solution

3 people are to be selected in order from a group of 20.

$$^{20}P_3 = \frac{20!}{(20-3)!}$$

$$= \frac{20!}{17!}$$

$$= 6840$$

Example 9

How many "words" of 4 letters can be selected from the word ABDUCTIONS.

Solution

$$^{10}P_4 = \frac{10!}{(10-4)!}$$

$$= \frac{10!}{6!}$$

$$= 5040$$

Example 10

A successful golf team has 3 male and 4 female members. They are going to be photographed. Find how many ways the following groups could be arranged.

a)   all 7 together.

b)   the 3 males on the right and the 4 females on the left.

c)   a group of 4.

d)   a group of 2 females on the left and 2 males on the right.

Solution

a)   all together = 7!

$$= 5040$$

b)   4 males = 4!

$$= 24$$

          3 females = 3!

$$= 6$$

   combined group = groups of males × groups of females

$$= 6 \times 24$$

$$= 144$$

c) $^7P_4 = \frac{7!}{(7-4)!}$

$$= 840$$

d)   two each sex = $^4P_2 \times {}^3P_2$

$$= 12 \times 6$$

$$= 72$$

Problems

Find the number of possible arrangements for each of the following problems.

15. I take 6 books from my collection of 30 books in my bookcase to read in the order they are selected. How many different ways can these 6 books be selected.

16. A television competition requires contestants to select the 3 best catches in order from 10. How many entries would you have to make to be sure of winning.

17. If you have only the digits 1, 2, 4, 5, 6, 8, and 9 how many numbers of 4 or less digits can be made.

4 digits

3 digits

2 digits

1 digit

total

18. A trifecta on a horse race requires that you pick the first 3 horses in order. How many bets would you need on a 17 horse race if you knew one particular horse would be in the first 3, in order to be certain that you would win.

19. You wish to select five letter "words" from the word MACINTOSH. How many different ways can this be done if

   a)   there are no restrictions.

   b)   each word contains the word IN.

a)

b)

20. In a horse race there are 15 starters. How many different ways can the first 3 positions be filled if

   a)   there are no dead heats.

   b)   there is a dead heat for third.

a)

b)

4.4 Combinations

Prescription

Exploring equations and expressions

Find numbers of distinct arrangements or selections from a given number of objects (permutations and combinations)

- cases where repetition is permissible such as selecting the two letters for New Zealand vehicle number plates

 ## Selecting Without Order

Often when a selection is made, the order the items are selected in is not important. If students were being selected to go on a trip it would not matter what order they were selected but whether they were selected or not.

From the work in section 4.3 we know the number of ways that a small group can be selected from a large group IN ORDER is

No. of ways in order $= {^nP_r}$

$$= \frac{n!}{(n-r)!}$$

where n is the size of the large group and r is the size of the selected group.

For each group of r objects selected, has $r!$ ways of being ordered (see the start of section 4.3) so if we divide the number of ways the group of r can be selected in order, by the number of ways this group can be ordered we get the number of unique groups.

No. of different groups $= \dfrac{\text{No. ways in order}}{\text{No. ways } r \text{ can be ordered}}$

$$= \frac{{^nP_r}}{r!}$$

$$= \frac{\frac{n!}{(n-r)!}}{r!}$$

$$= \frac{n!}{(n-r)!\,r!}$$

This is the definition of **Combination**.

The number of distinct groups size r that can be selected from a group size n is given by n Combination r

$$^nC_r = \frac{n!}{(n-r)!\,r!}$$

This formula is in the tables sheet given to you in the examination.

There is also a table of values for ^nC_r which will be explained shortly.

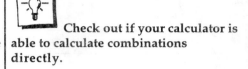 Check out if your calculator is able to calculate combinations directly.

_____

_____

_____

_____

 The symbol for combination appears in two forms. Both are correct and you need to recognise both.

n Combination r is represented by

$$^nC_r = \binom{n}{r}$$

 Using the definition

$$^nC_r = \frac{n!}{(n-r)!\,r!}$$

then we can see that $^nC_{n-r}$ gives

$$^nC_{n-r} = \frac{n!}{(n-r)!\,r!} \quad \text{also}$$

so selecting a group of r from n objects gives the same result as selecting a group of $n-r$ objects from the same group.

Binomial Coefficients

A table of Binomial coefficients is supplied to candidates in the examination. A copy of this table is available below and in the set of tables at the end of this book.

n \ r	0	1	2	3	4	5	6	7	8	9	10
0	1										
1	1	1									
2	1	2	1								
3	1	3	3	1							
4	1	4	6	4	1						
5	1	5	10	10	5	1					
6	1	6	15	20	15	6	1				
7	1	7	21	35	35	21	7	1			
8	1	8	28	56	70	56	28	8	1		
9	1	9	36	84	126	126	84	36	9	1	
10	1	10	45	120	210	252	210	120	45	10	1
11	1	11	55	165	330	462	462	330	165	55	11
12	1	12	66	220	495	792	924	792	495	220	66
13	1	13	78	286	715	1287	1716	1716	1287	715	286
14	1	14	91	364	1001	2002	3003	3432	3003	2002	1001
15	1	15	105	455	1365	3003	5005	6435	6435	5005	3003

To find a particular Binomial coefficient find the row for your particular value of n and place your ruler along this row. You now read the value in the column directly under your value for r.

Example 11

Find the Binomial coefficient corresponding to $^{13}C_5$

Solution

We go down to the ROW that starts with n = 13 ie.

1   13   78   286   715   1287   1716   1716 . . . .

and across to the column headed with 5. The number in that column is 1287.

© Robert Lakeland & Carl Nugent

Example 12

A group of 5 students from a music class of 28 is going to go on a trip to the Smoke Free Rock Quest. How many different ways can this group be selected.

Solution

$$^{n}C_r = \frac{n!}{(n-r)!\ r!}$$

$$^{28}C_5 = \frac{28!}{(28-5)!\ 5!}$$

$$= \frac{28!}{23!\ 5!}$$

$$= \frac{28 \times 27 \times 26 \times 25 \times 24}{120}$$

$$= 98280$$

Example 13

A school has 17 staff and they do duty 4 times a day. The school attempts to send a distinctly different duty team of 5 staff members each time they send out staff for duty. Find

a) the number of ways a duty team of 5 staff could be selected.

b) how long will it be before a duty team is repeated. A year is 180 school days.

c) the school has a policy that there must always be 3 male and 2 female staff on duty. If there are 10 male and 7 female staff how many ways can they now have distinctly different duty teams.

Solution

a) $^{17}C_5 = 6188$

b) 1 year gives 180 times 4 slots (ie. 720) so there would be no need to repeat a team for almost 8.6 years during which time they would probably have changed staff members.

c) selecting each sex separately then we use the multiplication principle to combine them.

male $^{10}C_3 = 120$

female $^{7}C_2 = 21$

teams $= 2520$

Extra Examples

Problems

21. In a pack of 52 cards how many different hands of 5 cards are possible.

22. In LOTTO you need to select 6 winning numbers out of 40 to win. How many different ways can this be done.

23. 10 people are to cross a river by waka. If 5 can fit in the waka find

   a) the number of ways of filling the waka for the first trip.

   b) the number of distinctly different ways of distributing the people between two wakas.

a)

b)

24. A parents support group of 4 is being selected to accompany a primary school group on an overnight trip. Find the number of ways the support group can be made up if it is made up from 5 married couples and it must consist of

   a) 2 men and 2 women.

   b) if a husband <u>and</u> wife cannot be selected.

a)

b) select one from each couple first

select which of each partner should go

25. There are 20 desks in a classroom, 10 at the front and 10 at the rear. How many ways can a statistics class of 8 be seated in the room if 2 refuse to sit in the front and 3 refuse to sit in the back.

There could be 6, 5, 4, or 3 at the front.

26. Find the number of ways 30 students can be assigned to two classes if each class must have 13 students in it.

Remember classes could have 13, 14, 15, 16 or 17 students.

How many in the 1st class.

27. 10 chairs are placed in a row. Find the number of ways

a) 2 people can sit on the chairs.

b) 8 people can sit on the chairs.

c) 2 people can sit so there is always at least one chair between them.

a)

b)

c)

28. Use your factorial definitions for combinations to prove

$$^nC_r + {}^nC_{r-1} = {}^{n+1}C_r$$

4.5 Mixed Permutations and Combinations

Prescription

Exploring equations and expressions

Find numbers of distinct arrangements or selections from a given number of objects (permutations and combinations)

- straightforward applications such as choosing a sample of 3 girls and 4 boys from a class of 16 girls and 12 boys

- cases where repetition is permissible such as selecting the two letters for New Zealand vehicle number plates

Example 14

A photographer wishes to arrange students for a photograph. There are 12 girls and 7 boys in the class. The boys and girls are lined up in descending order of height and then the two sexes are to be merged together for the group photograph. How many ways can they be arranged if

a) no two boys are to stand together.

b) there are no restrictions on groupings of either sex.

Solution

As the order of either sex can not change we are working with combinations only.

a) If no two boys are together then each boy can fit into one of the 11 gaps between girls or at either end (ie. in one of 13 positions)

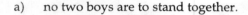

l g l gbg l g l gbgbg l gbgbg l gbgb

so we are distributing the 7 boys among the 13 gaps

$$^{13}C_7 = 1716$$

b) It is easier to think of the 19 positions that the class are going to occupy. Now the girls (or boys) are to be distributed among the 19 positions giving

$$^{19}C_{12} = 50388$$

The boys take the positions left.

© Robert Lakeland & Carl Nugent

Example 15

Three sets of identical twins are being arranged for a photograph. How many ways can they be arranged.

Solution

The six people can be arranged 6! ways where order is important but as we cannot tell the difference between each pair of twins so the number of ways is

$$\text{ways} = \frac{6!}{2! \times 2! \times 2!}$$
$$= 90$$

Example 16

In using flags for a signal, it is possible to have a number of flags on a single pole. The order the flags are on a flag pole is important. If a particular signal consists of hoisting 5 flags (with at least one flag up each pole), find the variations possible if there is

a) two poles

b) three poles

Solution

Find the number of ways 5 flags can be placed in order which is 5!.

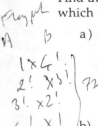

a) with two poles for each of the 5! ways of arranging the flags we can have between 1 and 4 up the first pole

$$\text{ways} = 4 \times 5!$$
$$= 480$$

b) with three poles you have to now divide the flags into three groups

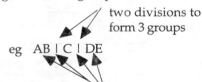

two divisions to form 3 groups

with four possible positions for these divisions

with the flags in each group going up one pole. These two division can be arranged in any of the four gaps between the five flags

$$\text{ways} = {}^4C_2 \times 5!$$
$$= 720$$

handwritten notes:

flag pole

A B

1 × 4!
2! × 3!
3! × 2!   72
4! × 1

5 × 4.

Problems

Simplify the following factorial problems leaving your answer in factorial form if appropriate

29.

A person walking from S to F moves up or moves to the right. How many different routes are there.

They will go up 4 times and right 6 times

_____

_____

_____

_____

30. A person has to enter a 4 letter password (not a numerical digit) when logging on to a computer. How many different combinations are possible if

a) repeats are allowed.

b) no letter is used twice.

a)
_____

_____

b)
_____

_____

31. How many different ways can $30 in dollar coins be divided among 4 people if

a) each person gets something.

b) no restrictions on who gets what.

a)
_____

_____

b)
_____

_____

32. The word MATHEMATICS has two A's, M's, and T's. How many distinctly different four letter arrangements (words?) are possible from it.

_____

_____

_____

_____

_____

_____

4.6 Binomial Expansion

Prescription

Expand binomial expressions for positive integral exponents

- Pascal's triangle and the notation ^nC_r or $\binom{n}{r}$

Pascal's Triangle

Pascal's Triangle is an array of numbers in the form of a triangle, where each number is the sum of the two numbers immediately above it.

```
            1
          1   1
        1   2   1
      1   3   3   1
    1   4   6   4   1
  1   5  10  10   5   1
  .   .   .   .   .   .
```

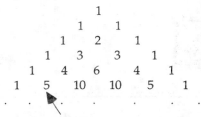

Each number is the sum of
the two numbers above it

The numbers in Pascal's Triangle equate exactly with the Binomial Coefficients (see below), where the values of n and r are the row number and the item number respectively.

$$\binom{0}{0}$$
$$\binom{1}{0} \quad \binom{1}{1}$$
$$\binom{2}{0} \quad \binom{2}{1} \quad \binom{2}{2}$$
$$\binom{3}{0} \quad \binom{3}{1} \quad \binom{3}{2} \quad \binom{3}{3}$$
$$\binom{4}{0} \quad \binom{4}{1} \quad \binom{4}{2} \quad \binom{4}{3} \quad \binom{4}{4}$$
$$\binom{5}{0} \quad \binom{5}{1} \quad \binom{5}{2} \quad \binom{5}{3} \quad \binom{5}{4} \quad \binom{5}{5}$$

Extra Notes

Problems

Use Pascal's triangle above to answer the following questions

33. Find $^5C_2$ $[= \binom{5}{2}]$

Answer

34. For what value of r is $^4C_r = 4$

Answer

Binomial Coefficients

If we expand the expression $(a + b)^n$ then the coefficients (the number in front of the each of the terms) match exactly with the rows in Pascal's Triangle and hence the Binomial Coefficients.

$(a + b)^0 = 1$		1
$(a + b)^1 = a + b$		$1 \quad 1$
$(a + b)^2 = a^2 + 2ab + b^2$		$1 \quad 2 \quad 1$
$(a + b)^3 = a^3 + 3a^2b + 3ab^2 + b^3$		$1 \quad 3 \quad 3 \quad 1$

Hence if we are required to expand any binomial in this form we can either calculate the Binomial Coefficients or read them from the table.

In summary

$$(a + b)^n = {}^nC_0 a^n b^0 + {}^nC_1 a^{n-1} b^1 + {}^nC_2 a^{n-2} b^2 + \ldots\ldots$$

$$\ldots\ldots + {}^nC_{n-1} a^1 b^{n-1} + {}^nC_n a^0 b^n$$

or

$$(a + b)^n = \binom{n}{0} a^n b^0 + \binom{n}{1} a^{n-1} b^1 + \binom{n}{2} a^{n-2} b^2 + \ldots\ldots$$

$$\ldots\ldots + \binom{n}{n-1} a^1 b^{n-1} + \binom{n}{n} a^0 b^n$$

For the expansion of $(a + b)^n$, the power a is raised to decreases by one each term while the power of the second term b is increased by one. The powers of a and b for each term always add to n. We use this to check we have the correct powers.

Example 17

Expand $(3x^2 - 4)^5$ completely using the Binomial expansion.

Solution

The row from the Binomial coefficients from the table corresponding to n = 5 is

n = 5   1   5   10   10   5   1

using these and the general expansion above gives

Coefficients from the Binomial table

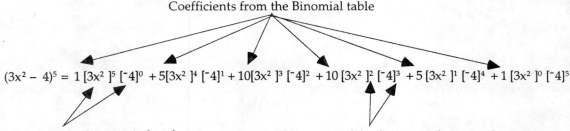

$$(3x^2 - 4)^5 = 1[3x^2]^5[{}^-4]^0 + 5[3x^2]^4[{}^-4]^1 + 10[3x^2]^3[{}^-4]^2 + 10[3x^2]^2[{}^-4]^3 + 5[3x^2]^1[{}^-4]^4 + 1[3x^2]^0[{}^-4]^5$$

We keep both terms in brackets to eliminate errors from raising the whole term to a power.

The power of the first term decreases by one while the power of the second increases by one. The total powers add to n.

$$(3x^2 - 4)^5 = 3^5 x^{10} + 5 \times 3^4 x^8 \times {}^-4^1 + 10 \times 3^3 x^6 \times 4^2 + 10 \times 3^2 x^4 \times {}^-4^3 + 5 \times 3^1 x^2 \times 4^4 + {}^-4^5$$

$$= 243 x^{10} - 1620 x^8 + 4320 x^6 - 5760 x^4 + 3840 x^2 - 1024$$

Example 18

Find the 4th term of the expansion $(3x^3 - 2y^{-2})^7$.

Solution

Using $T_{r+1} = \binom{n}{r} a^{n-r} b^r$ [see tables]

To find the fourth term we substitute $r = 3$

$\therefore \ T_{3+1} = \binom{7}{3} [3x^3]^{7-3} [-2y^{-2}]^3$

$\therefore \ T_4 = (35).(81 \ x^{12})(-8y^{-6})$

$\therefore \ T_4 = {}^-22680 \ x^{12} \ y^{-6}$

Example 19

Find the coefficient of x^3 in the expansion $\left(\dfrac{3}{x^2} - x^3\right)^6$.

Solution

Using $T_{r+1} = \binom{n}{r} a^{n-r} b^r$

We need to find which term gives us a coefficient of x^3.

$\binom{6}{r} [3x^{-2}]^{6-r} [-x^3]^r = kx^3$

$\therefore \ [x^{-12+2r}][x^{3r}] = x^3.$ (ignoring constant values)

$\therefore \ x^{-12+5r} = x^3$

$\therefore \ -12 + 5r = 3$

$\therefore \ 5r = 15$

$\therefore \ r = 3$

Substituting $r = 3$ into $T_{r+1} = \binom{n}{r} a^{n-r} b^r$ we obtain

$T_4 = 20 [3^3 x^{-6}][-1^3 x^9]$

$\therefore \ T_4 = {}^-540 \ x^3$

$\therefore$ coefficient of $x^4 = {}^-540$

Problems

Use the Binomial expansion to answer the following problems

35. Expand $(3x - 5)^6$ completely.

36. Expand $(\frac{2}{y} - 5y^2)^5$ completely.

Note: $\frac{2}{y} = 2y^{-1}$

37. Find the x^5 term in the expansion of

$(2x^3 + \frac{5}{x})^7$

Note we need the term not just the coefficient

38. Find the term independent of x in

the expansion of $(2x^2 - \frac{4}{x^2})^6$

The term independent of x is the constant term (x^0)

Problems continued

39. Find the 5th term in the expansion of $(2x^3 - 3x^{-1})^{10}$

40. Find the $x^4 y^3$ term in the expansion of $(3x^2 - y)^5$

41. Find the coefficient of the x^6 term in the expansion of $(2x^2 + \frac{5}{x})^9$

Note we need just the coefficient.

42. Use the first four terms of the binomial expansion of $(1 + 3x)^{11}$ to approximate $(1.03)^{11}$.

Find the first four terms of the expansion

Now let x = 0.01 and substitute.

5.0 Calculus

Introduction

In modelling situations we are often concerned with the rate by which a given quantity changes. If we are able to represent the quantity by a mathematical equation then this rate of change is found by differentiating the expression.

Prescription

Developing concepts of rate and change

Solve problems in context requiring differentiation of polynomials, e^{ax}, x^n for rational values of n

- **rates of change (chain rule not required)**
- **problems involving maxima and minima**

Solve problems in which the rate of change of a quantity is proportional to the value of the quantity (eg. $y' = ky$)

- **showing by differentiating that $y = Ae^{ax}$ is the solution to $y' = ky$**
- **exponential growth and decay (eg. population growth, radioactive decay, interest)**

5.1 Rate of Change

Average Rate of Change

The average rate at which an expression changes is given by

$$\text{Av. Rate of Chg} = \frac{\text{change in the value of the expression}}{\text{change in the dependent variable}}$$

For an expression $y = f(x)$ from $x = x_A$ to $x = x_B$ this is

$$\text{Av. Rate of Chg} = \frac{\text{change in } f(x)}{\text{change in } x}$$

$$= \frac{f(x_B) - f(x_A)}{x_B - x_A}$$

Alternatively this could be expressed as

$$= \frac{y_2 - y_1}{x_2 - x_1}$$

Extra Notes

Average Rate of Change cont...

Graphically the average rate of change is the gradient of the chord from A to B.

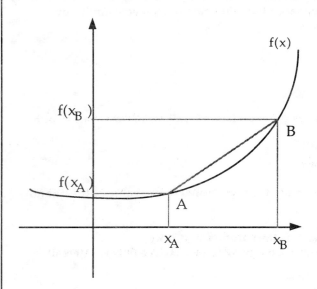

Figure 1

Similarly in a practical application the average rate of change is the change per time interval.

If you wanted to find the average rate of change of a person's salary over the last four and half years you would proceed as below.

$$\text{Av. Rate of Chg} = \frac{\text{change in salary}}{\text{change in time}}$$

$$= \frac{\text{salary at end} - \text{salary at start}}{\text{time period}}$$

which could give a result such as

$$\text{Av. Rate of Chg} = \frac{47300 - 43000}{4.5}$$

$$= \$956 \text{ per year} \qquad (0 \text{ dp})$$

Example 1

Find the average rate of change of the expression

$$y = x^2 + x + 3$$

from $x = 1$ to $x = 3$

Solution

When $x = 1$ $\quad y = 1^2 + 1 + 3$

$\qquad = 5$

When $x = 3$ $\quad y = 3^2 + 3 + 3$

$\qquad = 15$

We require the rate of change from $(1, 5)$ to $(3, 15)$.

Av. Rate of Chg $= \dfrac{f(x_B) - f(x_A)}{x_B - x_A}$

$\qquad = \dfrac{15 - 5}{3 - 1}$

$\qquad = 5$

Problems

Find the average rate of change for the following problems.

1. Find the average gradient from $x = {}^-2$ to $x = 5$ for the expression $y = 2e^{(x-1)}$.

2. The consumer price index increased from 647 in March 1986 to 944 in June 1990. Find the average rate of change of the index.

5.2 Instantaneous Rate of Change

Prescription

Developing concepts of rate and change

The Instantaneous Rate of Change

The rate of change between two points A and B is the gradient of the chord that joins the two points.

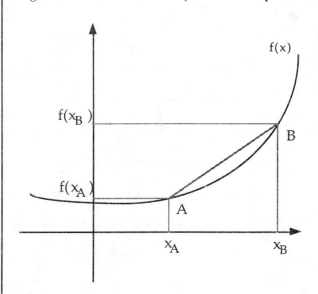

Figure 2

As the point B gets closer and closer to A, the gradient of the chord approaches the gradient at A.

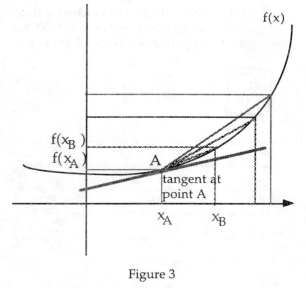

Figure 3

The Instantaneous Rate of Change cont…

Let the distance between A and B be h, then our expression for the rate of change becomes

Rate of Change $= \dfrac{\text{change in } f(x)}{\text{change in } x}$

$= \dfrac{f(x_B) - f(x_A)}{x_B - x_A}$

$= \dfrac{f(x_A + h) - f(x_A)}{(x_A + h) - x_A}$

$= \dfrac{f(x_A + h) - f(x_A)}{h}$

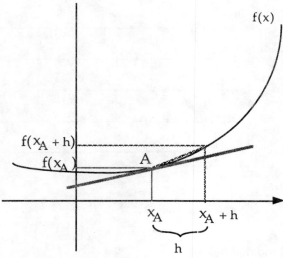

Figure 4

To find the instantaneous rate of change (gradient) we let the distance h become smaller and smaller.

Rate of Change $= \displaystyle\lim_{h \to 0} \dfrac{f(x_A + h) - f(x_A)}{h}$

We can use this definition to find expressions for the rate of change (called the Derivative) of polynomials by finding the rate of change at the point $(x, f(x))$ rather than the point $(x_A, f(x_A))$.

Instantaneous Rate of Change (or Derivative) is defined as

$f'(x) = \displaystyle\lim_{h \to 0} \dfrac{f(x + h) - f(x)}{h}$

Using this definition is called differentiating from first principles.

Example 2

Differentiate from first principles the expression

$$f(x) = x^2 + 3x - 1$$

Solution

Using the definition

Rate of Change $= \lim\limits_{h \to 0} \dfrac{f(x + h) - f(x)}{h}$

$f(x) = x^2 + 3x - 1$

$f(x + h) = (x + h)^2 + 3(x + h) - 1$

$\qquad = x^2 + 2xh + h^2 + 3x + 3h - 1$

Rate of Change or derivative

$= \lim\limits_{h \to 0} \dfrac{x^2 + 2xh + h^2 + 3x + 3h - 1 - (x^2 + 3x - 1)}{h}$

$= \lim\limits_{h \to 0} \dfrac{2xh + h^2 + 3h}{h}$

$= \lim\limits_{h \to 0} 2x + h + 3$

as h get closer to 0 then the derivative approaches

$\qquad = 2x + 3$

Problems

Find the derivative by first principles for each polynomial below.

3. $f(x) = x^2 - 5x - 1$

4. $f(x) = x^3 - 2x^2 + 5$

Note that $(x+h)^3 - 2(x + h)^2 + 5$

$= x^3 + 3x^2 h + 3xh^2 + h^3 - 2(x^2 + 2xh + h^2) + 5$

Calculus

5.3 Differentiation of Polynomials

Prescription

Solve problems in context requiring differentiation of polynomials x^n for rational values of n

 ## Differentiation of Polynomials

A polynomial is a mathematical expression in the form

$$a_n x^n + a_{n-1} x^{n-1} + a_{n-2} x^{n-2} + \ldots + c$$

Examples could be

$$5 x^3 + 3 x^2 - 8 x + 11$$

or $\quad 5 x^{-2} - 3 x^{-1} + 11$

If we differentiate terms systematically we soon note a pattern.

polynomial	derivative
x^5	$5x^4$
x^4	$4x^3$
x^3	$3x^2$
x^2	$2x^1 = 2x$
x^1	$1x^0 = 1$

In differentiating polynomials such as

$$x^n$$

we get

and reduce the power by one

multiply by the original power 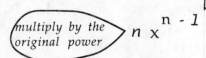 $n\, x^{n-1}$

Notation for the derivative

For any expression f(x) then the derivative is indicated by f ´(x).

Example 3

Differentiate the polynomial

$$f(x) = x^3 + 3x^2$$

Solution

$$f(x) = x^3 + 3x^2$$

$$f'(x) = 3x^2 + 2 \times 3x^1$$

$$= 3x^2 + 6x$$

Example 4

Differentiate the polynomial

$$f(x) = \frac{1}{x^3} + 3x - 5$$

Solution

Note that $\frac{1}{x^3} = x^{-3}$ and $3x = 3x^1$ so f(x) becomes

$$f(x) = x^{-3} + 3x^1 - 5$$

The constant 5 has no rate of change and has a derivative of 0.

$$f'(x) = {}^-3x^{-4} + 1 \times 3x^0 - 0$$

$$= {}^-3x^{-4} + 3 \qquad \text{as } x^0 = 1$$

$$= \frac{-3}{x^4} + 3$$

Problems

Differentiate the following polynomials

5. $f(x) = x^3 - 6x - 7$

Extra Examples

Multiply by the old power and reduce the power by one.

The derivative of a constant is always zero. This could also be shown by

$$5 = 5x^0$$

as x^0 is 1. This differentiates to give

$$(5x^0)' = 0 \times 5x^{-1}$$

$$= 0$$

6. $f(x) = 3x^3 - 2x^2 + 5x^{-2}$

7. $f(x) = \dfrac{2}{x^4} - 6\sqrt{x}$

We note that $\dfrac{2}{x^4} = 2x^{-4}$ and $\sqrt{x} = x^{0.5}$ (or $x^{\frac{1}{2}}$)

8. $f(x) = 3(x - 2)^2$

multiply out $3(x - 2)^2$

9. $f(x) = \dfrac{3x^2 + 5x - 6}{x^2}$

divide through by x^2

10. $f(x) = x^{2.5} - 6x^{-0.5}$

11. $f(x) = (4x + 3)(x - 5)$

multiply out $(4x + 3)(x - 5)$ first

12. $f(x) = \sqrt{x^3} - \dfrac{1}{x} + \dfrac{3}{\sqrt{x}}$

rewrite each term in the form kx^n

5.4 Differentiation of the Exponential Function

Prescription

Solve problems in context requiring differentiation of the exponential function e^{ax}

 ## Differentiation of e^{ax}

The exponential function e^x can be represented by the infinite series

$$f(x) = e^x$$

$$= 1 + \frac{x}{1!} + \frac{x^2}{2!} + \frac{x^3}{3!} \cdots$$

If we differentiate term by term we get

$$f'(x) = 0 + 1 + \frac{2x^1}{2!} + \frac{3x^2}{3!} \cdots$$

which simplifies to

$$f'(x) = 1 + \frac{x}{1!} + \frac{x^2}{2!} \cdots$$

$$= e^x$$

Similarly it can be shown that if

$$f(x) = e^{2x}$$

$$= 1 + \frac{(2x)}{1!} + \frac{(2x)^2}{2!} + \frac{(2x)^3}{3!} \cdots$$

then

$$f'(x) = 0 + 2 + \frac{4(2x)^1}{2!} + \frac{6(2x)^2}{3!} \cdots$$

$$= 2e^{2x}$$

In general, for the exponential function

$f(x)$	$f'(x)$
e^x	e^x
e^{2x}	$2e^{2x}$
e^{ax}	ae^{ax}

the derivative of e^{ax} is ae^{ax}

Example 5

Differentiate

$$f(x) = 7e^{3x}$$

Solution

$$f(x) = 7e^{3x}$$

$$f'(x) = 3 \cdot 7e^{3x}$$

$$= 21e^{3x}$$

Problems

Differentiate the following expressions.

13. $f(x) = 3e^{2x}$

14. $f(x) = 3x^2 - 2e^{2x} + 5e^{-2x}$

15. $f(x) = \dfrac{5}{e^x}$

16. $f(x) = \sqrt{e^{4x}}$

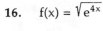 Use $\sqrt{e^{4x}} = (e^{4x})^{0.5}$

5.5 Applications of Differentiation - Rates of Change

Prescription

Solve problems in context requiring differentiation of polynomials x^n for rational values of n

- rates of change (chain rule not required)

Gradient of a curve

As differentiation gives us the instantaneous rate of change we can use it to find the gradient of a curve as well as the gradient of a tangent to the curve.

For any curve represented by the equation y = f(x), the gradient is given by f´(x) for any value of x.

eg. $f(x) = 3x^2 + 5x - 2$

has a gradient function

$f´(x) = 6x + 5$

and by substituting in values of x we can find the gradient of the curve f(x) for those values.

Example 6

Find the gradient of the curve $f(x) = \dfrac{1}{x^3} + 3x^2 - 5x$ at the point x = 2.

Solution

$$f(x) = \frac{1}{x^3} + 3x^2 - 5x$$

Differentiate to get the gradient function

$$f(x) = x^{-3} + 3x^2 - 5x$$

$$f´(x) = {}^-3x^{-4} + 2 \times 3x^1 - 5$$

$$= {}^-3x^{-4} + 6x - 5$$

at x = 2 $f´(2) = {}^-3(2)^{-4} + 6 \times 2 - 5$

$$= 6.8125$$

Example 7

Find the equation of the tangent to the curve

$$f(x) = 3x + \frac{2}{x}$$

through (2, 7).

Solution

For

$$f(x) = 3x + \frac{2}{x}$$

$$= 3x + 2x^{-1}$$

$$f'(x) = 3 - 2x^{-2}$$

at $x = 2$

$$f'(2) = 3 - 2(2)^{-2}$$

$$= 2.5$$

So tangent is given by

$$y - y_1 = m(x - x_1)$$

$$y - 7 = 2.5(x - 2)$$

This form of the straight line is fine but it could be rearranged to

$$y - 7 = 2.5x - 5$$

$$y = 2.5x + 2$$

Problems

Use differentiation to solve the following problems.

17. For the parabola

$$f(x) = x^2 + 5x - 3$$

find the gradient at $x = {}^-1$.

18. For the cubic

$$f(x) = \frac{1}{3}x^3 - 2x^2 + 3x + 3$$

find the gradient of the tangent at $x = 2$ and $x = 3$. Explain your answer for $x = 3$.

19. For the curve

$$f(x) = (2x + 1)(2x - 5)$$

find the gradient at (0, -5) and (1, -9).

20. Find the equation of the tangent at x = 3 for the cubic

$$f(x) = \frac{1}{3}x^3 - 3x^2 + 8x + 1$$

21. The sales of a new toy can be modelled by the expression

$$sales(t) = {}^-3t^2 + 36t + 39$$

where t represents the weeks since the toy was launched.

a) Find the rate of sales after 1, 4, and 9 weeks.

b) After how many weeks do the sales stop increasing.

a)

b)

22. A group of students start to excavate a hole for their new swimming pool. If the amount of soil excavated is v m^3 in t minutes where the relationship between v and t is given by

$$v(t) = 1.25\, t - \frac{t^2}{80}$$

a) Find the rate at which they are excavating the soil after 5, 12 and 25 minutes.

b) How much soil is removed in the first 25 minutes.

a)

b)

5.6 Applications of Differentiation - Max/Min Points

Prescription

Solve problems in context requiring differentiation of polynomials x^n for rational values of n

- problems involving maxima and minima

 ## Maximum and Minimum Points

When any curve reaches a turning point (a maximum or minimum point) then the gradient of that curve is instantaneously zero.

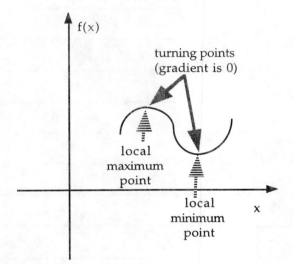

Figure 5

As we can find the gradient function for any polynomial we are able to set this equal to zero to find the x ordinates of all turning points.

 In summary

For any polynomial   f(x)

the gradient function
is its derivative   f´(x)

and the points with
a gradient of zero
are given by   f´(x) = 0

Example 8

Find the turning points of $f(x) = \frac{1}{3}x^3 + 3x^2 - 7x + 3$

Solution

$$f(x) = \frac{1}{3}x^3 + 3x^2 - 7x + 3$$

Differentiate to get the gradient function

$$f'(x) = x^2 + 6x - 7$$

and set the derivative equal to zero

$$f'(x) = 0 \qquad \text{for turning points}$$

$$x^2 + 6x - 7 = 0$$

$$(x + 7)(x - 1) = 0$$

$$x = 1, \; ^-7$$

when $x = 1$ $f(1) = \frac{1}{3}(1)^3 + 3(1)^2 - 7(1) + 3$

$$= \frac{^-2}{3}$$

and $x = ^-7$ $f(^-7) = \frac{1}{3}(^-7)^3 + 3(^-7)^2 - 7(^-7) + 3$

$$= 84\frac{2}{3}$$

The turning points are $(1, \frac{^-2}{3})$ and $(^-7, 84\frac{2}{3})$

Identifying Turning Points

To identify a turning point as a maximum or a minimum point we can use one of the tests which your teacher will probably go over.

Often the context of the problem or a knowledge of the shape of the graph of the polynomial is sufficient for us to identify the polynomial.

The example above (Example 8) is of a positive

cubic as the coefficient of the x^3 is positive.

Therefore the first x value ($x = ^-7$) is going to give the maximum and the second value ($x = 1$) would give us the minimum.

Alternative Approach

An approach that often works is to inspect the y value. When $x = ^-7$ the y value is $84\frac{2}{3}$ while when $x = 1$ the y value is less at $\frac{^-2}{3}$.

Example 9

Find and identify the turning points of

$$f(x) = {}^{-}x^2 - 8x + 4$$

Solution

$$f(x) = {}^{-}x^2 - 8x + 4$$

Differentiate to get the gradient function

$$f'(x) = {}^{-}2x - 8$$

and set the derivative equal to zero

$$f'(x) = 0 \qquad \text{for turning points}$$

$$-2x - 8 = 0$$

$$x = {}^{-}4$$

when $x = {}^{-}4$

$$f({}^{-}4) = {}^{-}({}^{-}4)^2 - 8({}^{-}4) + 4$$

$$= {}^{-}16 + 32 + 4$$

$$= 20$$

As $f(x)$ is a negative parabola , $(-4, 20)$ is a maximum.

Problems

Use differentiation to find and identify the turning points for the following functions.

23. $f(x) = x^2 + 4x + 5$ (note only 1 TP)

24. $f(x) = \frac{1}{3}x^3 - 2x^2 + 3x + 3$

25. $f(x) = 8x - x^2$

26. $f(x) = x^3 - 3x^2 - 9x + 3$

27. $f(x) = 2 + x + \dfrac{4}{x}$

$f(x) = 2 + x + 4x^{-1}$

Note: two answers

28. $f(x) = {}^-x^3 + 12x + 3$

Note: negative cubic

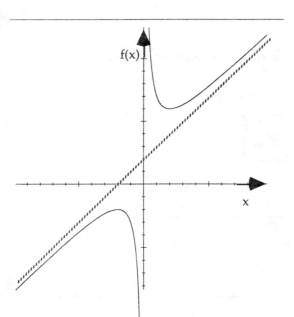

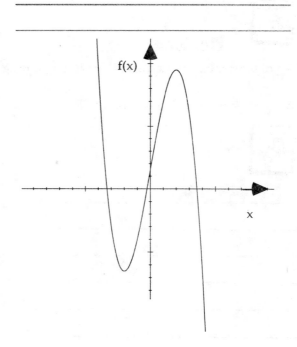

Practical Applications of Differentiation to find Maximum and Minimum values

It is possible to apply differentiation to solve practical problems. To do so, a mathematical expression will need to be identified and differentiated in order to solve the problem. Often this will involve

Drawing a diagram if possible.

Express the problem that needs to be maximised or minimised (often in terms of two variables).

Link the two variables above with an equation.

Substitute for one variable using this link above.

Differentiate.

Equate to zero so that you can find the turning points.

Back substitute into the original problem to find the maximum or minimum value.

Test your answer by re-reading the question.

The mnemonic **DELS DEBT** may help you remember these steps.

Example 10

A glass fish tank with a square base must have a volume of 0.1 cu metres. Find its dimensions so that a minimum amount of glass is used in its construction.

Solution

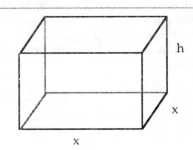

Figure 6

Using **DELS DEBT**

Draw a diagram.

(see Figure 6 on the right)

Express the problem that needs to be maximised or minimised (often in terms of two variables).

$$SA = \text{area bottom} + 4 \text{ sides}$$
$$= x^2 + 4xh$$

Link the two variables above with an equation.

$$\text{volume} = 0.1$$
$$\therefore \quad 0.1 = x^2 h$$

Substitute for one variable using this link above.

$$h = \frac{0.1}{x^2}$$

but

$$SA = x^2 + 4xh$$
$$\therefore \quad = x^2 + 4x \frac{0.1}{x^2}$$
$$= x^2 + \frac{0.4}{x}$$

Differentiate.

$$SA = x^2 + \frac{0.4}{x}$$
$$= x^2 + 0.4x^{-1}$$
$$\therefore \quad SA' = 2x - 0.4x^{-2}$$

Equate to zero so that you can find the turning points.

$$2x - 0.4x^{-2} = 0 \qquad \text{For Max / Min points}$$
$$2x^3 - 0.4 = 0$$
$$\therefore \quad x^3 = 0.2$$
$$x = 0.584$$

Back substitute into the original problem to find the maximum or minimum value.

$$SA = 1.026$$

Test your answer by re-reading the question.

No. The original question called for the dimensions so the correct answer is

Square base 0.584 m by 0.584 with height given by

$$h = 0.1 / (0.584^2)$$
$$= 0.292 \text{ m}$$

Problems

Solve the following maximum and minimum differentiation problems.

29. The sum of two numbers is 30. Find the maximum value of their product.

D   Diagram not needed

E   Prod = xy

L   x + y = 30

30. A right angled triangle's two shorter sides add to 13 cm. Find the maximum area of the triangle.

31. A paddock is made with an electric fence on three sides. The fourth side is formed by an existing fence. If there is 1 km of electric fence find the dimensions of the maximum area of paddock.

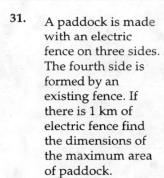
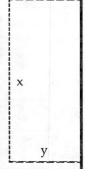

32. A square sheet of tin has sides length 10 cm. Small equal squares (side h) are cut from each corner and the resulting flaps folded up to form an open box. Find the maximum volume of the open box.

© Robert Lakeland & Carl Nugent

5.7 Differential Equations

Introduction

A differential equations is an equation containing a derivative (eg. y'). At this level we solve differential equations by knowing what differentiates to produce a particular differential equation.

Prescription

Solve problems in which the rate of change of a quantity is proportional to the value of the quantity (eg. $y' = ky$)

- **showing by differentiating that $y = Ae^{ax}$ is the solution to $y' = ky$**
- **exponential growth and decay (eg. population growth, radioactive decay, interest)**

 Differential Equations

We solve differential equations by working out what differentiates to produce them.

The differential equation

$$y' = 3x^2 + 4x$$

has a solution

$$y = x^3 + 2x^2 + c$$

where c is any constant.

If we differentiate $y = x^3 + 2x^2 + c$ we get the initial differential equation.

Similarly the differential equation

$$y' = 3e^{3x}$$

has a solution

$$y = e^{3x} + c$$

where c is any constant.

 Example 11

Solve the differential equation

$$y' = 12x^3 + e^x$$

 Solution

We guess what differentiates to give $12x^3$ and test it

Test $\qquad y = 3x^4 + k$

$\Rightarrow \quad y' = 12x^3$

similarly $\quad y = e^x$

$\Rightarrow \quad y' = e^x$

so the solution for the differential equation

is $\qquad y = 3x^4 + e^x + k$

 As any constant differentiates to 0, we are unable to identify any constant that may have been present in the original equation so we always add a constant c or k.

Problems

Match the differential equation in the left hand column with a possible solution on the right.

33.

	f´(x)	f(x)
a)	$f'(x) = 5x^4 + 2x$	$f(x) = 4x^3 + 4x + k$
b)	$f'(x) = 12x^2 + 4$	$f(x) = {}^-4e^{-3x} + x^4 - 5$
c)	$f'(x) = 12x^3 + 6x^2$	$f(x) = 6e^{4x} + 9$
d)	$f'(x) = 12e^{-3x} + 4x^3$	$f(x) = 3x^4 + 2x^3 + 11$
e)	$f'(x) = 24e^{4x}$	$f(x) = x^5 + x^2 + c$

	f´(x)	f(x)
a)	$f'(x) = 5x^4 + 2x$	
b)	$f'(x) = 12x^2 + 4$	
c)	$f'(x) = 12x^3 + 6x^2$	
d)	$f'(x) = 12e^{-3x} + 4x^3$	
e)	$f'(x) = 24e^{4x}$	

Solve the differential equations to get a general solution.

34.

a) $f'(x) = 8e^{2x}$

b) $f'(x) = 6e^{3x}$

c) $f'(x) = 4x^3 + 3x^2$

d) $f'(x) = 12e^{-3x}$

e) $f'(x) = 15x^4 + 2$

f) $f'(x) = 24e^{4x} - 6x + 2$

5.8 Exponential Differential Equations

Introduction

Sometimes in attempting to model real life situations it is found that the rate of change of a variable depends upon how much of that variable is present. An example would be the rate you are saving money (in dollars per time period) depends upon how much money you have invested.

Prescription

Solve problems in which the rate of change of a quantity is proportional to the value of the quantity (eg. $y' = ky$)

- **showing by differentiating that $y = Ae^{ax}$ is the solution to $y' = ky$**

Differential Equations in the form $y' = ky$

From the work in section 5.7 the differential equation

$$y' = 12 e^{3x}$$

could have a solution

$$y = 4e^{3x}$$

as this solution differentiates to give the differential equation.

If the original equation is now re-written as

$$y' = 3 \times 4 e^{3x}$$

and y is substituted for $4 e^{3x}$ the differential equation becomes

$$y' = 3 \times y$$

$$y' = 3y$$

In general any differential equation in the form

$$y' = k \times A e^{kx}$$

has a solution

$$y = A e^{kx}$$

By substituting $A e^{kx} = y$ the original differential equation becomes

$$y' = k y$$

and it has a **general solution**

$$y = A e^{kx}$$

Example 12

Solve the differential equation giving the general solution.

$$y' = 6y$$

Solution

General solution for

$$y' = ky$$

gives $\quad\quad y = Ae^{kx}$

$\therefore \quad y' = 6y$

gives $\quad\quad y = A e^{6x}$

Problems

Find the general solution for the following differential equations.

35. $\quad\quad y' = 12\,y$

Using $y' = k\,y$ has a solution $y = A\,e^{kx}$ then

36. $\quad\quad y' = {}^-3\,y$

37. $\quad\quad y' = \frac{1}{2}\,y$

38. $\quad\quad y' = {}^-0.45\,y$

Specific solutions for y´= ky

It has been established that a differential equation in the form $y´ = k y$ has a solution $y = A e^{kx}$ where A is a constant. To evaluate A, additional information about the problem is required.

Example 13

Solve the differential equation

$$y´ = 0.45 y$$

Given that y depends upon the variable t and that when $t = 0$, $y = 4535$.

Solution

$$y´ = 0.45 y$$
$$\therefore \quad y = A e^{0.45t}$$

If (0, 4535) is one solution then

$$4535 = A e^{0.45t}$$
$$A = 4535$$

So the solution is

$$y = 4535 e^{0.45t}$$

Problems

Find the specific solution for the following differential equations which depend upon t.

39. $y´ = 0.05y$
Given that when t = 0, y = 41.68

Using $y´ = k y$ has a solution $y = A e^{kx}$ then

Substitute (0, 41.68) to find A

40. $y´ = ^-0.13 y$
Given that when t = 2, y = 3152

5.9 Applications of Differential Equations in the form y′ = ky

Introduction

As stated in section 5.8, in modelling real situations, it is found that the rate of change of a variable often depends upon how much of that variable is present. Examples could be

- Depreciation where the rate of decrease (dollars per time period) depends upon the value of the object.

- Population growth where the rate of change (population per time period) depends upon the population level.

- Radioactive decay where the rate of decay (mass per time period) depends upon the radioactive mass.

Prescription

Solve problems in which the rate of change of a quantity is proportional to the value of the quantity (eg. y′ = ky)

- **exponential growth and decay (eg. population growth, radioactive decay, interest)**

Notes

Growth and Decay

When the rate of change over time of an object depends upon a proportion of the object present

$$y' = r \times y$$

where r is the proportion then the solution is

$$y = A e^{rt}$$

With population growth and inflation, r is the rate per time period expressed as a decimal.

With radioactive decay and depreciation, r is the rate per time period expressed as a negative decimal. It is negative as the object is decreasing.

Extra Notes

Example 14

A piece of machinery depreciates at 12.5% per annum. If it was initially worth $64 500 find its value in 5 years.

Solution

The rate (in $ per annum) it depreciates depends upon its value

$$V' = {}^-r\,V$$

V' is negative as the machine is decreasing in value and r = 0.125 (ie 12.5%).

$$V' = {}^-0.125\,V$$

The solution is

$$V = A\,e^{-\,0.125t}$$

At t = 0, V = 64 500

$$\therefore\ 64500 = A\,e^0$$
$$A = 64500$$
$$\therefore\quad V = 64500\,e^{-\,0.125t}$$

At t = 5

$$V = 64500\,e^{-\,0.625}$$
$$= \$34500 \qquad (3\ \text{sig fig})$$

Example 15

Inflation should increase the value of an art work, If inflation is 3.1 % find the price it should attract in 15 years if it is valued at $21 000 now.

Solution

$$V' = 0.031\,V$$

The solution is

$$V = A\,e^{0.031t}$$

At t = 0, V = 21 000

$$\therefore\ 21000 = A\,e^0$$
$$A = 21000$$
$$\therefore\quad V = 21000\,e^{0.031t}$$

At t = 15

$$V = 21000\,e^{0.465}$$
$$= \$33000 \qquad (2\text{sig fig})$$

Extra Examples

Example 16

The population of Palmerston North is growing steadily at 2.3 % per annum. Find the number of years it will take for the population to double.

Solution

The rate (in people per annum) it increases depends upon the population

$$P' = 0.023\,P$$

The solution is

$$P = A\,e^{0.023t}$$

The initial population ($t = 0$) is

$$P = A\,e^0$$
$$= A$$

When the population is doubled then $P = 2A$ solve

$$2A = A\,e^{0.023t}$$
$$2 = e^{0.023t}$$

Taking natural logs of both sides

$$\ln 2 = \ln(e^{0.023t})$$
$$0.6931 = 0.023t$$
$$t = 30.1 \text{ years}$$

Problems

Solve the following problems.

41. A business expects to make 2.5% real capital gain on an investment of $133 000. If the rate of return is proportional to the investment, find an equation that models this investment. After 14 years what would you expect this investment to be worth.

_____

_____

_____

_____

_____

_____

42. A population of rats is increasing at 23% per month. If the local population was originally 6 rats find the population in two years.

_____

_____

_____

_____

_____

_____

43. A radioactive substance is decaying with a half life of 125 years. If one particular sample start at a level of 1350 curies, how long will it take to decay to 100 curies.

_____

use (125, 0.5A) to work out k

_____

_____

then solve for t

_____

_____

_____

44. Assuming inflation has been constant at 2.5% for the past ten years, find the price of a house ten years ago if it now sells for $175000.

_____

_____

use $t = {}^-10$

_____

_____

_____

_____

6.0 Sequences and Series

Introduction

In this section we look at describing the behaviour of different sequences and series, specifically arithmetic, geometric and exponential, and identifying whether they converge. We investigate the use of sequences and series to model real situations, and interpret the findings.

Prescription

Explore patterns and relationships

Use graphing and calculator techniques to describe the behaviour of sequences and series, including the exponential series

- **informal treatment of convergence**

Use sequences and series to model situations and interpret the findings

- **arithmetic and geometric sequences and series**

6.1 Definitions

Definitions

A **sequence** is a list of numbers separated from each other.

eg.   1, 2, 4, 8, 16, 32, 64, 128, ...

A **series** is a sequence that has been 'added' together.

eg.   1 + 2 + 4 + 8 + 16 + 32 + 64 + 128 + ...

The **domain** of a sequence is the set of Natural numbers.

eg.

$$1 \quad 2 \quad 3 \quad 4 \quad 5 \quad 6 \quad 7 \quad 8...$$

$$\downarrow \quad \downarrow \quad \downarrow \quad \downarrow \quad \downarrow \quad \downarrow \quad \downarrow \quad \downarrow$$

$$1 \quad 2 \quad 4 \quad 8 \quad 16 \quad 32 \quad 64 \quad 128 ...$$

The **nth** term of a sequence is the rule for the sequence and we use $T(n)$ or t_n to denote it.

When we write the rule for a sequence inside diamond shaped brackets we are referring to the whole sequence.

eg. $< 2^{n-1} > = 1, 2, 4, 8, 16, 32, 64, ...$

A **recursive** sequence is one where each term is generated from the previous term by a 'rule'. The first or more terms is often needed to generate the sequence.

eg. $t_1 = 3$ and $t_{n+1} = 4t_n + 2$

gives 3, 14, 58, 234, 938, ...

Many series have alternating signs, that is they change from + to - to + to - etc.

eg. $<^-8, 4, ^-2, 1, ^-0.5, 0.25>$

To alternate the signs we put $(^-1)^n$ as the first part of our $T(n)$ formula.

eg. $T(n) = (-1)^n 2^{4-n}$

6.2 Arithmetic and Geometric Sequences

Prescription

- **arithmetic and geometric sequences and series**

In this section we revise much of the sixth form work on sequences and series.

Arithmetic Sequences

An **Arithmetic** sequence is recognisable, because the difference between successive terms is the same - this is called a 'common difference'

Consider the sequence   3, 5, 7, 9, 11, 13, ...

since $t_2 - t_1 = 5 - 3 = 2$

and $t_3 - t_2 = 7 - 5 = 2$

and $t_4 - t_3 = 9 - 7 = 2$ etc.

the sequence is arithmetic.

Formally, if we have an arithmetic sequence with first term 'a' and common difference 'd' then we can write:

$a, \ a + d, \ a + 2d, \ a + 3d, + \ ...... , + a + (n-1)d$

Therefore the rule for the nth term of an arithmetic sequence is given by

$$T(n) = a + (n-1)d$$

Adding up so many terms of an arithmetic sequence is finding a **partial sum.** To find the partial sum S_4 we would add up the first 4 terms of the sequence.

To find a formula for the nth partial sum of an arithmetic sequence, consider the partial sum

$$S_8 = 6 + 10 + 14 + 18 + 22 + 26 + 30 + 34$$

Notice that if we take the pairs of numbers

$$6 + 34 , 10 + 30 , 14 + 26 \text{ and } 18 + 22$$

and add them we obtain the same total '40'. Therefore

$$S_8 = 4 \times 40 = 160$$

Formally we can write this as

$$S_n = \frac{n}{2}(\text{ first } + \text{ last})$$

Since we do not always know the last term of the sequence we now replace 'last' with $a + (n-1)d$ and 'first' with 'a'.

$\therefore \qquad S_n = \frac{n}{2}[a + a + (n-1)d]$

and $S_n = \frac{n}{2}[2a + (n-1)d]$

We now have a formula which we can use to find the sum of 'n' terms of an arithmetic sequence.

Extra Notes

_____

_____

_____

_____

_____

_____

_____

_____

Note Well

This formula is in your tables.
Make sure you can locate it when needed.

_____

_____

_____

_____

_____

Note Well

This formula enables us to find the sum of the first 'n' terms of an AP.
It is in your tables. Make sure you can locate it when needed.

Geometric Sequences

A **Geometric** sequence is recognisable, because the ratio of one term divided by the previous term is always the same. It is said to have a 'common ratio'.

Consider the sequence 3, 6, 12, 24, 48, 96 ....

since $\dfrac{t_2}{t_1} = \dfrac{6}{3} = 2$

and $\dfrac{t_3}{t_2} = \dfrac{12}{6} = 2$

and $\dfrac{t_4}{t_3} = \dfrac{24}{12} = 2$ etc.

the sequence is geometric.

Formally, if we have a geometric sequence with first term 'a' and common ratio 'r' then we can write:

$$a,\ ar,\ ar^2,\ ar^3, +\ ......, + ar^{n-1}$$

Therefore the rule for the nth term of a geometric sequence is given by

$$T(n) = ar^{n-1}$$

This formula is in your tables. Make sure you can locate it when needed.

Adding up so many terms of a geometric sequence is finding a **partial sum.** To find the partial sum S_4 we would add up the first 4 terms of the sequence.

To find a formula for the nth partial sum of a geometric sequence, consider the partial sum

$$S_8 = 3 + 6 + 12 + 24 + 48 + 96 + 192 + 384$$

We now multiply this by the common ratio of 2

so $\quad 2S_8 = 6 + 12 + 24 + 48 + 96 + 192 + 384 + 768$

and $\quad S_8 = 3 + 6 + 12 + 24 + 48 + 96 + 192 + 384$

Subtracting the second line from the first.

$\therefore\quad S_8 = 768 - 3$

$\therefore\qquad S_8 = 765$

Formally we can write this as

$$rS_n = ar + ar^2 + ar^3 + ar^4 + ar^5 + ... + ar^n$$
$$S_n = a + ar + ar^2 + ar^3 + ar^4 + ... + ar^{n-1}$$

Subtracting the second line from the first.

$\therefore\ rS_n - S_n = ar^n - a$

$\therefore\ S_n(r-1) = a(r^n - 1)$

$\therefore\ Sn = \dfrac{a(r^n - 1)}{r - 1}$

This formula enables us to find the sum of the first 'n' terms of a GP. It is in your tables. Make sure you can locate it when needed.

Sum to Infinity

It is sometimes possible to find the **sum to infinity** of a Geometric sequence. For this to be possible we need to look at the ratio 'r' of the sequence.

If 'r' is between -1 and 1, that is $|r| < 1$, then when we raise 'r' to a high power it will become very small.

ie. as $n \to \infty$ then $r^n \to 0$.

Therefore as $\quad S_n = \dfrac{a(r^n - 1)}{r - 1}$

now as $n \to \infty$ then $r^n \to 0$ if $|r| < 1$

so $\qquad S_\infty = \dfrac{a}{1 - r}, \quad |r| < 1$

Extra Notes

_____

_____

_____

_____

Note Well

This formula is in your tables. Make sure you can locate it when needed.

Example 1   Find the nth term and the 20th term of the following two sequences.

a)   9, 4, ⁻1, ⁻6, ⁻11, ...

b)   16, 8, 4, 2, 1, ...

Solution

a)   Arithmetic sequence since it has a common difference d= -5 and first term a = 9

$\qquad$ Using $T(n) = a + (n-1)d$

$\qquad\qquad T(n) = 9 + (n-1)^-5$

$\qquad\qquad T(n) = {}^-5n + 14$

$\qquad$ Now $T(20) = -5(20) + 14$

$\qquad\qquad \therefore T(20) = -86$

Solution

b)   Geometric sequence since it has a common ratio $r = \frac{1}{2}$ and first term a = 16

$\qquad$ Using $T(n) = ar^{n-1}$

$\qquad\qquad T(n) = 16 . \dfrac{1}{2}^{n-1}$

$\qquad$ Now $T(20) = 16 . \dfrac{1}{2}^{20-1}$

$\qquad\qquad \therefore T(20) = \dfrac{1}{32768}$

Example 2   Find the sum of the first 10 terms of the sequences.

a)   2, 6, 10, 14, 18, 22, ...

b)   1, 3, 9, 27, 81, ...

Solution

a)   Arithmetic sequence since it has a common difference d= 4 and first term a = 2

$\qquad$ Using $\quad S_n = \dfrac{n}{2}[2a + (n-1)d]$

$\qquad \therefore \quad S_{10} = \dfrac{10}{2}[2(2) + (10-1)4]$

$\qquad \therefore \quad S_{10} = 5[4 + (9)4]$

$\qquad \therefore \quad S_{10} = 200$

Solution

b)   Geometric sequence since it has a common ratio r = 3 and first term a = 1

$\qquad$ Using $\quad S_n = \dfrac{a(r^n - 1)}{r - 1}$

$\qquad \therefore \quad S_{10} = \dfrac{1(3^{10} - 1)}{3 - 1}$

$\qquad \therefore \quad S_{10} = 29524$

Example 3

List the first 6 terms of the sequence $< (-1)^n \, 2^{3-n} >$

Solution

$t_1 = (^-1).2^2$ $t_2 = (1).2^1$ $t_3 = (^-1).2^0$

   $= -4$ $= 2$ $= ^-1$

$t_4 = (1).2^{-1}$ $t_5 = (^-1).2^{-2}$ $t_6 = (1).2^{-3}$

   $= \dfrac{1}{2}$ $= \dfrac{-1}{4}$ $= \dfrac{1}{8}$

Example 4

Give the first 6 terms of the sequence defined by

$$t_1 = 2, \ t_2 = ^-1 \ \text{ and } \ t_n = 3t_{n-1} + nt_{n-2}$$

Solution

$t_1 = 2,$ $t_2 = ^-1,$ $t_3 = 3t_2 + 3t_1$

                                                 $= 3$

$t_4 = 3t_3 + 4t_2 = 5$ $t_5 = 3t_4 + 5t_3$ $t_6 = 3t_5 + 6t_4$

   $= 5$ $= 30$ $= 120$

Example 5

A ball is dropped from a height of 9m. Each time it hits the ground it rebounds to only one third of the distance it last fell. What is the total distance that the ball travels before coming to rest.

Solution

Sequence is $9, \ 3, \ 1, \ \dfrac{1}{3}, \ \dfrac{1}{9}, \ \dfrac{1}{27}, \ ....,$ which is a geometric sequence. Since $r = \dfrac{1}{3}$, we can use the sum to infinity.

The total distance travelled by the ball is essentially made up of the sum of two sequences - the values when the ball is dropping and the values when the ball is bouncing back up.

Dropping sequence is $9, \ 3, \ 1, \ \dfrac{1}{3}, \ \dfrac{1}{9}, \ \dfrac{1}{27}, \ ....$ Bouncing back up sequence is $3, \ 1, \ \dfrac{1}{3}, \ \dfrac{1}{9}, \ \dfrac{1}{27}, \ ....$

Using $S_\infty = \dfrac{a}{1-r}$

Total distance travelled is $S_\infty = \dfrac{9}{1-\dfrac{1}{3}} + \dfrac{3}{1-\dfrac{1}{3}}$

$\therefore$ $S_\infty = 18m$

Problems

1. Find the nth term and the 20th term of the following sequences.

a) 2, 9, 16, 23, 30, ...

b) 120, 72, $43\frac{1}{5}$, $25\frac{23}{25}$, ...

_____

Arithmetic or Geometric

Find 'a' and 'd' OR 'r'

Use appropriate T(n) formula

Substitute 20 into formula

c) 10, -1, -12, -23, -34, ...

d) -3, $-6q^2$, $-12q^4$, ...

_____

Arithmetic or Geometric

Find 'a' and 'd' OR 'r'

Use appropriate T(n) formula

Substitute 20 into formula

2. Find the sum of the first 25 terms of the following.

a) 6, 14, 22, 30, 38, ...

b) 19, 38, 76, 152, ...

c) ‾6, ‾20, ‾34, ‾48, ‾62, ...

d) 2, $2\sqrt{2}$, 4, $4\sqrt{2}$

3. List the first 5 terms of the sequence defined by

a) $T(1) = {}^-5$, $T(2) = 4$,

   and $T(n+1) = -2(T(n))^2 - T(n-1)$

b) $T(1) = 4$, $T(2) = {}^-4$, $T(n + 1) = \dfrac{-2\,T(n)}{T(n - 1)}$

_____

_____

_____

_____

_____

_____

4. A crab is stranded 50 metres from a rocky pool. Between each wave it crawls 10 metres towards the pool. However every time a wave hits, it is washed backed 6m.

a) After how many waves has it reached the rocky pool.

a) _____

_____

_____

_____

b) What is the total distance travelled by the crab (forward and back) by the time it reaches the pool.

b) _____

_____

_____

_____

5. A pendulum successively swings through the following distances 40, 32, 25.6, 20.48, ... cm.

a) Find the total distance it travels before it comes to rest.

a) _____

_____

_____

_____

_____

b) How many swings must it have completed before it has travelled a total distance of at least 1.6 metres.

b) _____

_____

_____

_____

_____

6.3 Sigma Notation

Sigma Notation

In this section we look at a form of notation, called **Sigma Notation** which will enable us to represent the adding of a sequence of numbers.

The Greek letter sigma, drawn below, means the 'sum of'.

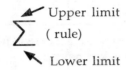

Upper limit

(rule)

Lower limit

The expression at the top represents the upper limit and the expression at the bottom the lower limit. The rule to generate the sequence is written immediately following the sigma sign.

Formally $\displaystyle\sum_{r=1}^{5} a_r = a_1 + a_2 + a_3 + a_4 + a_5$

Properties of Sigma Notation

1. Common factors can be removed.

$$\sum_{r=1}^{n} K a_r = K . \sum_{r=1}^{n} a_r$$

2. A constant term added n times is n times c.

$$\sum_{r=1}^{n} c = c + c + c + \dots + c = nc$$

3. $\displaystyle\sum_{r=1}^{n} (x_r + y_r) = \sum_{r=1}^{n} x_r + \sum_{r=1}^{n} y_r$

Extra Notes

Example 6

Evaluate $\displaystyle\sum_{r=1}^{6} (3r + 4)$

Solution

Lower limit $r = 1$. Upper limit $r = 6$. Rule $(3r + 4)$

$\therefore \displaystyle\sum_{r=1}^{6} (3r + 4) = (3 + 4) + (6 + 4) + (9 + 4) + (12 + 4) + (15 + 4) + (18 + 4)$

$= 7 + 10 + 13 + 16 + 19 + 22$

$= 87$

Example 7

Write the following in sigma notation.

$7 + 12 + 17 + 22 + 27 + 32 + 37 + 42$

Solution

Arithmetic sequence - first term $a = 7$, common difference $d = 5$

Using $T(n) = a + (n - 1)d$ to find the rule

$\therefore$ $T(n) = 7 + (n - 1)5$

$\therefore$ $T(n) = 5n + 2$

Using sigma notation with lower limit = 1 and upper limit = 8

$\therefore$ $\displaystyle\sum_{n=1}^{8} (5n + 2)$

Problems

6. Evaluate $\displaystyle\sum_{n=1}^{5} (2n^2 + 1)$

7. Evaluate $\displaystyle\sum_{n=3}^{7} (-1)^n \left(\frac{1}{2n + 3}\right)$

8. Write in sigma notation
    $20 + 17 + 14 + 11 + \ldots + -4$

9. Write in sigma notation
    $20 + 10 + 5 + \ldots + .15625$

10. Evaluate $\sum_{n=1}^{5} (2n+1)(3n-2)$

_____

_____

_____

_____

11. Evaluate $\sum_{n=1}^{4} (-1)^{n+1} 2^{n+1}$

_____

_____

_____

_____

12. Write in sigma notation

$\frac{1}{5} + \frac{1}{7} + \frac{1}{9} + \frac{1}{11} + ... + \frac{1}{51}$

_____

_____

_____

_____

13. Write in sigma notation

$3 \times 2 + 5 \times 4 + 7 \times 8 + 9 \times 16 + ... + 17 \times 256$

_____

_____

_____

_____

14. Evaluate $\sum_{x=1}^{4} (ax+b)$

_____

_____

_____

_____

15. Write in sigma notation

$\frac{1}{2} + \frac{3}{4} + \frac{9}{8} + \frac{27}{16} + ...$

_____

_____

_____

_____

6.4 Behaviour of a Sequence

Prescription

- use graphing and calculator techniques to describe the behaviour of sequences and series

Behaviour of a Sequence

To identify and describe the behaviour of a sequence it is often worthwhile to graph the sequence first. We usually represent T(n) on the y axis and n on the x axis. Some of the different properties of sequences are drawn and identified below.

Increasing - A sequence is said to be increasing if the current term is greater than or equal to the previous term ie. $t_{n+1} \geq t_n$

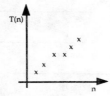

Strictly Increasing - A sequence is said to be strictly increasing if the current term is greater than the previous term ie. $t_{n+1} > t_n$

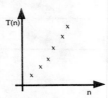

Decreasing - A sequence is said to be decreasing if the current term is less than or equal to the previous term ie. $t_{n+1} \leq t_n$

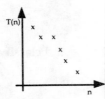

Strictly Decreasing - A sequence is said to be strictly decreasing if the current term is less than the previous term ie. $t_{n+1} < t_n$

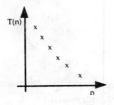

Behaviour of a Sequence cont...

Bounded Above - A sequence is said to be bounded above if all terms are less than or equal to a specific value ie. $t_n \leq u$, where u is the upper bound.

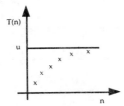

Bounded Below - A sequence is said to be bounded below if all terms are greater than a specific value ie. $t_n \geq b$, where b is the lower bound.

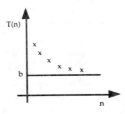

Constant - A sequence is constant if each successive term is the same ie. $t_n = c$

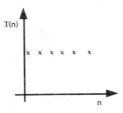

Example 8

Draw a graph of the sequence $<\frac{2n+1}{n+2}>$ and classify it by using the appropriate descriptors.

Solution

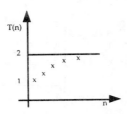

From the graph the sequence is
- strictly increasing
- bounded above by 2

Problems

After drawing graphs of the given sequences, classify them using appropriate descriptors.

16. $\left\langle \dfrac{3n+1}{n} \right\rangle$

_____

_____

_____

_____

_____

_____

17. $\left\langle \dfrac{2n+1}{n+5} \right\rangle$

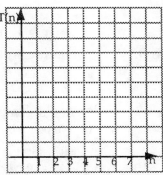

_____

_____

_____

_____

_____

18. Study the graph of the sequence below and describe it using appropriate descriptors.

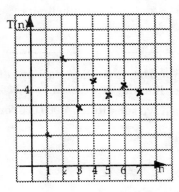

_____

_____

_____

_____

_____

6.5 Limit of a Sequence

Prescription

• informal treatment of convergence

Limit of a Sequence

Some sequences approach a definite value. These sequences are said to have a **limit**.

Sequences which have a limit are said to **converge**. Those that don't have a limit are said to **diverge**.

Consider the diagram of the sequence $< 2 + \dfrac{1}{2^n} >$ below

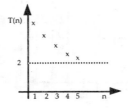

Obviously it is getting closer to the value 2, which we call the limit.

Example 9

A sequence is defined by $< \dfrac{4n + 2}{n + 1} >$. State the limit of the sequence.

Solution

To find the limit of the sequence we find another way of expressing it. We begin by dividing the denominator into the numerator.

$\therefore \ \lim\limits_{n \to \infty} \dfrac{4n + 2}{n + 1}$

$= \lim\limits_{n \to \infty} 4 - \dfrac{2}{n + 1}$ rewriting by dividing $4n + 2$ by $n + 1$

$\therefore$ as $n \to \infty, \ \dfrac{2}{n + 1} \to 0$ as n gets larger $\dfrac{2}{n + 1}$ tends to zero

$\therefore$ the limit of $< \dfrac{4n + 2}{n + 1} >$ is 4

Another approach to finding the limit of a sequence is to use the 'millionaire theory'. Substitute a very large number into the expression, ie. 1,000,000 and calculate what value the expression is close to. In Example 9 above if we substituted 1,000,000 for 'n' we would obtain $\dfrac{4,000,002}{1,000,001}$ which is very close to 4, the limit of the sequence.

Problems

19. Find the limit of $< \dfrac{1}{n^2} >$

20. Find the limit of $< \dfrac{6n+2}{2n+3} >$

21. Find the limit of $< \dfrac{n+4}{2n-1} >$

22. Find the limit of $< 3\left(1 - \left(\tfrac{1}{2}\right)^n\right) >$

6.6 Series

Prescription

- use graphing and calculator techniques to describe the behaviour of sequences and series, including the exponential series
- informal treatment of convergence

Series

In this section we take a closer look at **series**.

Since most series we will be dealing with are infinite, we need a technique that will enable us to identify whether the series converges or diverges.

Looking at what happens to the total as we add successive terms of the sequence, can give us information on the series itself.

This sequence of totals is called the sequence of partial sums.

We use the notation S_n to mean the sum of the first n terms, or nth partial sum.

eg.   Consider the series $16 + 8 + 4 + 2 + 1 + \ldots$

$S_1 = 16$ (1st partial sum)

$S_2 = 16 + 8 = 24$ (2nd partial sum)

$S_3 = 16 + 8 + 4 = 28$ (3rd partial sum)

$S_4 = 16 + 8 + 4 + 2 = 30$ (4th partial sum)

etc.

The sequence of partial sums is 16, 24, 28, 30, ...

Note Well

Remember a series is a sequence that has been 'added' together.

Note Well

If the sequence of partial sums converges to a particular value, then the series itself will converge.

Note Well

If the sequence of partial sums does not converge to a value then the series is said to diverge.

Example 10

$S_n = \dfrac{2n-3}{n+1}$ generates the partial sums of a series.

a) Find the first 4 **partial sums**.

b) Find the first 4 **terms** of the series.

c) Show that the series converges to a limit, and find the limit.

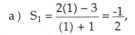

Solution

a) $S_1 = \dfrac{2(1)-3}{(1)+1} = \dfrac{-1}{2}$,

$S_2 = \dfrac{2(2)-3}{(2)+1} = \dfrac{1}{3}$,

$S_3 = \dfrac{2(3)-3}{(3)+1} = \dfrac{3}{4}$,

$S_4 = \dfrac{2(4)-3}{(4)+1} = 1$

Solution

b) $T_1 = S_1 = \dfrac{-1}{2}$,

$T_2 = S_2 - S_1 = \dfrac{5}{6}$,

$T_3 = S_3 - S_2 = \dfrac{5}{12}$,

$T_4 = S_4 - S_3 = \dfrac{1}{4}$

$\therefore$ series is $\dfrac{-1}{2} + \dfrac{5}{6} + \dfrac{5}{12} + \dfrac{1}{4} + \ldots$

Solution

c) For the series to converge

$\displaystyle\lim_{n \to \infty} S_n$ must exist.

Using the division technique.

$\therefore \displaystyle\lim_{n \to \infty} \dfrac{2n-3}{n+1} = \lim_{n \to \infty} 2 - \dfrac{5}{n+1}$

dividing $(n+1)$ into $(2n-3)$

$\therefore$ as $n \to \infty$, $\dfrac{5}{n+1} \to 0$

$\therefore$ limit is 2

(or by the "*millionaire theory*")

The limit of S_n is 2 (ie. it exists). Therefore the series
$\dfrac{-1}{2} + \dfrac{5}{6} + \dfrac{5}{12} + \dfrac{1}{4} + \ldots$ converges

Problems

23.   The partial sums of a series is given by $S_n = 5 + \dfrac{2}{n}$

a) Find S_1, S_2, S_3 and S_4

b) Find the first 4 terms of the series.

c) Show the series converges and find the limit of S_n.

a)

b)

c)

24.   The first 4 partial sums of a series are $S_1 = 1\frac{2}{3}$, $S_2 = 3\frac{13}{15}$, $S_3 = 6\frac{31}{105}$ and $S_4 = 8\frac{268}{315}$

a) List the first four terms of the original sequence.

b) Show that $T_n = \dfrac{6n-1}{2n+1}$ is the nth term of the sequence.

c) What is the limit of the sequence $\langle T_n \rangle = \dfrac{6n-1}{2n+1}$, for any natural number n.

a)

_____

_____

_____

_____

_____

_____

b)

_____

_____

_____

_____

_____

_____

c)

_____

_____

_____

_____

_____

_____

25.   The nth term of a sequence is given by $t_n = \dfrac{n+3}{2n}$

a)   Write down the first 4 terms of the sequence.

b)   Show, by graphing, that the sequence is decreasing and bounded below by $\frac{1}{2}$

c)   State the value of $\displaystyle\lim_{n \to \infty} t_n$

d)   Write down the first four terms of the sequence of partial sums.

e)   Is this sequence of partial sums converging.

a)

_____

_____

_____

_____

_____

_____

b)

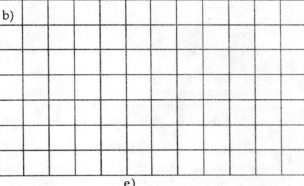

c)

_____

_____

_____

_____

d)

_____

_____

_____

_____

e)

_____

_____

_____

_____

6.7 The Exponential Series

Prescription

- the exponential series

The Exponential Series

Extra Notes

A function of the form $f(x) = a^x$, where 'a' is called the base and 'x' the exponent is called an exponential function or growth curve.

The **exponential function** $f(x) = e^x$ (see Figure 1) is a special growth curve in that it is, its own derivative. ie. the slope of the function at any point is the same as the functional value at the point.

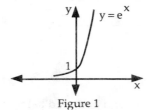

Figure 1

It is possible to express many mathematical functions as series. In this section we look at a series that approximates the exponential function.

$$\exp(x) \text{ or } e^x = 1 + x + \frac{x^2}{2!} + \frac{x^3}{3!} + \frac{x^4}{4!} + \dots$$

$$= \sum_{n=1}^{\infty} \frac{x^{n-1}}{(n-1)!}$$

Note Well

This series is in your tables. Make sure you can locate it when needed.

Some problems that are related to exponential series require a series to be written out in full. By substituting appropriately for x and using the expansion above we can obtain the necessary series.

The exponential series always converges, irrespective of the value for x, because ultimately the factorial values on the denominator will become larger than the numerator values - therefore we will start to add successively smaller values and the series will converge.

Example 11

Write down the first 4 terms of the series e^{3x}.

Solution

Using the exponential series.

$$e^x = 1 + x + \frac{x^2}{2!} + \frac{x^3}{3!} + \frac{x^4}{4!} + ...$$

and substituting 3x for x

$$\therefore \quad e^{3x} = 1 + (3x) + \frac{(3x)^2}{2!} + \frac{(3x)^3}{3!} + \frac{(3x)^4}{4!} + ...$$

$$\therefore \quad e^{3x} = 1 + 3x + \frac{9x^2}{2} + \frac{9x^3}{2} + \frac{27x^4}{8} + ...$$

Example 12

Write down the first 4 terms of $(1 + x)e^x$.

Solution

Using the exponential series.

$$e^x = 1 + x + \frac{x^2}{2!} + \frac{x^3}{3!} + \frac{x^4}{4!} + ...$$

$$(1 + x) e^x = (1 + x) \left(1 + x + \frac{x^2}{2!} + \frac{x^3}{3!} + \frac{x^4}{4!} + ...\right)$$

Multiplying out

$$(1 + x) e^x = \left(1 + x + \frac{x^2}{2!} + \frac{x^3}{3!} + \frac{x^4}{4!} + ...\right) + \left(x + x^2 + \frac{x^3}{2!} + \frac{x^4}{3!} + \frac{x^5}{4!} + ...\right)$$

$$= 1 + 2x + \frac{3x^2}{2} + \frac{2x^3}{3} + ...$$

Example 13

Use the exponential series to evaluate $\frac{1}{\sqrt[3]{e}}$ to four decimal places.

Solution   Using the exponential series and substituting $\frac{-1}{3}$ for x.

$$e^{\frac{-1}{3}} = 1 + \left(\frac{-1}{3}\right) + \frac{\left(\frac{-1}{3}\right)^2}{2!} + \frac{\left(\frac{-1}{3}\right)^3}{3!} + \frac{\left(\frac{-1}{3}\right)^4}{4!} + \frac{\left(\frac{-1}{3}\right)^5}{5!} \qquad \text{(note } \frac{1}{\sqrt[3]{e}} = e^{\frac{-1}{3}}\text{)}$$

$$e^{\frac{-1}{3}} = .7165 \text{ (4dp)}$$

Note: we stop at the sixth term in this example, since

$$\frac{\left(\frac{-1}{3}\right)^6}{6!} = .000001905...\text{is not required for accuracy to 4dp.}$$

Problems

26. Write down the first four terms of e^{5x}.

Substitute 5x into the exponential series

_____

_____

_____

_____

_____

27. Write down the first four terms of e^{x^2}

_____

_____

_____

_____

_____

28. Calculate the value of e^{-3} using the first 7 terms of the exponential series.

_____

_____

_____

_____

_____

29. Write down the first 4 terms of the series expansion $(2 + 3x)e^{2x}$.

_____

_____

_____

_____

_____

30. Write down the first 4 terms of the series expansion $(1 - 4x)e^{3x}$.

_____

_____

_____

_____

_____

31. Find the first three terms for the series expansion for $\dfrac{1 + x}{e^x}$.

_____

_____

_____

_____

_____

7.0 Graphs

Introduction

A graphical representation of a problem can often help us see where solutions are likely to occur.

Prescription

Exploring patterns and relationships

Use graphical techniques to illustrate

- $y = x^a$
- **piece-wise functions**

Choose an appropriate type of model for real data, analyse and interpret results

- **transforming variables (including log-log and semi-log techniques)**

Model situations using linear programming techniques, and obtain the optimal solution

7.1 The Power Function $y = x^a$

The Rules of Indices

We use the following terms for indices

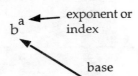

b^a ← exponent or index

base

From our work in previous years we have summarised the rules of indices as

$$x^a.x^b = x^{a+b} \qquad \frac{x^a}{x^b} = x^{a-b}$$

$$(x^a)^b = x^{ab} \qquad (x.y^a)^b = x^b.y^{ab}$$

$$x^{-a} = \frac{1}{x^a} \qquad x^{\frac{1}{a}} = {}^a\sqrt{x}$$

$$x^0 = 1 \ (\text{if } x \neq 0)$$

To understand the power functions $y = x^a$ we make use of these rules.

Extra Notes

© Robert Lakeland & Carl Nugent

Graphs of the Power Function

For the power function $y = x^a$, a is constant for each particular function.

1. If a < 0 then the resulting curve has asymptotes at right angles to each other.

In Figure 1 the power functions $y = x^{-0.4}$, $y = x^{-1.2}$ and $y = x^{-2.4}$ are plotted

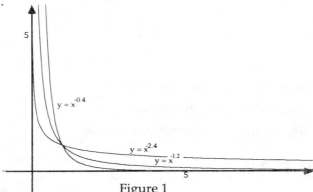

Figure 1

Unless 'a' in $y = x^a$ is an integer it is unlikely that we can plot negative values of x as we are unable to take the root of a negative number.

2. If a = 0 then $y = x^0$ simplifies to $y = 1$ as $x^0 = 1$. The graph of $y = 1$ is a straight line parallel to the x axis

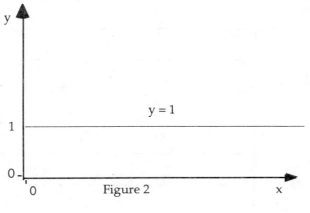

Figure 2

The Dynamic Graph facility on your graphics calculator (Casio CFX-9850G or Texas Instruments TI 83) enables you to sketch a number of graphs of the same form, eg. $y = x^k$. You specify a variable (ie. k) with start, finish and increment values and the various graphs are drawn on the same set of axis.

Extra Notes

Extra Notes

Graphs of the Power Function cont...

3. If $0 < a < 1$ we get the characteristic 'square root' function. In Figure 3 the power function $y = x^{0.6}$ is plotted.

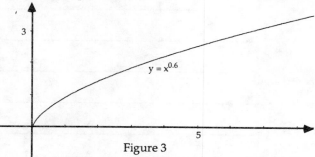

Figure 3

4. If $a > 1$ then we get the functions plotted in Figure 4.

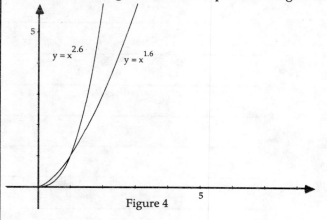

Figure 4

Example 1

Simplify the algebraic expression $(4x^2y^{-1})^{-2}$.

Solution

Using $(x.y^a)^b = x^b.y^{ab}$

$$(4x^2y^{-1})^{-2} = (4^{-2}x^{-4}y^2)$$

Now using $x^{-a} = \dfrac{1}{x^a}$

$$(4^{-2}x^{-4}y^2) = \dfrac{y^2}{4^2x^4}$$

$$= \dfrac{y^2}{16\,x^4}$$

Example 2

Graph the equation $y = x^{-1.1}$

Solution

By plotting points $x > 0$

x	y
0	~
0.2	5.87
0.4	2.74
0.6	1.75
0.8	1.28
1.0	1.00
1.2	0.82
2	0.47

Plotting these on a graph gives

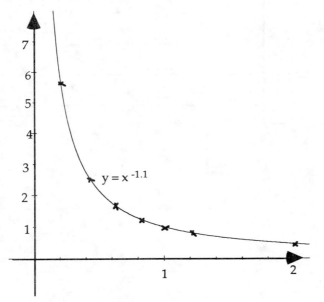

Figure 5

Extra Examples

<u>Problems</u>

Simplify the algebraic expressions. Your answer should always have positive indices.

1. $\dfrac{(4x^2)^3}{8x^{-2}}$

2. $\dfrac{x^{-3}(3y^3y^5)^0}{(x^5)^2}$

Graph the following power functions.

3. $y = x^{-0.5}$

4. $y = x^{1.5}$

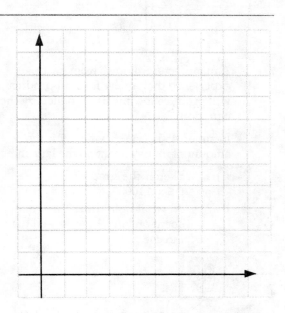

Sketch the family of curves as n takes values from the starting point (in steps of 1) to the end point.

5. $y = x^n$ for $1 \leq n \leq 4$
          using x values from ⁻3 to 3

x	$y_1 = x^1$	$y_2 = x^2$	$y_3 = x^3$	$y_4 = x^4$
⁻3				
⁻2				
⁻1				
0				
1				
2				
3				

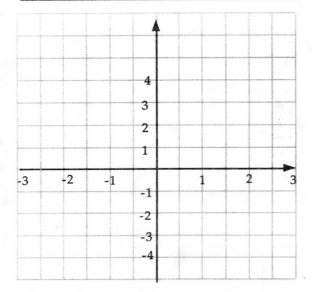

6. $y = x^{1/n}$ for $1 \leq n \leq 4$
          using x values from ⁻3 to 3

x	$y_1 = x^1$	$y_2 = x^{0.5}$	$y_3 = x^{0.33}$	$y_4 = x^{0.25}$
⁻3				
⁻2				
⁻1				
0				
1				
2				
3				

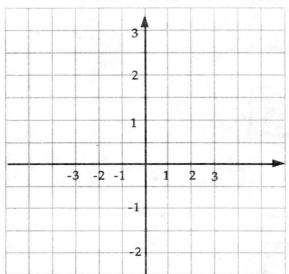

7. A manufacturer knows from past experience that a new fashion product will produce income as modelled by the equation.

Income= $450 \times (x)^{0.32}$ where x is the amount of money spent on the launching.

a) Sketch the graph for $0 \leq x \leq 10000$.

b) At what point does the money spent on launching exceed the income.

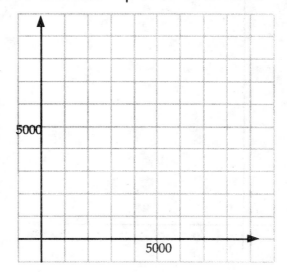

Answer from graph is_____

7.2 The Exponential Functions

Prescription

Exploring patterns and relationships

 Note Well

The exponential or growth function can be expressed in two forms which are mathematically equivalent. Your teacher will probably use one or the other and we would encourage you to consistently use the form taught by your teacher.

Either the equation is in the form

$$y = k\, e^{ax}$$

where e is an irrational number approximately equal to 2.71828.

An example is $y = e^{3x}$

or the equation is in the form

$$y = k\, c^x$$

This form appears to be different but is the same with $c = e^a$

An example is $y = 20^x$

For consistency problems in this book will follow the $y = k\, e^{ax}$ model but all problems can be solved by either model.

Notes

Growth Curves $(f(x) = ke^{ax})$

Growth curves are often the most appropriate mathematical model we can find for real data.
An exponential function can be in the form

$$f(x) = k\, e^{ax}$$

The constant k is a multiplying factor which stretches the graph parallel to the y axis (see Figure 6).

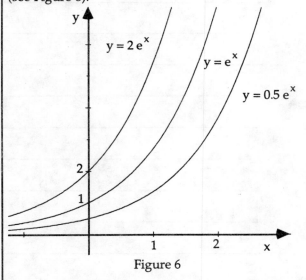

Figure 6

Extra Notes

© Robert Lakeland & Carl Nugent

Growth Curves cont...

Different values of a in $f(x) = k\,e^{ax}$ produce the family of possible curves in Figure 7.

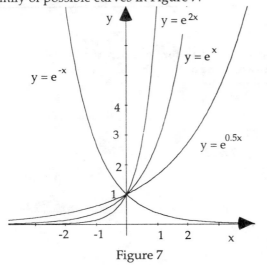

Figure 7

Example 3

Sketch the exponential function.

$$f(x) = 4\,e^{-0.5x}$$

Solution

Plot points from x = ⁻3 to x = 3.

x	y
-3	17.9
-2	10.9
-1	6.6
0	4
1	2.4
2	1.5
3	0.9

$$y = 4\,e^{-0.5x}$$

Example 4a

Express the exponential function.

$$f(x) = 3 e^{1.5x}$$

in the form $f(x) = k c^x$

Solution

$$e^{1.5} = 4.48$$

$$\therefore \quad f(x) = 3 \times 4.48^x$$

Example 4b

Express the exponential function.

$$f(x) = 3 \times 1.065^x$$

in the form $f(x) = k e^{ax}$

Solution

$$e^a = 1.065$$

$$\therefore \quad a = \log_e 1.065$$

$$a = 0.0630$$

$$f(x) = 3 e^{0.0630 x}$$

Problems

Sketch all the exponential functions.

8. $\quad f(x) = e^{0.45 x}$

9. $\quad f(x) = 1.85^x$

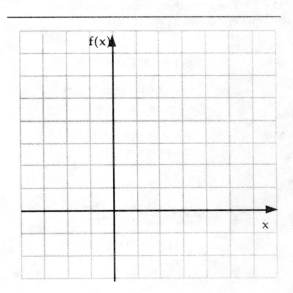

Sketch the exponential functions.

10. $f(x) = 3 e^{1.2x}$

_____

_____

_____

_____

_____

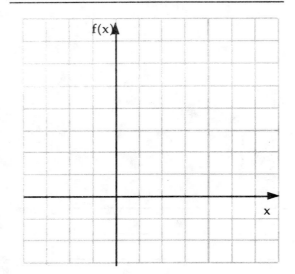

11. $f(x) = 8 e^{-0.45x}$

_____

_____

_____

_____

_____

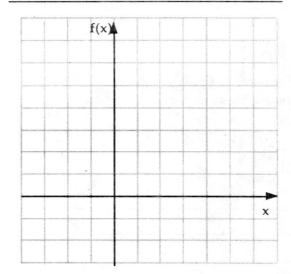

Graph the exponential function and use it to answer the following questions.

12. The growth of the population in Wanganui is described by the equation

$$p(t) = 32150 \, e^{0.0080t}$$

a) Sketch the graph $p(t)$ from $t = {}^-30$ to $t = 50$

b) What is the population in the year $t = 15$

$p(15) = \underline{\qquad}.$

c) In what year is the population = 40 000.

$p(t) = 40\,000$

$t = \underline{\qquad}.$

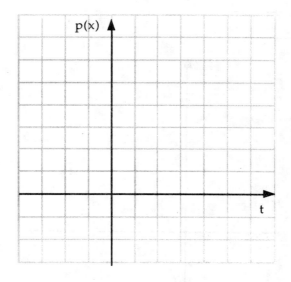

7.3 Piece-wise Functions

Prescription

Exploring patterns and relationships

Use graphical techniques to illustrate

- **piece-wise functions**

 Piece-wise Functions

A piece-wise function is described by different equations for different intervals of its domain or x values.

For example

$$f(x) = \begin{cases} x & \text{for } x < 0 \\ x^2 & 0 \le x < 2 \\ 8 - 2x & 2 < x \le 4 \end{cases}$$

is the line $f(x) = x$ for x less than 0

then it is $f(x) = x^2$ for x greater than or equal 0 to x less than 2

then it becomes $f(x) = 8 - 2x$ for x greater than 2 but less than or equal to 4.

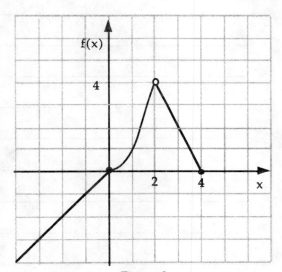

Figure 8

Where an end point is included we use a filled circle

● (see x = 0 and 4 in Figure 8) and where it is

excluded we use an empty circle ○

(see x = 2 in Figure 8).

 Extra Notes

Example 5

Sketch the piece-wise function.

$$f(x) = \begin{cases} 2-x & \text{for } x < 0 \\ x^{1.5} & 0 \le x < 4 \\ 8 & 4 < x \end{cases}$$

Solution

1. Draw the line $y = 2 - x$ for $x < 0$. Leave an open circle at $x = 0$.

2. Plot points of $y = x^{1.5}$ and join up from $x = 0$ to $x = 4$. Leave a closed circle at $x = 0$ but an open circle at $x = 4$.

x	y
0	0
1	1
2	2.83
3	5.20
4	8

3. Draw the line $y = 8$ for $x > 4$.

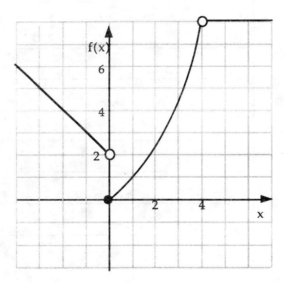

Problems

Sketch the piece-wise functions.

13.

$$f(x) = \begin{cases} 3 & \text{for } x < 0 \\ x^{0.5} & 0 < x \leq 4 \\ 2x - 6 & 4 < x \end{cases}$$

14.

$$f(x) = \begin{cases} 3 & \text{for } x = -1 \\ x^3 & -1 < x < 2 \\ -(x-2)^2 + 8 & 2 < x < 3 \end{cases}$$

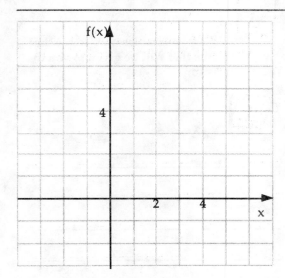

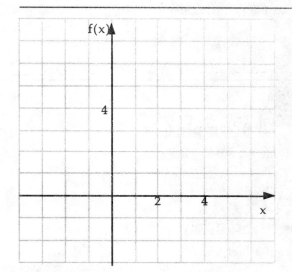

Use the piece-wise function on the right to answer the following questions.

15. The graph of f(x) is shown on the right. Use it to answer the following questions.

a) Find f(4), and f(⁻1.5)

b) If f(x) = 1 find x

c) Write the piece-wise equation for f(x)

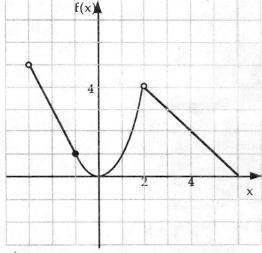

a) f(4) = _____   f(⁻1.5) = _____

b) for f(x) = 1 ⇒ x =

c)

$$f(x) = \begin{cases} \\ \end{cases}$$

7.4 Logarithms

Logarithms

To understand the theory behind the analysis of real data we need to revise our understanding of logarithms.

In the sixth form we learnt the equivalent exponent - logarithmic statement

$$b^y = x \quad \Leftrightarrow \quad y = \log_b x$$

and when the base is e.

$$e^y = x \quad \Leftrightarrow \quad y = \log_e x \quad \Leftrightarrow \quad y = ln\ x$$

and the log rules

1. $\log (A \times B) = \log A + \log B$

2. $\log (\frac{A}{B}) = \log A - \log B$

3. $\log A^n = n \log A$

With Natural Logarithms the log base e is usually abbreviated as *ln*.

$$y = \log_e x \quad \Leftrightarrow \quad y = ln\ x$$

Check your tables now to see the log statements that will be given to you in the examination.

Example 6

Rewrite $\quad 1.3010 = \log_{10} 20$

as an exponent statement.

Solution

We note that

$$y = \log_b x \quad \Leftrightarrow \quad b^y = x \quad \text{from our tables}$$

so $b = 10$, $x = 20$ and $y = 1.3010$ so

$$1.3010 = \log_{10} 20 \quad \Leftrightarrow \quad 10^{1.3010} = 20$$

Example 7

Rewrite the expression $2 \log 6 - \log 12$ as the logarithm of a single number.

Solution

Using $\log A^n = n \log A$ gives

$$2 \log 6 - \log 12 = \log 36 - \log 12$$

Using $\log (\frac{A}{B}) = \log A - \log B$ gives

$$\log 36 - \log 12 = \log 3 \quad \text{the answer}$$

Problems

Use the log rules to help you with the following problems.

16. Find the equivalent exponent statement to

$$\log_e (2y + 1) = 3x$$

---

17. Find the equivalent logarithmic statement to

$$2^3 = 8$$

---

18. Make t the subject of the equation by writing an equivalent natural log statement (log base e).

$$M = 45 \times e^{2t}$$

---

19. Write the following log equation as a simple exponent statement.

$$y = \log_{10} 4x + \log_{10} (x + 1)$$

---

20. The equation below describes the expected income from an investment. By rewriting it as a natural log statement find t when R = 49500

$$R = 35500 \times e^{0.055t}$$

---

21. The equation below describes the expected population of a small town. By rewriting it as a base 10 log statement find t when P = 17000

$$R = 12000 \times 1.015^{t}$$

7.5 Modelling Growth Data

Prescription

Choose an appropriate type of model for real data, analyse and interpret results

- transforming variables (including log-log and semi-log techniques)

 ## Modelling Growth Data

Data from real life is often modelled by exponential or power functions. We have an exponential function when the variable is part of the power.

Examples could be

$$f(x) = 4 \times 5^x$$

or $$f(x) = 3.45 \times e^{0.025x}$$

Our approach is to follow the $f(x) = 3.45 \times e^{0.025x}$ format.

To identify the modelling equation for exponential data we plot the $\log_e y$ (or $\ln y$) against x (or t). If the resulting graph is a straight line then the exponential function is an appropriate model.

 ## Identifying an Exponential Function $(f(x) = ke^{ax})$

The algebraic justification for the approach is

$$y = k e^{ax}$$

taking natural logs of both sides we get

$$\log_e y = \log_e (k e^{ax})$$
$$= \log_e k + \log_e e^{ax}$$
$$= \log_e k + ax \log_e e$$
$$= \log_e k + ax \quad (\text{as } \log_e e = 1)$$

as k is a constant then $\log_e k$ is also a constant.

let $\log_e k = K$

By comparing

$$\log_e y = ax + K$$

to the general equation of the straight line

$$y = mx + c$$

we can see that for an exponent statement, plotting the $\log_e y$ versus x should give you a straight line with y intercept $\log_e k$ and gradient a.

Extra Examples

Note Well

Learn this derivation as it could be required in the examination.

Example 8

The data on the right is known to be modelled by an equation in the form

$$P = C\,e^{kt} \quad \text{or} \quad P = C\,a^t$$

a), Plot the log of P against t.

b) Find the gradient of the resulting straight line.

c) Hence find the equation that models the data.

P	t
1168	0.8
1251	3.1
1411	7.1
1600	11.3
1820	15.6
2307	23.5
6360	57.3

Solution (using $P = C\,e^{kt}$)

a)

P	t	$\log_e P$
1168	0.8	7.06
1251	3.1	7.13
1411	7.1	7.25
1600	11.3	7.38
1820	15.6	7.51
2307	23.5	7.74
6360	57.3	8.76

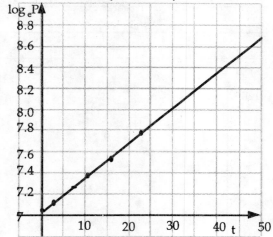

b)　Gradient $= \dfrac{\log_e P_2 - \log_e P_1}{t_2 - t_1}$

$$= \frac{8.76 - 7.06}{57.3 - 0.8}$$

$$= 0.0301$$

c) The equation is of the form

$$P = C\,e^{kt}$$

Substitute k = 0.0301, t = 0.8, P = 1168 to solve for C

$$1168 = C\,e^{0.0301 \times 0.8}$$

$$C = 1140$$

Answer　　　$P = 1140\,e^{0.0301\,t}$

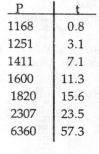

Problems

For the following problems the data is assumed to be modelled best by an equation in the form $P = C\,e^{kt}$.

22. Inflation (which is assumed to be constant) has produced the following market valuations for a piece of unimproved land.

year (t)	Value(V)
0	$53000
2	$59000
3	$62000
5	$69000
7	$77000
10	$95000

a) Plot t the against $\log_e$ of V.

b) Find the gradient of the resulting straight line.

c) Hence find the equation that models the data.

a)

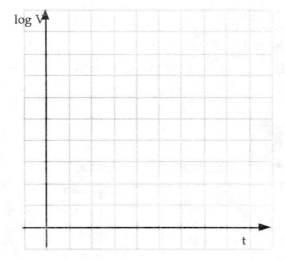

b) _____

_____

_____

_____

c) _____

_____

_____

_____

23. The population of a particular species is declining. The bi-annual census has shown the following numbers

year (t)	Number(P)
1986	460
1988	388
1990	327
1992	276
1994	233
1996	197

a) Plot t against the $\log_e$ of P.

b) Find the gradient of the resulting straight line.

c) Hence find the equation that models the data.

a)

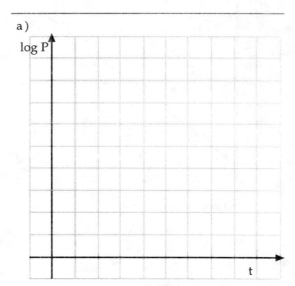

b) _____

_____

_____

c) _____

_____

_____

7.6 Modelling using semi-log Graph Paper
Prescription

Choose an appropriate type of model for real data, analyse and interpret results

- transforming variables (including log-log and semi-log techniques)

Modelling exponential functions using semi-log graph paper

It has already been established that an exponential function in the form

$$y = k\,e^{ax} \quad \text{or} \quad y = k\,c^x$$

will form a straight line when log y is plotted against x.

A quicker way of demonstrating that the straight line exists for a particular set of data is to plot y directly on a logarithmic scale.

Graph paper where one axis is a logarithmic scale and the other is linear is called semi-log graph paper.

To investigate real data that may be best modelled by an exponential function we

1. Label both axes so the graph is as large as possible.

2. Plot all the co-ordinates and check if you have a straight line.

3. Determine the gradient using

   $$\text{Gradient} = \frac{\text{change in vertical}}{\text{change in horrizontal}}$$

   $$a = \frac{\log P_2 - \log P_1}{t_2 - t_1}$$

   This gradient can be used to solve for a as per Section 7.5.

4. Substitute any point into the formula along with a and solve for k.

   $$y = k\,e^{ax}$$

Do not attempt to measure the gradient directly off the semi-log graph.

Note the following points

- The semi-log graph is only used to identify if the function is exponential or not.

- The log scale on semi-log graph paper works equally well irrespective of the form of the equation we are using.

- The mathematics to derive the equation does not use the graph.

Extra Notes

_____

_____

_____

_____

_____

_____

_____

_____

_____

_____

_____

_____

_____

_____

_____

Example 9   (this is the same problem as Example 8)

The data on the right is assumed to be modelled
by an equation in the form

$$P = k\,e^{at}$$

t	P
0.8	1168
3.1	1251
4.3	1297
7.1	1411
11.3	1600
15.6	1820
23.5	2307
57.3	6360

a) Plot P on the vertical ($\log_e$) scale against t

b) Find the gradient of the resulting
straight line.

c) Hence find the equation that models the
data.

Solution

a)

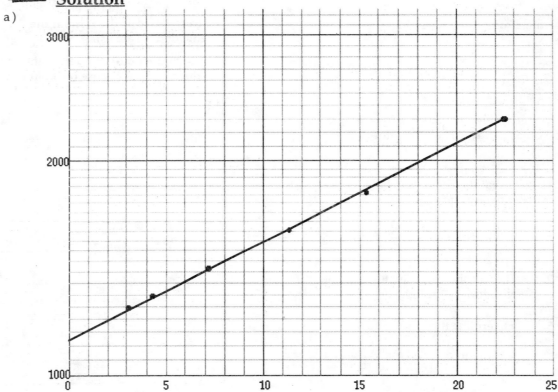

Approach using $P = k\,e^{at}$

b)   Gradient $= \dfrac{\log_e P_2 - \log_e P_1}{t_2 - t_1}$

$a = \dfrac{8.76 - 7.06}{57.3 - 0.8}$

$a = 0.0301$

c)   equation of the form $P = k\,e^{at}$

Solve for k given that when t = 0.8 P = 1140 gives

Answer $P = 1110\,e^{0.0301\,t}$

Problems

Use semi-log graph paper to investigate the following data.

24. A student suggested the height of a child would be best be modelled by a growth curve. Investigate if this is true for the following data.

Age (years)	Height	Age (years)	Height
3	0.85 m	8	1.34 m
4	0.91 m	12	1.61 m
6	1.09 m	17	1.74 m

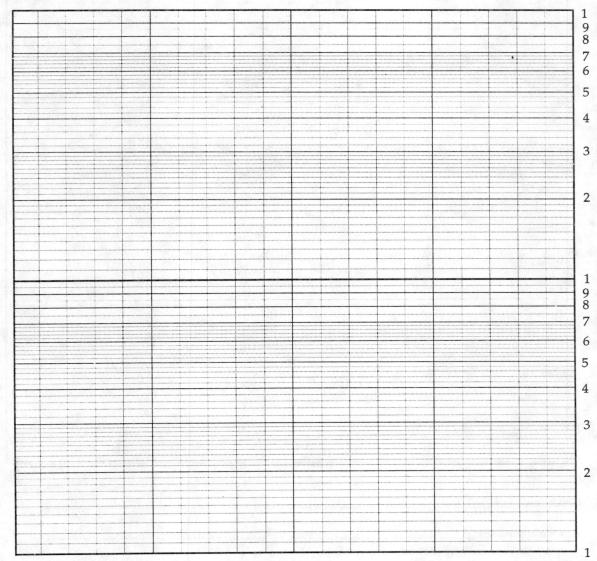

Conclusion _____

25. An investor suggests that a piece of art has appreciated at greater than the inflation rate of 3%. By plotting the data on an appropriate **graph** confirm that the data follows a growth curve and determine the rate it is appreciating.

Year of sale	Price paid	Year of sale	Price paid
1970	$10000	1987	$30000
1975	$14000	1990	$37000
1981	$21000	1995	$52000

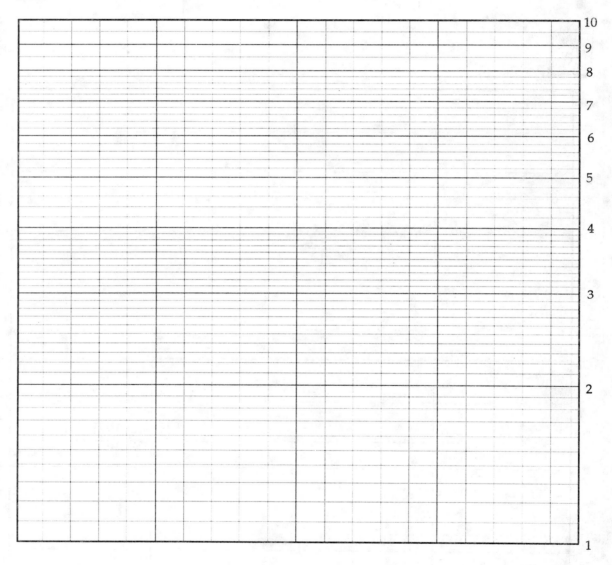

Conclusion _____

Rate it is appreciating _____

7.7 Modelling Power Functions

Prescription

Choose an appropriate type of model for real data, analyse and interpret results

- **transforming variables (including log-log and semi-log techniques)**

Modelling Power Functions

A power function is in the general form

$$y = Cx^n$$

and we approach it similar to the exponential function.

Examples could be

$$y = 4x^2$$

or $\quad f(x) = 3x^{0.5}$

or $\quad f(x) = x^{-2}$

The algebraic justification for the approach is

$$y = Cx^n$$

taking natural logs of both sides (base 10 logs also work) we get

$$\log_e y = \log_e (Cx^n)$$

$$= \log_e C + \log_e x^n$$

$$= \log_e C + n \log_e x$$

$$= n \log_e x + \log_e C$$

as C is a constant then $\log_e C$ is also a constant. By comparing to the general equation of the straight line

$$\log_e y = n \log_e x + \log_e C$$

$$y = mx + c$$

we can see that for an exponent statement, plotting the log y versus log x should give you a straight line with y intercept $\log_e C$ and gradient **n**.

Learn this explanation as it is examinable.

Extra Notes

Example 10

The data below is from a power function.

x	f(x)		x	f(x)
1.4	3.55		2.1	4.35
3.0	5.20		4.3	6.22
6.7	7.77		7.6	8.27
9.1	9.05		11.7	10.69

Plot log [f(x)] versus log x to determine the power function.

Solution

x	$\log_e x$		f(x)	$\log_e f(x)$
1.4	0.34		3.55	1.27
2.1	0.74		4.35	1.47
3.0	1.10		5.20	1.65
4.3	1.46		6.22	1.83
6.7	1.90		7.77	2.05
7.6	2.03		8.27	2.11
9.1	2.21		9.05	2.20
11.7	2.46		10.69	2.37

Both $\log_{10}$ and natural $\log_e$ (ie. *ln* x) could be used. It will not affect any of the calculations.

The gradient of the straight line gives the power for the power function.

$$\text{Gradient} = \frac{\text{change in vertical}}{\text{change in horrizontal}}$$

$$= \frac{\log f(x_2) - \log f(x_1)}{\log x_2 - \log x_1}$$

$$= \frac{2.37 - 1.27}{2.46 - 0.34}$$

$$= 0.519$$

$$f(x) = C\, x^{0.519}$$

substituting one point to solve for C

$$3.55 = C\,(1.4)^{0.519}$$

$$C = 2.98$$

The data is best modelled by the power function

$$f(x) = 2.98\, x^{0.519}$$

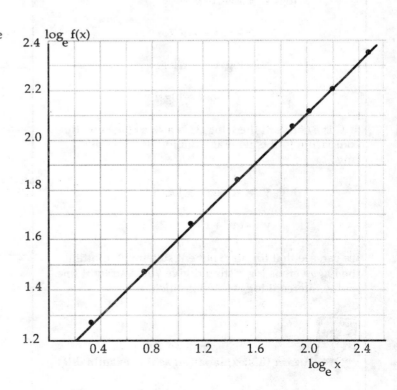

Problems

Find the function that best models the following data.

26. The intensity of sound decreases as illustrated by the following data.

Dist. (d)	Volume(V)
0.45	1480
0.71	595
1.21	205
1.78	95
2.14	65
3.65	23

Assuming the data is best modelled by a power function.

a) Plot log d against log V.

b) Find the gradient of the resulting straight line.

c) Hence find the equation that models the data.

a)

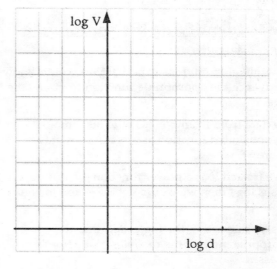

b) _____

_____

_____

c) _____

_____

_____

27. The sales per week of a popular workbook may be best modelled by a power functions. For the following data

Week (w)	Sales(S)
2	210
4	125
5	110
8	75
13	55
23	35

a) Plot log w against log S.

b) Find the gradient of the resulting straight line.

c) Hence find the equation that models the data.

a)

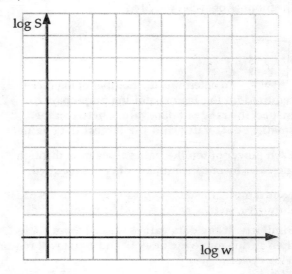

b) _____

_____

_____

c) _____

_____

_____

7.8 Modelling of Real Data

Prescription

Choose an appropriate type of model for real data, analyse and interpret results

- **transforming variables (including log-log and semi-log techniques)**

Identifying the appropriate function

It is unlikely with real data that you would know in advance the appropriate function to model the data.

The data from Example 7 is obviously modelled by an exponential function as already shown (see Figure 9).

If we treated it as a power function by plotting log P versus log t then we would get the graph in Figure 10.

It is by inspecting the log graph that the appropriateness of the modelling function is assessed.

Log-log graph paper

A quick assessment of the best modelling function can be made by using semi-log or log-log graph paper.

Log-log graph paper is used like semi-log graph paper. The range of each variable will determine the number of cycles required.

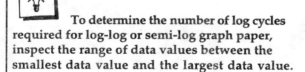

To determine the number of log cycles required for log-log or semi-log graph paper, inspect the range of data values between the smallest data value and the largest data value.

Each power of ten the data values pass through increases by one the number of cycles required.

For example, the data values from 0.3 to 9.5 pass through 1, so two cycles would be required.

Similarly, if the data values ranged from 7.4 to 234 then as this range includes 10 and 100 it will require 3 log cycles.

With real data neither will give a perfect straight line but a judgement has to be made as to how close to a straight line the resulting graph is on both the semi-log and log-log graph. This will determine which (if any) is the best model for the data.

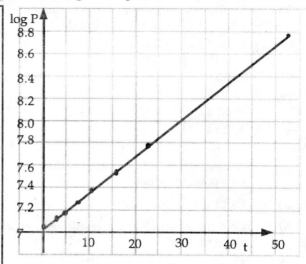

Figure 9

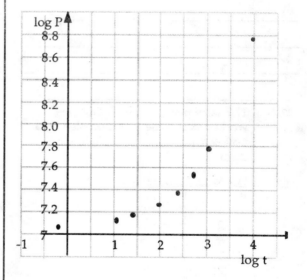

Figure 10

_____

_____

_____

_____

_____

_____

Example 11

The following data is of the share price for a new publishing company.

week(t)	3	5	11	24	39	73
price(P) in ¢	37	54	95	160	225	350

a) By plotting the data on either semi-log or log-log graph paper, determine the best model for the data.

b) Find the equation that best models the data.

Solution

a) Plotting the data on semi-log graph paper (Figure 11) and log-log paper (Figure 12) gives the graphs below.

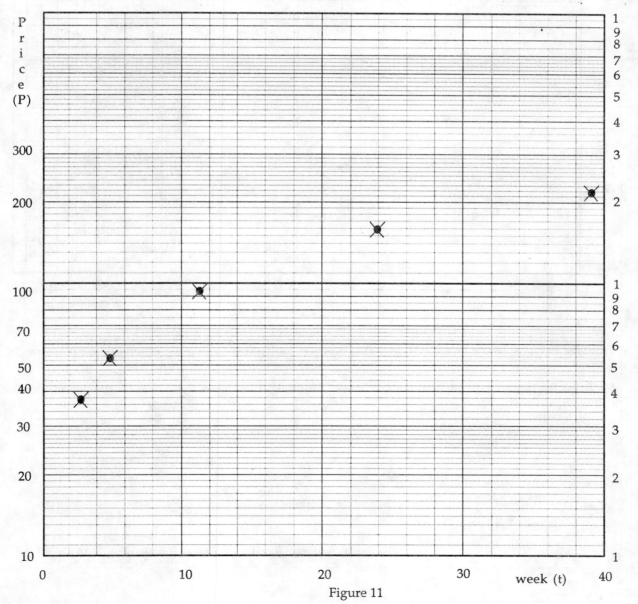

Figure 11

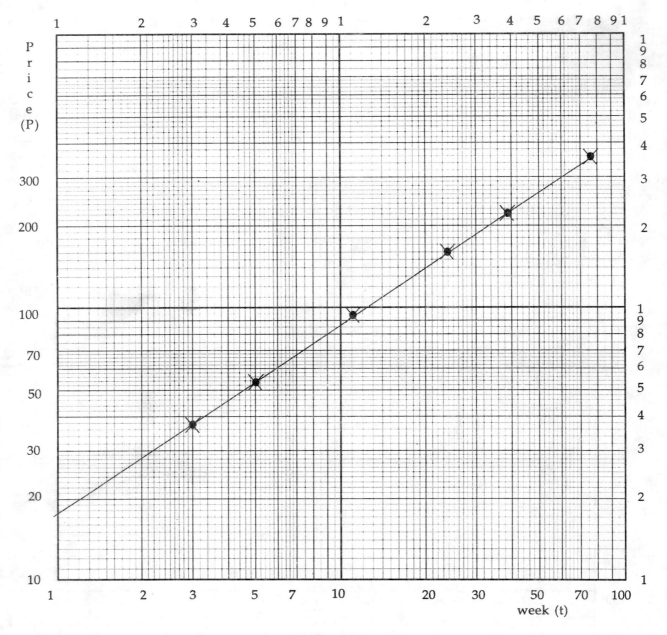

Figure 12

From the two graphs the best model is that of a power function as the log-log graph is close to a straight line.

b) To get the modelling equation, the gradient of the straight line gives the power for the power function.

$$\text{Gradient} = \frac{\log_e P_2 - \log_e P_1}{\log_e t_2 - \log_e t_1}$$

$$= \frac{5.86 - 3.61}{4.29 - 1.10}$$

$$= 0.71$$

$$P = C\, x^{0.71} \qquad \text{substituting one point to solve for C}$$

$$350 = C\,(73)^{0.71}$$

$$C = 16.6 \qquad \text{The data is best modelled by the power function } P = 16.6\, x^{0.71}$$

Problems

Select the best model by sketching on semi-log or log-log graph paper for each set of real data and hence find the modelling equation.

28. The concentration of bacteria on a plate were

day(t)	1	3	7	11	18	22
pop(P)	8	10	16	26	61	98

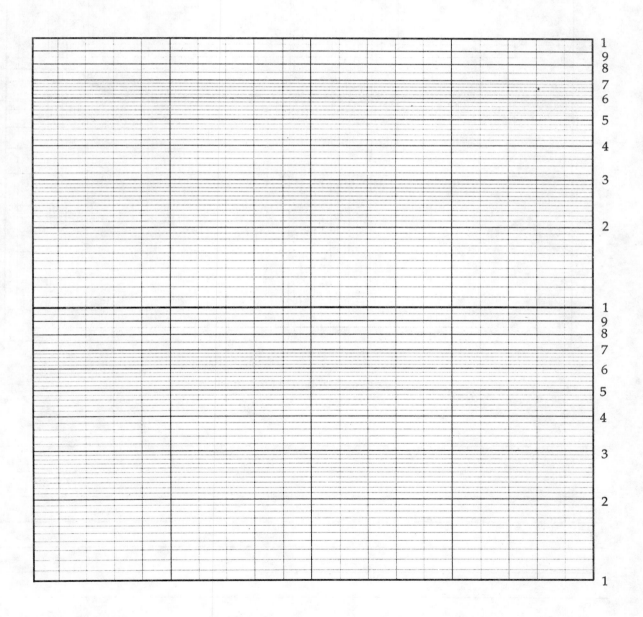

Semi-log graph paper for question 28.

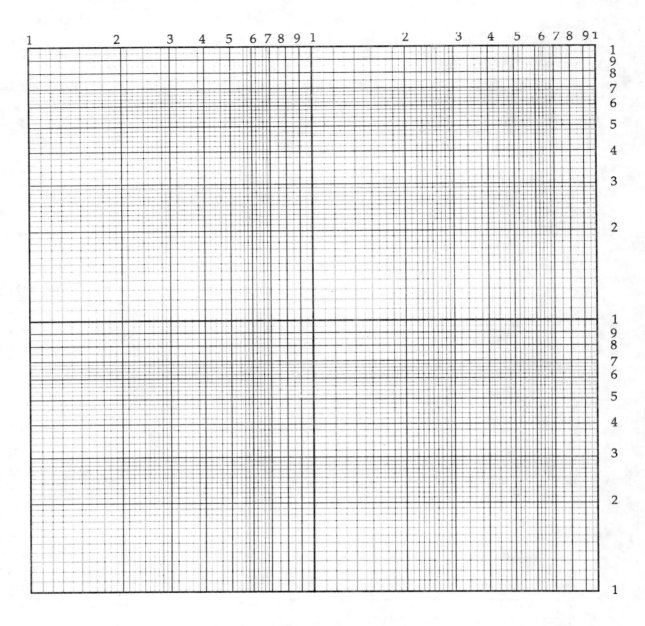

Log-log graph paper for question 28

29. The price paid for a work of art (time in years)

time (t)	1.2	4.5	8.7	14.5	35.7	46.5
price (P)	16	68	141	246	663	887

Semi-log graph paper for question 29

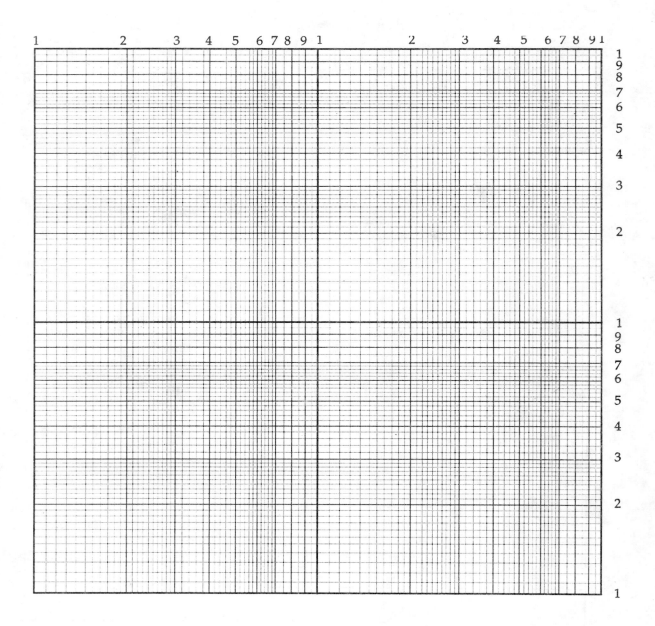

Log-log graph paper for question 29

7.9 Linear Programming

Introduction

Linear Programming is the graphical representation of a problem of two variables where we are given a number of constraints (linear inequalities) and we are trying to find an optimal solution for the region of the graph that satisfies the constraints.

Prescription

Model situations using linear programming techniques, and obtain the optimal solution

 ## Linear Inequalities

To graph a linear inequality such as

$$2y + x \geq 6$$

the general approach has been to lightly graph the straight line first.

$$2y + x = 6$$

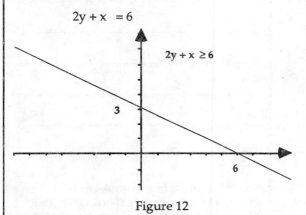

Figure 12

Then the correct side of the line is shaded. This is done by testing a point and checking if it satisfies the inequality. If it does, then the side that includes this point is shaded. If not, then the other side is shaded.

Finally the line is overwritten indicating whether the points on the line are included [$\leq$ or $\geq$ gives a **continuous line**] or excluded [< or > gives a **dotted line**]. An example is shown in Figure 13.

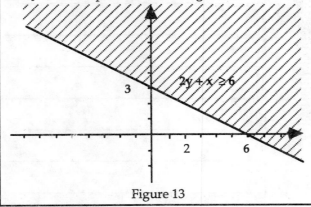

Figure 13

 The cover up method.
A quick way of graphing a straight line in the form

$$2y + x = 6$$

is to cover the y term to get the x intercept

$$\blacksquare + x = 6 \quad ie \quad x = 6$$

and cover the x term to get the y intercept

$$2y + \blacksquare = 6 \quad ie \quad y = 3$$

Linear Inequalities cont...

In linear programming we are required to plot several inequalities on the one set of axes. As we are shading the area required, the region that satisfies all inequalities becomes hopelessly crowded. In Figure 14 the inequalities

$$2y + x \geq 6$$
$$x + y < 8$$
$$y < 4 \qquad \text{are all plotted}$$

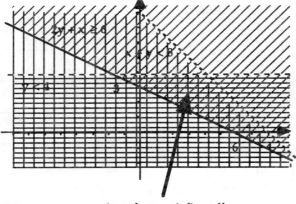

region that satisfies all three inequalities

Figure 14

Shading Out

To make sense of such diagrams with multiple inequalities, by convention we shade the area we do want. Shading the area NOT required is called **shading out**.

The inequalities in Figure 14 would then become;

$$2y + x \geq 6$$
$$x + y < 8$$
$$y < 4$$

are all plotted in Figure 15 with SHADING OUT.

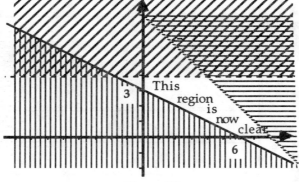

This region is now clear

Figure 15

The required region is now obvious.

It there is any doubt as to whether the shading is IN or OUT, then the graph should be endorsed with the phrase SHADING OUT.

Example 12

Plot the following inequalities on the same axes and indicate the region that satisfies all the inequalities.

$$2y - x < 6$$

$$y \geq 1$$

$$2y - 3x \geq {}^-6$$

Solution

Graphing the straight lines (by the cover up method)

Let $\qquad 2y - x = 6$

Cover y terms to get the x intercept

$$\blacksquare - x = 6 \quad \text{ie} \quad x = {}^-6$$

Cover the x term to get the y intercept

$$2y - \blacksquare = 6 \quad \text{ie} \quad y = 3$$

The procedure is repeated to get the other straight lines

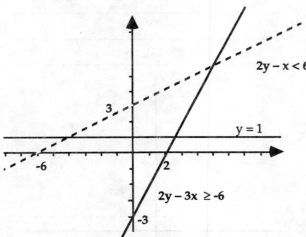

Now testing a point and **SHADING OUT**

Test $(0, 0)$ for $\quad 2y - x < 6$

Is $\qquad 0 - 0 < 6$ **yes** so shade other side

This is repeated for the other two inequalities. The resulting graph is shown on the right.

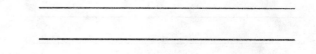

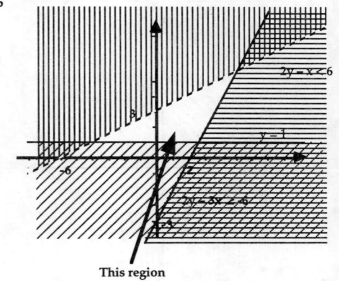

This region

<u>Problems</u>

Graph each set of inequalities on the same axes.

30.

$$3y + x > 6$$

$$x \leq 4$$

$$y - 2x \leq 4$$

31.

$$y - 4x \leq 8$$

$$y < 6$$

$$y + 5x \leq 6$$

$$y + x > 0$$

32.

$y > 2x + 3$

$y \leq 3 - x$

$x \geq -3$

_____

_____

_____

_____

_____

_____

_____

_____

_____

_____

_____

33.

$y \geq x^2$

$y < 9$

$y - x < 6$

_____

_____

_____

_____

_____

_____

_____

_____

_____

_____

_____

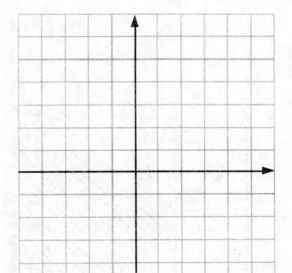

Linear Programming

Linear inequalities enable the region that satisfies the constraints to be identified.

Linear programming has in addition to these constraints an expression that must be maximised or minimised. All possible solutions for that expression are represented by the SHADED OUT polygon on the graph. The maximum or minimum solution will always be as close as possible to the vertex (ie. corner) of the SHADED OUT polygon.

After the SHADED OUT polygon has been identified then the nearest possible answer to each vertex is tested. Sometimes possible answers are limited to natural numbers.

 Example 13

A music shop makes $5 profit on each CD and $3 on each cassette. In a week it expects to sell at least 25 CDs and at least 30 cassettes, but no more than 80 in total of CDs and cassettes. Calculate the shops maximum and minimum possible profits.

 Solution

First express the conditions as inequalities
Let CDs be y and cassettes be x.

"In a week it expects to sell at least 25 CDs" gives

$$y \geq 25$$

and at least 30 cassettes gives

$$x \geq 30$$

while *" no more than 80 in total of CDs and cassettes."* gives

$$x + y \leq 80$$

which gives the graph on the right. The nearest natural number solution to each vertex is (30,50), (55, 25) and (30, 25). Testing each with *"A music shop makes $5 profit on each CD and $3 on each cassette"*

(30, 50)   profit $= 30 \times 3 + 50 \times 5$

$\qquad\qquad\quad = \$340$ MAXIMUM

(55, 25)   profit $= 55 \times 3 + 25 \times 5$

$\qquad\qquad\quad = \$290$

(30, 25)   profit $= 30 \times 3 + 25 \times 5$

$\qquad\qquad\quad = \$215$ MINIMUM

Answer. Max profit is $340 and min profit is $215.

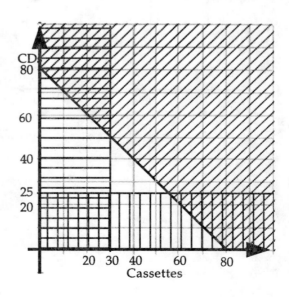

Problems

Solve each of the Linear Programming problems by first graphing the constraints and testing each vertex.

34. A company produces surf boards in two types, *Ryder* and *Performa*. Under existing contracts they must build 4 *Ryders* and 6 *Performa* per month. The facilities limit production to a total of 20 boards per month. The materials for boards cost $60 for the *Ryder* and $80 for the *Performa* come from a budget of $1440 per month.

   a) Graph this information

   b) If a profit is made of $40 per *Ryder* and $50 per *Performa* find the maximum profit that can be made per month

35. An grape grower wishes to establish a new vineyard of up to 10 hectares by planting either Pinot Noir or Sauvignon Blanc. She estimates that each hectare of Pinot will cost $40 000 and each hectare of Sauvignon Blanc will cost $10 000. She has only $200 000 to spend on development.

   She estimates that the profit for each hectare of Pinot Noir as $8 500 and $4 250 for Sauvignon Blanc.

   a) What is the maximum possible profit?

   b) How many hectares of each should she plant.

Answer b) _____

Answer a) _____

Answer b) _____

36. An exporter selling Kiwi clams overseas sells either trays of large or small clams. To purchase the clams from the grower costs the exporter, per tray $5 for small and $10 for large clams. He has $800 to spend on them. The airline will have space for up to 100 trays. Contracts exist for at least 25 small and 15 large trays.

a) Graph this information.

b) If a profit per tray of $15 for small and $20 for large, find the maximum and minimum profit.

_____
_____
_____
_____
_____
_____

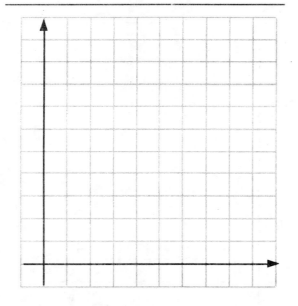

Max Profit is _____

Min Profit is _____

37. An agricultural college has 10 hectares to plant in corn or pumpkins. The cost of planting corn is $125 / Ha while pumpkins cost $75. The budget is $1125 for planting. The teacher estimates that over two weeks they have 240 pupil periods while corn requires 15 pupil periods per Ha and pumpkin 30 pupil periods.

a) Graph this information

b) If the profit for corn is $240 per Ha and for is $300 per Ha find the area of each they should plant for best return to their school.

_____
_____
_____
_____
_____

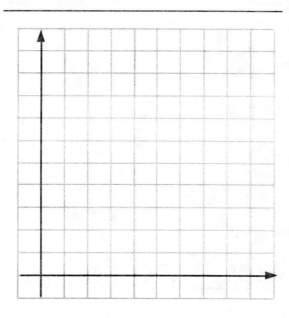

Area of corn is _____

Area of pumpkin is _____

8.0 Equations

Introduction

Algebraic equations are tools we use to solve problems. In this section we extend our knowledge of equations to 2 and 3 variable simultaneous equations and the numerical solution of equations.

Prescription

Exploring equations and expressions

Use simultaneous equations to solve problems in context

- **2 x 2 and 3 x 3 linear systems**

- **consistency and uniqueness of solutions**

Use bisection method or Newton-Raphson method to solve non-linear equations

- **advantages and disadvantages of these methods**

- **geometric understanding of these methods**

8.1 Simultaneous Equations

Simultaneous equations are equations with more than one variable. The term *simultaneous* refers to the condition that any solution must be simultaneously true for all equations. Graphically it is the single point through which all the straight lines pass.

2 x 2 Simultaneous Equations

2 x 2 simultaneous equations are a pair of equations with two unknowns. An example could be

$$2y + x = 8$$
$$y - 2x = ^-1$$

These linear equations are shown in Figure 1.

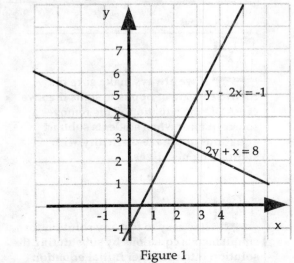

Figure 1

© Robert Lakeland & Carl Nugent

2 x 2 Simultaneous Equations cont...

There are a number of different methods for solving simultaneous equations. These include substitution, elimination, graphs and matrices.

In this *Workbook*, only the elimination method will be presented, for simplicity. The single requirement to use elimination is that both equations should be in the same form, such as

$$ax + by = c$$

$$dx + ey = f$$

To be in the same form, both equations should have their x, y, and constant terms in the same relative position.

If the equations are not in the same form then we have to manipulate them prior to starting.

For example

$$y = 3x + 5$$

and $$2y - x = 5$$

would be rearranged as

$$y - 3x = 5$$

and $$2y - x = 5$$

The method of elimination is to multiply one or other of the equations by a constant so that you are able to ADD one equation to the other in order to eliminate one variable. In selecting the constant to multiply by we are attempting to get the coefficient of x (or y) the same but of opposite sign. Multiplying the first equation above by negative 2 would give

$$^-2y + 6x = {}^-10$$

and $$2y - x = 5$$

Adding these two equation vertically gives

$$5x = {}^-5$$

The resulting equation with one variable is then easily solved.

$$x = {}^-1$$

This result is substituted into either of the first two equations to get the solution of y = 2.

If we always make sure the coefficients are of opposite signs then we can ADD the equation. This removes a source of error when students subtract equations and have difficulty with subtracting negatives.

It is easy to test any solution for simultaneous equations by substituting the solution into the other initial equation and checking that is true.

Example 1

Solve the simultaneous equations.

$$3x + 2y = 3$$
$$^-2x + 4y = 14$$

Solution

Assign each equation a label

$$3x + 2y = 3 \qquad (1)$$
$$^-2x + 4y = 14 \qquad (2)$$

Multiply (1) by 2 and equation (2) by 3.

$$2*(1) \qquad 6x + 4y = 6 \qquad (3)$$
$$3*(2) \qquad ^-6x + 12y = 42 \qquad (4)$$

Now combine both equations by adding down.

$$(3) + (4) \qquad 0 + 16y = 48 \qquad (5)$$
$$\therefore \qquad y = 3$$

Substituting back $\quad 3x + 2.3 = 3$

$$\therefore \qquad x = {}^-1$$

The solution to the equations is ($^-$1, 3)

Example 2

Solve the simultaneous equations.

$$2.04x + 1.72y = 1.68$$
$$2.45x + 4.02y = 6.84$$

Solution

$$2.04x + 1.72y = 1.68 \qquad (1)$$
$$2.45x + 4.02y = 6.84 \qquad (2)$$

To eliminate x multiply (1) by 2.45 and equation (2) by $^-$2.04 so the coefficients of x are the same in both equations but of opposite sign.

$$2.45_\times(1) \qquad 4.998x + 4.214y = 4.116 \qquad (3)$$
$$^-2.04 \,_\times(2) \;\; ^-4.998x + {}^-8.2008y = {}^-13.9536 \qquad (4)$$

Now combine both equations by adding down.

$$(3) + (4) \qquad 0 + {}^-3.9868y = {}^-9.8376 \qquad (5)$$
$$\therefore \qquad y = 2.468 \qquad (4 \text{ sig fig})$$
$$2.04x + 1.72.2.468 = 1.68$$
$$\therefore \qquad x = {}^-1.257$$

The solution to the equations is ($^-$1.26, 2.47) 3 sig fig.

If the answer is required to 3 significant figures we must be careful to always work to at least 4 significant figures throughout the problem.

<u>Problems</u>

Solve the following simultaneous equations.

1.
$$3x + y = 3$$
$$x - 2y = 8$$

2.
$$4.15x + 1.23y = 7.25$$
$$1.42x - 5.35y = 11.25$$

Find the point of intersection of these two straight lines

3.

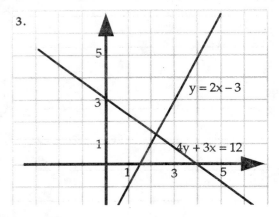

$y = 2x - 3$

$4y + 3x = 12$

4.

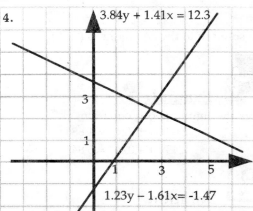

$3.84y + 1.41x = 12.3$

$1.23y - 1.61x = -1.47$

8.2 Consistency and Uniqueness of solutions

Prescription

Use simultaneous equations to solve problems in context

- **consistency and uniqueness of solutions**

Inconsistency of Simultaneous Equations

A pair of 2x2 simultaneous equations is inconsistent when they represent a pair of parallel lines. A pair of parallel lines never meet, so they have no simultaneous solution.

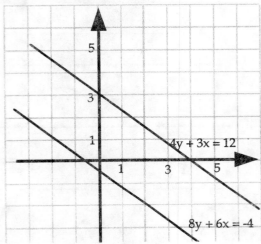

Figure 2

Algebraically, we recognise inconsistent equations because, when an attempt is made to solve inconsistent equations, a contradictory statement is formed.

$$4y + 3x = 12 \qquad (1)$$

$$8y + 6x = {}^-4 \qquad (2)$$

$${}^-2 \times (1) \quad {}^-8y + {}^-6x = {}^-24 \qquad (3)$$

$$(2) + (3) \qquad 0 = {}^-28 \qquad (4)$$

As 0 is not equal to $^-$28 we know the two equations are inconsistent.

Uniqueness of Solutions

If our two equations represent the same straight line then we have an infinite number of solutions. This will happen when one equation is an exact multiple of the other (eg. $y + 2x = 5$ and $3y + 6x = 15$).

We will recognise this, when if we attempt to solve the equation algebraically, we end with a statement that is always true (eg. $4 = 4$). In such a situation we have no unique solution.

Example 3

Identify if the following has a consistent and unique answer.

$$1x - 2y = 4$$
$$^{-}2x + 4y = ^{-}8$$

Solution

$$1x - 2y = 4 \qquad (1)$$
$$^{-}2x + 4y = ^{-}8 \qquad (2)$$

We multiply (1) by 2 so the coefficients are the same but of opposite signs.

$$2*(1) \qquad 2x - 4y = 8 \qquad (3)$$
$$^{-}2x + 4y = ^{-}8 \qquad (2)$$

Adding down.

$$(3) + (2) \qquad 0 + 0 = 0$$

which is always true and does not lead to a solution for x or y.

There is <u>no unique solution</u>. One equation is a multiple of the other.

Problems

Identify if the following simultaneous equations have consistent and unique answers.

5. $x + 3y = 3$

         $^{-}3x - 9y = 8$

6. $1.25x + 0.45y = ^{-}0.70$

        $^{-}4.25x - 1.53y = 2.38$

8.3 3 x 3 Simultaneous Equations

Prescription

Use simultaneous equations to solve problems in context

- 3 x 3 linear systems
- consistency and uniqueness of solutions

3 x 3 Simultaneous Equations

An equation with three variables could represent a plane in three dimensions. The intersection of two planes in three dimensions produces the line of intersection. Where this line intersects a third plane would be the simultaneous solution to all three equations.

The three equations below are simultaneously equal (all true) at the point $x = 2$, $y = {}^-1$ and $z = 3$.

$$x + 2y + z = 3$$

$$2x - y - 2z = {}^-1$$

$${}^-2x + 3y + 3z = 2$$

Algebraically we use the method of elimination as we did with 2 x 2 simultaneous equations.

Consistency of Solution

If the line of intersection between two of the planes runs parallel to the third plane then there is no solution. The equations are inconsistent.

If we attempt to solve a pair of inconsistent equations algebraically, we would get a mathematically contradictory statement such as $0 = 4$.

Uniqueness of Solutions

If the line of intersection lies on the third plane then there are an infinite number of solutions. There is no unique solution.

We will recognise this if, when we attempt to solve the equation algebraically, we end with a statement that is always true (eg. $4 = 4$).

Example 4

Solve the 3 x 3 simultaneous equations.

$$x - 2y + z = 0$$
$$2x + 2y + 3z = 7$$
$$^-3x + 8y + 2z = ^-7$$

Solution

Label each equation

$$x - 2y + z = 0 \qquad (1)$$
$$2x + 2y + 3z = 7 \qquad (2)$$
$$^-3x + 8y + 2z = ^-7 \qquad (3)$$

Eliminate x using the first two equations and then the first and third equation.

Our method is still to get the coefficients the same but of opposite sign with equation (1) and (2).

$$^-2_x(1) \quad ^-2x + 4y - 2z = 0 \qquad (4)$$
$$2x + 2y + 3z = 7 \qquad (2)$$
$$(4) + (2) \qquad 6y + z = 7 \qquad (5)$$

Now the same approach with (1) and (3).

$$3_x(1) \qquad 3x - 6y + 3z = 0 \qquad (6)$$
$$^-3x + 8y + 2z = ^-7 \qquad (3)$$
$$(6) + (3) \qquad 2y + 5z = ^-7 \qquad (7)$$

Now we use equations (5) and (7) to eliminate y to solve for z.

$$6y + z = 7 \qquad (5)$$
$$2y + 5z = ^-7 \qquad (7)$$
$$^-3_x(7) \qquad ^-6y - 15z = 21 \qquad (8)$$
$$6y + z = 7 \qquad (5)$$
$$(8) + (5) \qquad ^-14z = 28$$
$$z = ^-2$$

Back substitute in (5) [or (8)].

$$6y + ^-2 = 7$$
$$y = 1.5$$

Back substitute both values in any of (1), (2) or (3).

$$x - 2_x1.5 + ^-2 = 0 \qquad (1)$$

gives $\qquad x = 5$

therefore the final answer is x = 5, y = 1.5 and z = $^-$2.

Problems

Solve the following simultaneous equations if possible. If a solution is not possible state whether the equations are inconsistent or there is no unique answer.

7.
$$x + y + 2z = 6$$
$$3x + 2y + 4z = 9$$
$$^-2x + 3y - 6z = 3$$

label eqns.

$^-3x(1)$

8.
$$2x + 3y + z = 5$$
$$x - 2y + 2z = 4$$
$$2x + 17y - 5z = ^-1$$

9.
$$2.1x + 2.8y + 0.9z = 5.7$$
$$1.1x - 1.8y + 2.3z = 4.2$$
$$2.3x + 16.3y - 5.4z = ^-1.3$$

10.
$$3.14x + 1.67y = 5.76$$
$$2.76x - 1.75y + 3.65z = 3.89$$
$$4.17x - 5.87z = ^-1.23$$

8.4 Applications of Simultaneous Equations

Prescription

Use simultaneous equations to solve problems in context

Applications

Practical applications of simultaneous equations have the additional step of identifying the simultaneous equations from the mass of information given in the question. The approach is to state what your two or three variables represent and then attempt to form the equations.

With the problem

On the first day an upholsterer covers 4 couches, 8 seats and 4 foot rests after working 8.4 hours. The next day he works 8.1 hours and covers 6 couches, 2 seats and a foot rest. In the third day he covers 2 couches, 6 seats and 11 foot rests in only 8.3 hours. How long does it take him to cover each piece of furniture?

You would define the time to cover each piece of furniture as your variable as that is what is asked for in the question.

Let the time to cover a couch be c.

Let the time to cover a seat be s.

Let the time to cover a foot rest be f.

The first equation would then become

$$4c + 8s + 4f = 8.4$$

where 4c would be the time to cover 4 couches.

This problem is completed as Example 5 on the next page.

Check the end of the question as to what is being asked for and consider using them as your variables.

If possible use a relevant symbol for each variable rather than always use x, y, or z.

Example 5

In the first day an upholsterer covers 4 couches, 8 seats and 4 foot rests after working 8.4 hours. The next day he works 8.1 hours and covers 6 couches, 2 seats and a foot rest. In the third day he covers 2 couches, 6 seats and 11 foot rests in only 8.3 hours. How long does it take him to cover each piece of furniture?

Solution

Let the time to cover a couch be c.

Let the time to cover a seat be s.

Let the time to cover a foot rest be f.

The equations would then become

$$4c + 8s + 4f = 8.4 \qquad (1)$$
$$6c + 2s + f = 8.1 \qquad (2)$$
$$2c + 6s + 11f = 8.3 \qquad (3)$$

To eliminate c from (1) and (2) we get their coefficients.

$^-3_\times (1) \quad ^-12c - 24s - 12f = ^-25.2 \qquad (4)$

$2_\times (2) \qquad 12c + 4s + 2f = 16.2 \qquad (5)$

$(4) + (5) \qquad ^-20s - 10f = ^-9 \qquad (6)$

Similarly we eliminate c from (1) and (3)

$4c + 8s + 4f = 8.4 \qquad (1)$

$^-2_\times (3) \quad ^-4c - 12s - 22f = ^-16.6 \qquad (7)$

$(1) + (7) \qquad ^-4s - 18f = ^-8.2 \qquad (8)$

Now using equations (6) and (8) we can eliminate s.

$^-4s - 18f = ^-8.2 \qquad (8)$

$^-20s - 10f = ^-9 \qquad (6)$

$^-5_\times (8) \qquad 20s + 90f = 41 \qquad (9)$

$(6) + (9) \qquad 80f = 32$

$\therefore \qquad f = 0.4$

Back substitute in (8) [or (9) or (6)].

$^-4s - 18_\times 0.4 = ^-8.2$

$s = 0.25$

Back substitute both s and f in any of the first 3 gives c.

$c = 1.2$

Time to cover a couch is 1.2 hours, a seat is 0.25 hours and a foot rest is 0.4 hours.

Extra Examples

Problems

Express each problem as a set of simultaneous equations and hence solve the problem.

11. A health conscious man was concerned about his intake of two different vitamins, A and B2. He needs 5000 units of A and 1.7 units of B2 daily. Two foods are good sources of these but the person wants to find the minimum he should consume to get the daily intake. Liver gives 120 units of A per gram and 0.013 units of B2. Spinach gives about 7.2 units of A per gram and 0.0046 units of B2. How many grams of each does he need?

12. An women is trying to earn her living by doing *piecework* at home. In the first week she completed 11 hours working on job A, 16.5 hours on job B, and 4 hours on job C. That week she was paid $134.55. The next week she spent 6 hours on job A, 21 hours on job B and 7 hours on job C. For this she was paid $138.75. In the third week she spent 4 hours on job A, 27 hours on job B and 12 hours on job C. For this she was paid $172.50. What is the effective hourly rate of pay for each of the jobs?

Let *L* be the quantity of liver.

13. When shopping at the local store, a man buys only apples, spinach, and potatoes. In the last three visits he purchased;

1st - 1.7 kg of apples, 0.855 kg of spinach and 3.2 kg of potatoes at a cost of $15.43.

2nd - 3.2 kg of apples, 1.6 kg of spinach and 1.4 kg of potatoes at a cost of $23.12.

3rd - 1.4 kg of spinach and 6.1 kg of potatoes at a cost of $17.58.

On a fourth visit his purchases of 4 kg of apples, no spinach and 5.2 kg of potatoes came to $19.20. Is he right to suspect a price increase? Justify your answer.

14. A triathlete is doing a programme of exercises as she builds up to a race. Each day's mix of events means she covers 156.5 km.

On the first day she runs for 1.5 hours, cycles for 2.4 hours and paddles for 1.4 hours.

The next training day she runs for 0.7 hours, cycles for 1.3 hours and paddles for 3.9 hours.

The third variation has her running for 1.2 hours, cycles for 3.1 hours and paddles for 0.4 hours.

What is the effective speed she reaches in each of her three disciplines (events).

8.5 Numerical Solutions to Non-Linear Equations

Introduction

Real life problems are often modelled by equations that are difficult to solve algebraically. An alternative approach is to use a numerical method which can find an approximation to the true solution. There are a number of different numerical methods but the approach in this course is to study just two of them.

Prescription

Use the bisection method or Newton-Raphson method to solve non-linear equations

- **advantages and disadvantages of these methods**
- **geometric understanding of these methods**

8.6 The Bisection Method

 ## The Bisection Method

In previous years we used algebraic methods to solve linear ($2x + 3 = 7$) and quadratic ($x^2 + 3x + 2 = 0$) equations.

Finding a numerical solution to an equation is an alternative approach to algebraic manipulation. It leads to an approximation of the roots or solutions of the equation.

Bisection Method

This method relies on starting with an interval that contains a root to the equation

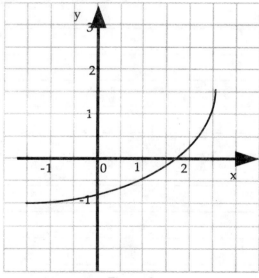

Figure 3

From Figure 3, it can be seen that this function has a root or solution between 1 and 2.

Bisection Method cont...

From the graph in Figure 3 we can see the y value at x = 1 is negative and at x = 2 it is positive.

If we could not see the graph it would seem reasonable that the graph crosses the x axis in the interval x = 1 to x = 2 given that the y values corresponding to these points are of opposite sign.

We now bisect the two x values (find the mid point between them) and check the y value.

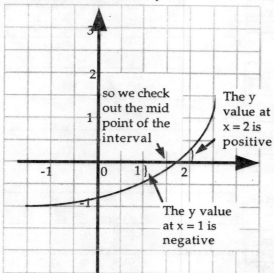

so we check out the mid point of the interval

The y value at x = 2 is positive

The y value at x = 1 is negative

Figure 4

In Figure 4 it can be seen that at x = 1.5 the function is negative so we now concentrate on the interval x = 1.5 to x = 2 as it is in this interval that the y value changes sign.

This method of successively bisecting the interval as you close in on the root of the function, is the basis of the bisection method.

Note Well

Each time the x value which has the same sign as the midpoint x value is discarded. In this example as y is negative, when x = 1.5, (see Figure 4) we discard x = 1.

The method continues until the interval which contains the root or solution is reduced to the required degree of accuracy. If the answer is required to n decimal places then the two x values(top and bottom of the interval) need to round to the same answer when rounding to n decimal places.

Example 6

Find a root of the equation $\sin x - \ln x = 0$ (sin x in radians) between x = 2 and x = 2.5 accurate to 2 dp.

Solution

Set up a table with the two x values accurate to 3 dp (one more than the required accuracy).

x_0	y_0	x_1	y_1	x_m	y_m
2.000		2.500			

Calculate the y ordinates at 2 and 2.5.

x_0	y_0	x_1	y_1	x_m	y_m
2.000	0.216	2.500	-0.318		

Find the x and y ordinates of the mid point.

x_0	y_0	x_1	y_1	x_m	y_m
2.000	0.216	2.500	-0.318	2.250	-0.033

As the y value at the mid point is negative we discard the other negative producing x value and replace it with the midpoint (so we still have points either side of the x axis.

x_0	y_0	x_1	y_1	x_m	y_m
2.000	0.216	2.500	-0.318	2.250	-0.033
2.000	0.216	**2.250**	**-0.033**	2.125	0.097

As the new midpoint 2.125 produces a positive y value we discard the x_0 value by replacing with the mid point

x_0	y_0	x_1	y_1	x_m	y_m
2.000	0.216	2.500	-0.318	2.250	-0.033
2.000	0.216	**2.250**	**-0.033**	2.125	0.097
2.125	**0.097**	2.250	-0.033	2.1875	0.033

This process is repeated until the x values all round to the same value when rounding to 2 dp.

x_0	y_0	x_1	y_1	x_m	y_m
2.000	0.216	2.500	-0.318	2.250	-0.033
2.000	0.216	**2.250**	**-0.033**	2.125	0.097
2.125	**0.097**	2.250	-0.033	2.1875	0.033
2.1875	**0.033**	2.250	-0.033	2.219	.00011
2.219	**.00011**	2.250	-0.033	2.235	-0.017
2.219	.00011	**2.235**	**-0.017**	2.227	-0.008
2.219	.00011	**2.227**	**-0.008**	2.223	-0.004
2.219	.00011	**2.223**	**-0.004**	2.221	-0.002
2.219	.00011	**2.221**	**-0.002**		

As both x_0 and x_1 round 2.22 to 2 decimal places the answer is 2.22.

Example 7

Find which of the roots or solutions (R_1, R_2 or R_3) of the function shown in Figure 5 would be identified by using the bisection method starting with the interval $x = 0$ to $x = 4$.

Figure 5

Solution

At $x = 0$ the y value is negative and at $x = 4$ the y value is positive. At the mid point $x = 2$ the y value is positive so discard the other x value generating a positive y value and continue with the interval $x = 0$ to $x = 2$.

As there is only one solution in the interval $x = 0$ to $x = 2$ the bisection method will identify it.

The answers R_1 .

Problems

Use the bisection method to solve the equation to two decimal places.

15. Find a solution to f(x) = 0 for
f(x) = 2x − tan x (tan x in radians)
in the interval x = 1 to x = 1.5.

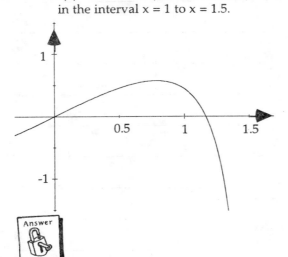

16. Find a solution to f(x) = 0 for
f(x) = x sin x − 1 (sin x in radians) in
the interval x = 2 to x = 3 .

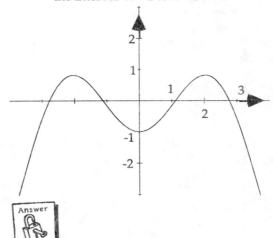

17. Find a solution to f(x) = 0 for
f(x) = $\sqrt{x} - 3\ln x$ in the interval
x = 1.3 to x = 1.7.

---

18. Find a solution to f(x) = 0 for
f(x) = $\sin(x^2)$ (in radians) from
x = 1.6 to x = 2.

     The number of iterations required by the
bisection method can be calculated in advance.

As the interval halves each iteration we can calculate
the number of iterations required to find an answer to a
specified error by solving the equation

$$\text{error} \ \geq \frac{\text{Interval}}{2^n}$$

Where *error* is the degree of accuracy required, the
interval is the initial interval that you start with and
n is the number of iterations.

Rearranging this formula gives

$$2^n \ \geq \frac{\text{Interval}}{\text{error}}$$

The bisection method is reliable but slow. To converge
to 4 decimal places where the initial interval is 1 unit
takes

$$2^n \ \geq \frac{1}{0.001}$$

$$\geq 1000$$

$$n \ \geq 10$$

8.7 The Newton Raphson Method
Prescription

Use the Bisection method or Newton-Raphson method to solve non-linear equations

- advantages and disadvantages of these methods
- geometric understanding of these methods

The Newton Raphson Method

As already stated the bisection method is reliable but slow.

The Newton Raphson method starts with a single estimate of a solution to the equation. At the point on the curve corresponding to the estimate the tangent is drawn. Where this tangent crosses the x axis is a better estimate.

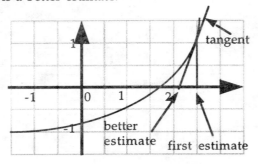

Figure 6

The process or iteration is repeated over and over again until the solution is established to the required degree of accuracy.

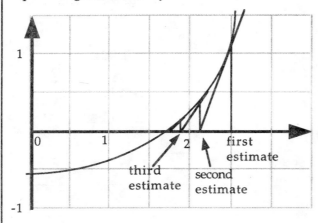

Figure 7

In order to find the gradient of the tangent at each estimate, a gradient function or derivative is required.

This may be supplied as part of the question or if it is a polynomial or exponential function you may be required to differentiate the original function to get the derivative.

The Newton Raphson Method cont...

The iterative formula for the Newton Raphson method relies upon the general equation of a straight line (in this case the tangent)

$$y - y_0 = m(x - x_0)$$

where (x_0, y_0) is a point on the line and m is the gradient

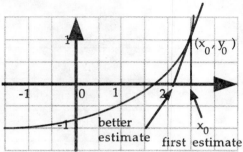

Figure 8

The y_0 value is found by substituting our estimate into the original equation to get $f(x_0)$.

The gradient of the tangent is found by substituting the original estimate into the gradient function or derivative $f'(x_0)$. The equation then becomes

$$y - f(x_0) = f'(x_0) \times (x - x_0)$$

To find where this tangent strikes the x axis again we set y = 0 and make x the subject.

$$0 - f(x_0) = f'(x_0) \times (x - x_0)$$

$$x = x_0 - \frac{f(x_0)}{f'(x_0)}$$

As this is a particular value for x we change the notation to

$$x_1 = x_0 - \frac{f(x_0)}{f'(x_0)}$$

Where x_1 is the improved estimate for the solution to the equation $f(x) = 0$. This is the Newton Raphson formula

This formula is in the tables that are given to you when you sit Bursary. Look up these tables now so you are confident where to look for the formula later on.

Example 8

Use the Newton Raphson method to find a solution accurate to 2 dp to the function $f(x) = 0$ where

$$f(x) = \log_e x - \sin x \quad (\sin x \text{ in radians})$$

and $f'(x) = \dfrac{1}{x} - \cos x \quad (\cos x \text{ in radians})$

Using the initial estimate of $x = 2.5$.

Solution

Using

$$x_1 = x_0 - \frac{f(x_0)}{f'(x_0)}$$

$$x_1 = x_0 - \frac{\ln x_0 - \sin x_0}{\dfrac{1}{x_0} - \cos x_0}$$

Calculate the new estimate by substituting in $x_0 = 2.5$ into the above equation.

$$x_1 = 2.5 - \frac{\ln 2.5 - \sin 2.5}{\dfrac{1}{2.5} - \cos 2.5}$$

$$= 2.235$$

This is the improved estimate of the solution of the equation. State each improved estimate we do to one more decimal place than we are required by the question.

It is best not to round, at all, this value for x but to place it into the memory of your calculator and continue using MR (as per the bright idea on the right).

This iterative process is repeated until two consecutive estimates of the solution agree to the required number of decimal places. In this case we get the values below.

iteration	x_0	x_1
1	2.5	2.235
2	2.235	2.219
3	2.219	2.219

As both x_0 and x_1 round 2.22 to 2 decimal places then the answer is 2.22. (This is the same problem as Example 6)

 To restrict possible errors it is easier to put the estimate for x_0 into the memory of the calculator. Then just hit MR (or memory recall) where appropriate instead of re-entering the estimate x_0 five times for each iteration. When you generate a new value for x_0 you store the new value in the memory.

Example 9

Explain with the aid of diagrams what would happen if an attempt was made using the Newton Raphson method with an initial estimate of x_0 to solve the equation $f(x) = 0$ for the function shown in Figure 9.

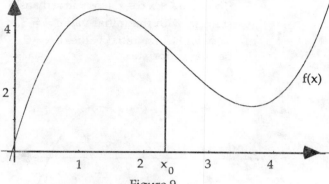

Figure 9

Solution

Sketch in the tangent at $x = x_0$ for our improved estimate of the solution. The improved estimate is where the tangent crosses the x axis.

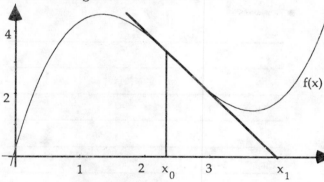

Figure 10

This process is repeated as shown in Figure 11

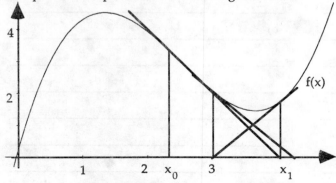

Figure 11

This shows the estimates oscillating around $x = 3$ and failing to converge.

Problems

Use the Newton Raphson method to solve the equation to the specified degree of accuracy.

19. Find a solution accurate to 3 decimal places to $f(x) = 0$ for

$f(x) = 2x - \tan x$ (tan x in radians)

$f'(x) = 2 - \dfrac{1}{(\cos x)^2}$ (cos x in radians)

starting $x = 1$.

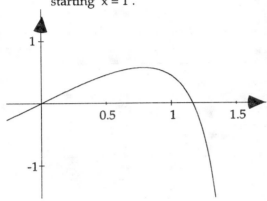

20. a) Find a solution accurate to 3 decimal places to $f(x) = 0$ for

$f(x) = x \sin x - 1$ (in radians)

$f'(x) = \sin x + x \cos x$ (cos x in radians)

starting with the initial value $x = 3$.

b) Why would an initial value of $x = 2$ be inappropriate.

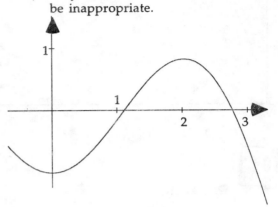

a)

b)

21. Starting with the initial value of $x = 2$, find a solution accurate to 2 decimal places to $f(x) = 0$ for

$f(x) = x^2 - 3x + 1$

by first finding the derivative $f'(x)$.

22. Starting with the initial value of $x = {}^-1$, find a solution accurate to 3 decimal places to $f(x) = 0$ for

$f(x) = e^x - x^2$

by first finding the derivative $f'(x)$.

23. Starting with the initial value of $x = 3$, find a solution accurate to 4 decimal places to $f(x) = 0$ for

$f(x) = 0.5 x^2 + e^x - 9x$

by first finding the derivative $f'(x)$.

24. Starting with the initial value of $x = 3$, find a solution accurate to 4 decimal places to $f(x) = 0$ for

$f(x) = x^4 - 3x^3 + 2x$

by first finding the derivative $f'(x)$.

9.0 Display of Data

Introduction

An integral part of statistics is the display of data. Although not formally mentioned in the prescription, the need for students to be able to represent data in appropriate forms that best reveals patterns, trends and differences is essential. Most students will have been exposed to a wide variety of statistical graphs and in this chapter we present only those introduced in the sixth and seventh form.

There is much disagreement on the different ways of representing a number of graphs and in this text we attempt to draw on the commonly accepted conventions with our primary objective being to reveal the key patterns and trends etc. that are present in the data.

9.1 Stem and Leaf Graph

Stem and Leaf Graph

In most statistical investigations the collection of data is one of the key factors. The organisation of this data as it is collected can make much of the later work easier. A Stem and Leaf graph achieves this by giving the person undertaking the experiment an impression or 'feeling' for the data as it is collected.

A Stem and Leaf graph is composed of a 'stem', which is usually the first significant digit of the numbers or data being collected and a 'leaf' which is the fractional or remaining significant figures of the data.

The 'stem' figures are represented vertically with the 'leaf' figures being written horizontally to the right hand side. It is possible to draw back to back stem and leaf graphs, where the stem is drawn vertically in the middle of the page and one set of data is represented on the right hand side and the other set of data on the left hand side. Back to back stem and leaf graphs are ideal for gaining an impression or feeling for the differences between two sets of data.

Stem and Leaf graphs essentially order the data for us as it is collected and make the calculation of such parameters as median and quartiles relatively straight forward. They are usually regarded as an interim graph in the creation of more formal statistical graphs such as Box and Whisker plots.

Example 1

The number of spark plugs that where issued each day from the parts department in a large city workshop to the mechanics for the first 20 days of a month were 12, 23, 13, 6, 42, 34, 55, 26, 29, 32, 37, 41, 28, 22, 33, 50, 4, 25, 44, 30. Draw a stem and leaf graph to represent this data.

Spark plugs issued in 20 days (unordered)

0	6, 4
1	2, 3
2	3, 6, 9, 8, 2, 5
3	4, 2, 7, 3, 0
4	2, 1, 4
5	5, 0

Spark plugs issued in 20 days (ordered)

0	4, 6
1	2, 3
2	2, 3, 5, 6, 8, 9
3	0, 2, 3, 4, 7
4	1, 2, 4
5	0, 5

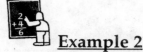

Example 2

The weights of 20 fourth form girls and 20 fourth form boys were taken to the nearest kg.

Girls: 62, 54, 55, 52, 33, 48, 49, 36, 37, 42, 41, 44, 47, 45, 40, 43, 53, 38, 39,46

Boys: 62, 61, 69, 38, 66, 48, 47, 42, 57, 53, 52, 49, 46, 45, 51, 54, 52, 58, 59, 64

Draw a back to back stem and leaf graph of this data and comment on any obvious differences between the weights of fourth form girls and fourth form boys.

Weights fourth form girls (kg)		Weights fourth form boys (kg)
3	3	
9, 8, 7, 6	3	8
4, 3, 2, 1, 0	4	2, 5
9, 8, 7, 6, 5	4	6, 7 ,8, 9
4, 3, 2	5	1, 2, 2, 3, 4
5	5	7, 8, 9
2	6	1, 2, 4
	6	6, 9

From the stem and leaf graph it is fairly obvious that the weight of fourth form boys tends to be greater than that of fourth form girls.

Note Well

Each number on the stem has been repeated so the data can be spread out a little more. If the second significant figure is between 0 and 4 inclusive it goes along side the first occurrence of the number. If it is between 5 and 9 inclusive it goes along side the second occurrence of the number.

Note Well

All statistical graphs should have a clear title and any axes should be graduated, numbered and labelled. By plotting back to back Stem and Leaf graphs a direct comparison between the data can be observed.

Note Well

It is easy to calculate the medians and quartiles from a stem and leaf graph, since the data has been ordered. Remember the median is the middle value and in the example above lies between the 10th and 11th numbers. The lower quartile lies halfway between the minimum value and the value one less than the median (between 5th and 6th values). The upper quartile lies halfway between the value one more than the median and the maximum value (between 15th and 16th values).   Make sure you can calculate the medians and quartiles from Example 2. Check your answers with the results below.

	Girls	Boys
Lower Quartile	39.5	47.5
Median	44.5	52.5
Upper Quartile	50.5	60.0

Problems

1. a)   The retail price of 30 late model cars is collated from a local second hand car sales
            yard. Draw a stem and leaf graph to represent this data.

            22400, 27500, 19450, 26000, 26995, 19500, 22000, 24350, 25750, 21800, 22350, 24100, 23200,
            22750, 23400, 24950, 25100, 23995, 20900, 21350, 23700, 22800, 27000, 19330, 22900, 25600,
            20100, 21300, 24220, 23750

    b)   From the stem and leaf graph calculate the median, lower quartile, upper quartile and
            inter quartile range.

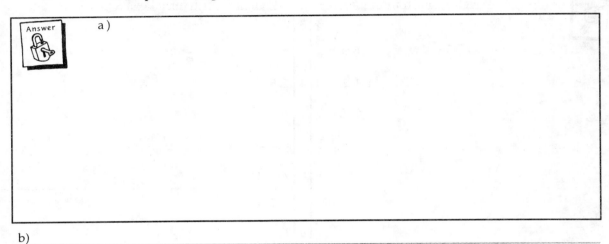

a)

b) _____
_____
_____

2. a)   The number of runs scored by two batsmen over a season of 20 completed innings are listed
            below.

            Batsman 1:   82, 62, 45, 41, 57, 22, 21, 1, 13, 10, 0, 28, 24, 43, 34, 37, 34, 35, 35, 32

            Batsman 2:   61, 64, 42, 36, 0, 14, 0, 20, 44, 47, 51, 53, 74, 73, 87, 57, 58, 84, 45, 36

            Draw a back to back stem and leaf graph to represent this data.

    b)   From the stem and leaf graph comment on which of the players appears to be a better
            batsman and why.

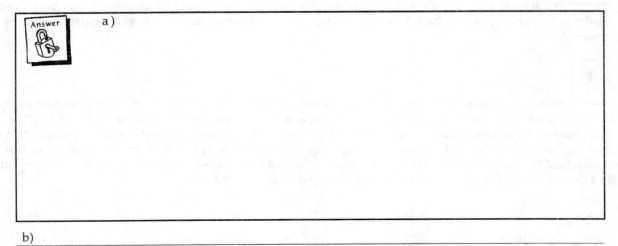

a)

b) _____
_____
_____

9.2 Box and Whisker Plot

Box and Whisker Plot

Box and Whisker plots are a visual way of representing the median, quartiles, minimum and maximum values of a set of data.   They are best used when you wish to compare two sets of similar data or when you wish to represent the spread of data.

The 'box' part of the graph represents the middle values of the distribution while the 'whiskers' extending from the box show the extreme values.   The width of the box has no significance for us, but it should be noted that if two box and whisker plots are drawn on the same axes then they should be drawn with the same width box in order that one is not emphasised more than the other.

Box and Whisker plots can be drawn either vertically or horizontally - in this text we have drawn them horizontally.

A graphical calculator can quickly calculate the median, quartiles, minimum and maximum as well as draw the graph so you can concentrate on the interpretation rather than just on drawing it. The Casio CFX- 9850 G and TI 83   require you to enter the data into a table while in statistics mode. They will then calculate the sample (or population) statistics and plot a box and whisker graph.

Example 3

The net take home pay ($ per week) of 15 employees from a manufacturing plant are listed
470, 350, 280, 520, 490, 650, 570, 290, 320, 530, 490, 190, 700, 430, 375
Draw a box and whisker plot to represent this data.

Putting the data in order to calculate the median and quartiles we obtain
190, 280, 290, 320, 350, 375, 430, 470, 490, 490, 520, 530, 570, 650, 700

Median	= 470	Lower Quartile	= 320
Upper Quartile	= 530	Top	= 700
Bottom	= 190		

Nett take home pay ($ per week)

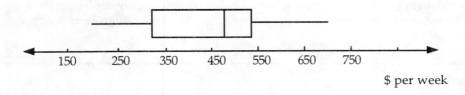

$ per week

When drawing statistical graphs you need to select a scale on the axes so that the graphs is big enough that differences and or trends of the graph(s) are clearly visible.

Example 4

Results in Calculus and Statistics

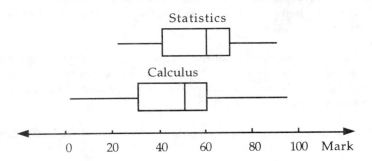

Above are drawn two box and whisker plots which represent a class of 30 students exam results in both Statistics and Calculus.

a)   Read off the quartile and median values from the graphs for Calculus and Statistics.

b)   Comment on the extreme values for both Calculus and Statistics.

c)   Interpret and make comparisons between the two subjects.

a)   Calculus: Median   = 50

                      Lower Quartile = 30

                      Upper Quartile = 60

       Statistics   Median   = 60

                      Lower Quartile = 40

                      Upper Quartile = 70

b)   The extremes for Calculus are greater than the extremes for Statistics since both whiskers in the Calculus plot are longer.

c)   It would appear from the two box and whisker plots that this class of 30 students find Calculus more difficult than Statistics. Three quarters of the Calculus class (upper quartile) obtain a result below the median of the Statistics class.   All 3 parameters, median, lower quartile and upper quartile are higher in Statistics.

> To compare two sets of data, it is effective to plot side by side Box and Whisker Plots. The same scale is used for both sets of data and direct comparisons can then be made between them.

Problems

3. **a)**   The temperature in a town is taken at 3pm every day for one month. The temperatures to the nearest °C where.

13, 17, 22, 18, 25, 23, 16, 24, 22, 20, 19, 17, 17, 16, 21, 27, 22, 25, 24, 19, 17, 15, 22, 24, 23, 26, 24, 23, 22, 21. Draw a box and whisker plot to represent this data.

    b)   Comment on your box and whisker plot.

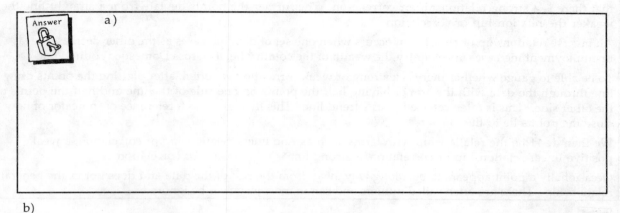

a)

b)
_____

_____

_____

4. **a)**   The length of life of two different brands of light bulbs was to be investigated. A sample of 20 light bulbs of each brand was taken. Their life (to the nearest hour) was

Brand A: 200, 170, 310, 150, 280, 165, 190, 245, 230, 168, 175, 420, 185, 170, 210, 225, 245, 280, 205, 225

Brand B: 120, 150, 190, 185, 210, 250, 135, 350, 340, 190, 210, 205, 196, 198, 304, 175, 205, 210, 220, 230

Draw side by side box and whisker plots to represent this data.

    b)   From the box and whisker plots comment on which of the brands of light bulb was better than the other and why.

a)

b)
_____

_____

_____

9.3 Scatter Graph

Scatter Graph

A scatter graph enables us to investigate whether there is a relationship between two sets of data. By pairing the data and plotting the coordinates on a Cartesian plane we can obtain a visual indication of the relationship between the data.

If the points on a scatter graph do not fall exactly along a straight line, but lie within a narrow belt we say that there is a strong relationship or correlation. The further the points deviate from a straight line the weaker the relationship or correlation.

An inverse relationship or correlation occurs when one set of data increases as the other decreases ie. as unemployment increases in a country the wealth of the country (ie. its Gross Domestic Product) falls.

To be able to gauge whether there is a strong or weak correlation we often, after plotting the points draw a line through the data with the aim of having half the points on one side of the line and half the points on the other side. This is often referred to as a trend line. This then gives us a reference or indicator of how close the points lie to the line.

We then describe the relationship with terms such as - no linear relationship or correlation, a weak positive linear relationship or correlation, a strong linear relationship or correlation etc.

Occasionally a point appears to be a long way away from the rest of the data and does not fit the general relationship. These are often called outliers and can in most instances be ignored.

Example 5

Over a ten year period a country keeps a record of the total number of vehicles on the road and the total number of road accidents. The data is represented below

Year	1	2	3	4	5	6	7	8	9	10
Vehicles (1,000,000's)	2.5	3.0	3.4	3.6	4.0	4.5	4.6	4.9	5.4	5.6
Accidents (1000's)	135	160	165	150	178	200	220	215	230	220

a) Draw a scatter graph of this data.
b) Describe the relationship between the two sets of data.

a)

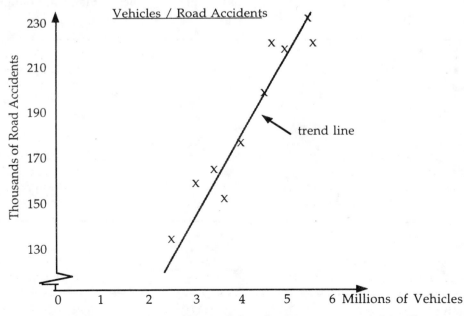

b) The points are close to the trend line indicating that there is a strong positive linear correlation between the number of vehicles on the road and the number of accidents in a year.

Example 6

A researcher decided to see whether there was a relationship between the height of males and blood pressure. He obtained the following results for 10 males.

	1	2	3	4	5	6	7	8	9	10
Blood Pressure (mm Hg)	116	120	118	125	120	134	150	140	144	150
Height (cm)	180	178	176	175	172	170	169	165	162	161

a) Draw a scatter graph of this data.

b) Describe the relationship between the two sets of data.

  a)

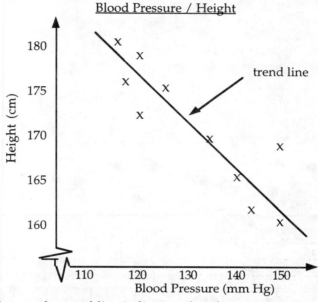

b) The points are reasonably close to the trend line indicating that there is a good negative linear correlation between height and blood pressure.

It is easy, when using scatter graphs, to draw a conclusion that there is some form of relationship between two sets of data. Ten pairs of figures on their own do not substantiate a claim even though they form a near straight line when displayed on a scatter graph. Further investigation is probably indicated to see if their is truly a relationship.

It is possible to calculate a correlation coefficient using a mathematical formula that gives us a value for r, the correlation coefficient. The closer $|r|$ is to 1 the stronger the relationship between the two sets of data. This formula is beyond the scope of this course. Students could explore this further in the internal assessment part of the course.

Again most Graphical Calculators will allow you to enter both sets of data into a list in the statistics mode and plot a scatter graph. The calculator will also calculate the equation of the trend line. For the data above a TI 83 or a Casio 9850 G gives the usual statistics as well as the linear regression (or x regression parameters) of a = ⁻0.45 , b = 230 and r = ⁻0.92 (figures rounded 2 sig. fig.) which means the trend line is Height = ⁻0.45 times (Blood Pressure) + 230   and the correlation coefficient is r = ⁻0.92 which implies a strong negative relationship between the sets of data.

Problems

5.   A class of 10 students are asked to record the total amount of time they spent revising for their Calculus exam. Below in the table this value is presented as well as their final Calculus mark.

Student	1	2	3	4	5	6	7	8	9	10
Revising (hours)	2	1	3	4	12	6	10	7	5	4
Final Mark (%)	20	40	54	50	80	80	60	62	70	65

a)   Draw a scatter graph of this data.
b)   Describe the relationship between the two sets of data and comment.

a)

b)

6.   a)   Plot the following the following data on a scatter graph

No.	1	2	3	4	5	6	7	8	9	10
x	20	18	16	14	12	10	8	6	4	2
y	4	8	1	5	2	10	4	4	10	6

b)   Describe the relationship between the two sets of data and comment.

a)

b)

9.4 Histogram

Histogram

Most students are very familiar with Histograms as they are commonly used to display grouped continuous data.

However it is often forgotten when dealing with Histograms that the area of the bar drawn, represents the frequency, NOT the height of the bar. It is therefore essential when dealing with intervals of differing widths to make the appropriate adjustment to the height of the bars to represent the correct area.

Grouped discrete data can also be represented in a Histogram, however it is essential when labelling the x-axis to be able to distinguish between grouped discrete data and grouped continuous data. We do this by labelling the entire interval, rather than the midpoint value or a single endpoint value.

Example 7

A student wished to investigate the mobility of earthworms. They took a sample of 104 earthworms and measured (cm) how far each had travelled from a fixed line after 30 minutes. Their results are represented in the table below.

interval	0 -	25 -	50 -	75 -	100 -	125 -	150 -	200 - 225
frequency	20	18	16	14	12	10	8	6

Draw a histogram to represent this data.

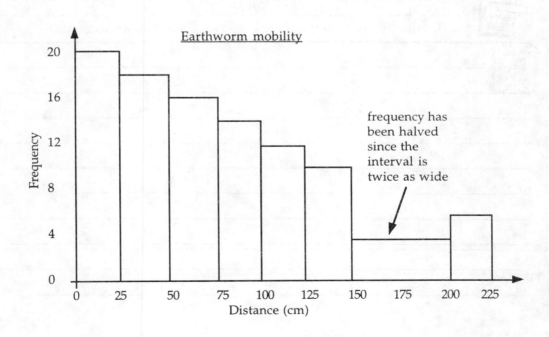

frequency has been halved since the interval is twice as wide

Example 8

A class of 32 students sat the end of year Calculus exam with the following results (%).

interval	0 - ≤ 20	21 - ≤ 40	41 - ≤ 60	61 - ≤ 80	81 - ≤100
frequency	1	5	13	9	4

Draw a histogram to represent this data.

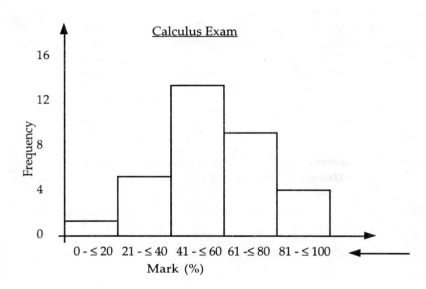

the entire
interval has
been labelled to
show the data
is grouped
discrete

Problems

7.   A retailer of men's clothing, over a one week period, recorded the chest measurement of those customers requiring a new shirt.   The results are displayed in the table below.

Chest (cm)	90-	100 -	110 -	120 -	130 -	140 -	160 -	190 -
Frequency	2	1	3	4	12	6	10	7

Draw a histogram to represent this data.

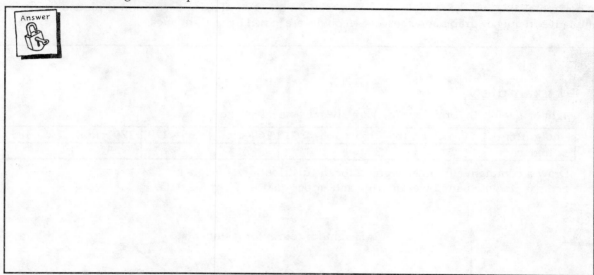

8.   A sample of 50 long life light bulbs are tested and their life in hours recorded. The results are displayed in the table below.

Hours	601 - 800	801 - 1000	1001 - 1200	1201 - 1400	1401 - 1600	1601 - 2000
Frequency	4	7	18	10	6	5

Draw a histogram to represent this data.

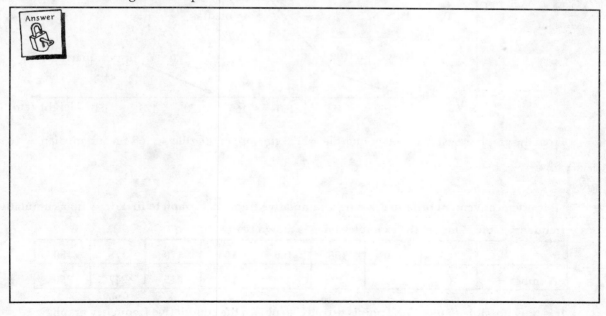

9.5 Cumulative Frequency Graph

Cumulative Frequency Graph

With grouped data, either continuous or discrete, we can use a Cumulative Frequency Graph or Ogive curve to estimate values for the median and quartiles. It is also possible using the Cumulative Frequency Graph to estimate other percentiles.

The Cumulative Frequency is the total frequency up to a point. The upper class boundaries are displayed on the horizontal axis and the cumulative frequencies on the vertical axis. Each point is plotted on the cumulative frequency graph and consecutive points are joined by straight lines.

Example 9

The height of 250 fourth form boys (cm) are given in the table below

height(cm).	145-<150	150-<155	155-<160	160-<165	165-<170	170-<175	175 - 180
frequency	6	23	60	74	52	32	3

a) Draw a cumulative frequency graph for the distribution of heights.
b) Estimate the median, lower quartile and upper quartile from the data.

a)

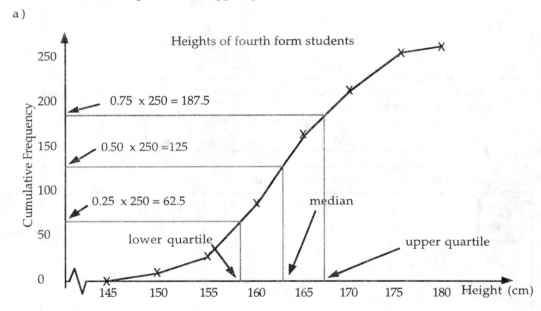

b) From the graph we estimate lower quartile = 158 cm, upper quartile = 168 cm and median = 163 cm

It is often convenient prior to drawing a cumulative frequency graph to first draw up a cumulative frequency table. One for the example above is drawn below.

x	145	150	155	160	165	170	175	180
Number < x	0	6	29	89	163	215	247	250

It is now possible to plot these points directly to obtain the cumulative frequency graph.

Problems

9   A retailer of men's clothing, over a one week period, recorded the chest measurement of those customers requiring a new shirt.   The results are displayed in the table below.

Chest (cm)	90- < 100	100 - <110	110 - <120	120 - <130	130 - <140	140 - < 160	160 - < 190	190 - < 200
Frequency	2	4	6	10	8	7	5	1

a)   Draw a cumulative frequency graph for the distribution of heights.

b)   Estimate the median, lower quartile and upper quartile from the data.

10.   A sample of 50 long life light bulbs are tested and their life in hours recorded. The results are displayed in the table below.

Hours	601 - 800	801 - 1000	1001 - 1200	1201 - 1400	1401 - 1600	1601 - 2000
Frequency	4	7	18	10	6	5

a)   Draw a cumulative frequency graph for the distribution of heights.

b)   Estimate the median, lower quartile and upper quartile from the data.

Practice Exam

SECTION A: COMPULSORY

QUESTION ONE: COMPULSORY (28 marks)
Show all working in each part.

(a)   From the frequency distribution below find the upper quartile.

Length (cm)	40	41	42	43	44	45
Frequency	4	3	5	6	3	3

(1 mark)

(b)   A bag contains 5 red and 7 black counters. Find the probability of drawing 2 black counters in two draws if

   1.   the counters drawn are not replaced.   (1 mark)

   2.   the counters are replaced after each draw.   (1 mark)

(c)   If the random variable Z has a standard normal distribution, find $P(1.2 < Z < 2.3)$ (1 mark)

(d)   Consider the expansion $\left(3x^3 + \frac{2}{x}\right)^8$. Find the term independent of x.   (1 mark)

(e)   Consider the piecewise function $f(x) = \begin{cases} x^2 + 2 & \text{for } 0 \leq x < 2 \\ -2x + 8 & \text{for } 2 \leq x \leq 4 \end{cases}$

   1.   Sketch the graph of f(x).   (1 mark)

   2.   Calculate f(2.3).   (1 mark)

(f)   If the random variable Z has a standard normal distribution, find the value of *a* if

   $P(Z > a) = 0.28$.   (1 mark)

(g)   The random variable X has a probability distribution defined by

$$P(X = x) = \frac{2x + 3}{56}, x = 4, 5, 6, 7$$

$$= 0, \text{ otherwise}$$

   1.   Find E(X)   (1 mark)

   2.   Find SD(X)   (1 mark)

   3.   Find $P(X \neq 5)$ (1 mark)

(h)   Differentiate the expression $f(x) = 7x^2 - 3e^{-2x}$ (1 mark)

(i)   **1.**   Solve the simultaneous equations $3x + y = 3$

                              $x - 2y = 8$ (1 mark)

   2.   The simultaneous equations in part **1.** are unique and consistent. Give a pair

         of simultaneous equations that are not consistent.   (1 mark)

(j)   Represent the series $64 + 60 + 56 + 52 + ... + 8$ in sigma notation.   (1 mark)

(k)   **1.**   Express $3 \log 4 - 3 \log 2$ as the logarithm of a single number.   (1 mark)

      2.   Solve $\log_{0.5} x = 2$ (1 mark)

(l)   Simplify $\begin{pmatrix} n \\ n-2 \end{pmatrix}$ (1 mark)

(m)   A person randomly draws a card from a pack of 52. What is the probability that the card drawn is a King or a red card.   (1 mark)

(n)   The graph of a function is drawn below

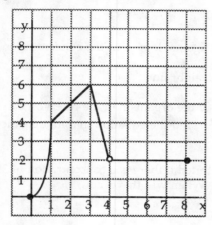

      1.   Find $f(3)$ (1 mark)

      2.   When does $f(x)$ not exist.   (1 mark)

      3.   Find when $f(x) = 4$.   (1 mark)

(o)   A certain mountain erupts on average once every five years. Assuming the number of eruptions per year is X, and models a Poisson distribution.

      1.   State the value of the parameter of the distribution X.   (1 mark)

      2.   Find the probability that in a particular year there are more than 2 eruptions   (1 mark)

(p)   Simplify $\dfrac{\sqrt[3]{a^{13}}}{a^4 \times \sqrt{a}}$ (1 mark)

(q)   **1.**   Show that the equation $x^3 - 10x + 11 = 0$ has a root between $x = 1$ and $x = 2$.   (1 mark)

      2.   Explain your reasoning.   (1 mark)

(r)   X is a random variable having a binomial distribution with $n = 60$ and $\pi = 0.45$. Find the mean and standard deviation of this distribution.   (1 mark)

SECTION B: OPTIONAL QUESTIONS
(Choose any **TWO** of questions TWO to FOUR)

Each question is worth 18 marks.

You should spend about 30 minutes on each question.

QUESTION TWO: (18 marks)

(a)   As part of the testing of a small towns water reservoir a bacterial organism was identified in the supply. It was first detected at the rate of 14 units per litre. Further measurements were taken at day 10, 15, 23 and day 30 resulting in the following concentrations being identified, 61 units/litre, 127 units/litre, 413 units/litre and 1155 units/litre.

   1.   On the Cartesian plane plot time (t) against $\log_e$ of C, the concentration.   (2 marks)

   2.   Find the gradient of the resulting straight line.   (1 mark)

   3.   It is assumed that the concentration of the organism in the reservoir can be modelled by the equation $C = C_0 \, e^{kt}$. Find the equation that models the data.   (1 mark)

   4.   The reservoir is defined as being polluted if there is a concentration of 3850 units/litre of the organism present. When will this occur.   (2 marks)

(b)   Consider the function $f(x) = 2x - e^x + 2$

   1.   Use differentiation to identify the coordinates and nature of the turning point of the function f(x).   (2 marks)

   2.   Using an appropriate starting value, perform two iterations of the Newton Raphson method to find the positive root of the equation f(x) = 0. Clearly show all your steps.   (4 marks)

   3.   Draw a graph of f(x) clearly labelling the turning point, the positive root and an estimate of the second root of the equation.   (2 marks)

   4.   Explain why when using the method in **(b) 2**, it is necessary to select a starting value relatively close to the positive root.
Relate your answer to the function f(x).   (1 mark)

(c)   The population of the small town in part **(a)** is falling at the rate of 2.4% per annum as a consequence of the water pollution. This can be modelled by the differential equation $\frac{dP}{dt} = -kP$. How long will it take for the population of the small town to half.   (3 marks)

QUESTION THREE: (18 marks)

(a) A new export company plans to export New Zealand grown bonsai to Japan. They initially plan to send two different products.

- Radiata pine which cost $10 to produce and ship and when packed occupies a volume of 0.020 m^3 .

- Pohutukawa which cost $21 to produce and ship and when packed occupies a volume of 0.012 m^3 .

Represent the number of Radiata pine with the letter r and the number of Pohutukawa with the letter p.

1. Give the four inequalities which describe the following;

- The firm's transport contracts allows them to send up to 1.2 m^3 per month.

- The firm's cash flow allows then to purchase up to $1200 worth of products each month.

- The company has firm commitments to sell at least 15 Radiata and 25 Pohutukawa per month.

2. Graph this system of inequalities.

3. The firm expects to make a profit of $7.50 for each Radiata and $11.25 for each Pohutukawa. How many of each bonsai tree should be sent?

4. What is the maximum monthly profit? (9 marks)

(b) A squad of 11 students is training for a netball team. Find the number of possible ways the team could be picked if;

1. All 11 students can play in any of the 7 positions.

2. 3 students are vying for the 2 goal attack positions, 4 students for the 3 wing/centre positions and 4 students are contesting the two defence positions.

In each game the team members get points for the MVP competition. At the end of the season, the first, second and third highest points gain prizes

3. In how many ways could the 11 students fill the first three places. (4 marks)

(c) A square with area = 1 has another square inscribed in it by joining the midpoints of the sides. The corner triangle is then painted, as shown in diagram 1. The process is repeated again and again, giving diagrams 2, 3, 4 and so on.

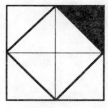 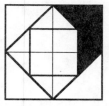 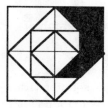 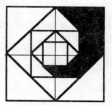

Diagram 1　　　　Diagram 2　　　　Diagram 3　　　　Diagram 4

1. What is the connection between areas of successive SQUARES?

2. What proportion of the square is the first triangle.

3. Write down a geometric sequence for the area being added in each diagram in the painting process.

4. If the process is continued there is a limit to the size of the area painted. What is this limit? (5 marks)

QUESTION FOUR: (18 marks)

(a) A scientist investigating a chemical reaction noted that the time (*time*) in seconds taken for completion was dependent upon the starting temperature (TEMP) in °C. The following experimental results were obtained

TEMP °C	7.2	9.1	11.2	17.8	23.3
time sec	86	58	41	20	12

It is required to find an appropriate mathematical model relating the Temperature to the time.   The two possible models are;

Exponential function $time = A\,e^{k\,TEMP}$

or a Power function $time = A\,(TEMP)^{k}$

USE THE SHEET PROVIDED AT THE END OF THIS EXAM TO ANSWER THIS QUESTION.

1. Copy and complete the following table by adding the $\log_e$ of each value.

TEMP °C	4.6	7.2	11.2	18.0	23.3
$\log_e$ (TEMP)					
time sec	180	86	41	20	12
$\log_e$ (*time*)					

(2 marks)

2. Using the axes provided, draw the semi - log graph of the $\log_e$ (*time*) on the y axis against TEMP on the x axis. (1 mark)

3. Using the next axes , draw the log - log graph of the $\log_e$ (*time*) on the y axis against $\log_e$ (TEMP) on the x axis. (1 mark)

4. From your graph explain, with clear reasoning, as to how TEMP and *time* are related (3 marks)

5. From your graph or raw data, find values for A and k . Show all working. (3 marks)

6. Use your formula to predict the *time* when the starting temperature is 30°C. (1 mark)

(b) A sketch graph of

$$y = 1.06x\,lnx - 2.62$$

is on the right. It is required to find a solution for

$$1.06x\,lnx - 2.62 = 0$$

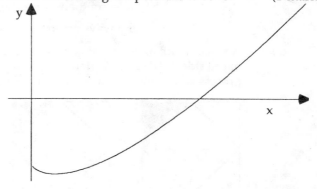

1. Accurately draw the graph of

$$y = 1.06x\,lnx - 2.62$$

for $0 < x \le 5$.

and use it to estimate one solution (1dp)

USE THE SHEET PROVIDED AT THE END OF THIS EXAM (3 marks)

2. It is required to find the solution to

$$1.06x\,lnx - 2.62 = 0$$

Given that $f(x) = 1.06x\,lnx - 2.62$ use the Bisection numerical method to find the solution accurate to 2 decimal places. For your starting values use 2.500 and 3.000. (4 marks)

SECTION C: OPTIONAL QUESTIONS
(Choose any **TWO** of questions FIVE to SEVEN)

Each question is worth 18 marks.

You should spend about 30 minutes on each question.

QUESTION FIVE: (18 marks)

(a) In the foyer of its offices a large company has a coffee dispensing machine. It is set so that on average it discharges 140 ml of coffee per cup with a standard deviation of 12 ml. Assume that the dispensing of coffee from this machine is normally distributed.

    1. If the machine consistently dispenses less than 115 ml of coffee per cup, employees at the company complain to the management. What is the probability that a cup filled at random from the machine dispenses less than 115 ml. **(2 marks)**

    2. On an average day 430 cups of coffee are dispensed from the machine. The capacity of each cup is 150 ml. How many of the 430 cups are over-filled. **(2 marks)**

    3. The manufacturer of the machine is concerned that a significant amount of coffee is being wasted due to over filling. They decide to adjust the mean fill of the cup so that only 5% of the cups are overfilled. What would be the new mean fill per cup in millilitres. **(2 marks)**

    4. The manufacturer of the machine now resets it to the new mean calculated in **(a) 3**. In order to ensure that it is working properly they decide to take a sample of so many cups of coffee. What size sample is required if the manufacturer wishes to be 95% confident that the machine is accurate to within 2 ml of the correct setting. **(2 marks)**

(b) As part of an ongoing study and promotion by the coffee machine manufacturer, two demonstration machines were set up in a shopping mall. Coffee machine A dispensed 130 cups in a single day and machine B dispensed 115 cups. The data below was collected from the machines at the end of the day.

	Machine A	Machine B
Sample size	130	115
Mean dispensed	132 ml	128 ml
Standard deviation dispensed	14 ml	12 ml

    1. One of the executives at the coffee machine manufacturing company claims that there is no significant difference between the mean coffee per cup dispensed from the two machines. To check this assertion, calculate the probability of obtaining a difference between the means at least as large as that obtained from the data in the table above. **(3 marks)**

    2. Calculate a 95% confidence interval for the difference between the mean coffee dispensed from the two machines. **(2 marks)**

    3. What conclusions can you draw about the mean coffee dispensed at the two machines. What assumptions do you have to make about the two machines. **(3 marks)**

    4. Is this study of two machines undertaken by the manufacturer sufficient to base their conclusions on. Explain. **(2 marks)**

QUESTION SIX: (18 marks)

A branch of an insurance company has found that 15% of its clients will claim against its *All Risks* policy in any year. It is assumed that the probability that one client claiming is independent of any other client claiming. A sample of 10 policies is selected.

1. Justify why this can be considered a Binomial distribution. (1 mark)

2. Find the probability that there is exactly one client who has claimed in the past year in this sample. (1 mark)

3. Find the probability that there is greater than one claimant in this sample. (2 marks)

The branch has 180 clients with this All Risks policy. They require to know the probability that there are 30 or more claimants in the next 12 months.

4. Explain why this problems meets the criteria for the Normal approximation to the Binomial distribution. (1 mark)

5. Find the probability that there are 30 or more claimants in the next 12 months. (3 marks)

This branch also handles other types of insurance and responds to on average 17.6 phone calls every 8 hour day. These calls are randomly distributed and are independent of each other. They require to know the probability that they will get a set number of calls over a specified time period.

6. What distribution is most appropriate for this problem? (1 mark)

7. Find the probability that in a specific two hour period they will get exactly 4 calls. (1 marks)

8. Find the probability that there are exactly 2 calls in each of two consecutive hours. (2 marks)

9. Find the probability that there is at least 1 call in a 15 minute time period. (2 marks)

The company is concerned about claims made against its *Automobile* policy.

Over the last 24 months they have had the following claims.

An analysis of their 200 policies produced the results on the Venn diagram on the right.

Use the Venn diagram to answer the following questions.

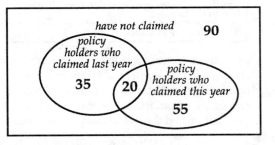

10. Find the number of claims against the policy this year. (1 mark)

11. The probability that a policy holder had made claim in the last two years. (1 mark)

12. Find the probability that a person claims against the policy this year given that they claimed last year. (2 marks)

QUESTION SEVEN: (18 marks)

(a)   The following table gives the School Certificate results for a sample of 30 students
(15 of each sex) for both Geography and Physics.

MALE	Geography	Physics
1	45	57
2	56	47
3	38	70
4	68	40
5	59	45
6	49	57
7	58	49
8	68	39
9	64	43
10	78	33
11	82	28
12	45	55
13	65	42
14	34	65
15	28	65
Mean	**55.8**	**49**

FEMALE	Geography	Physics
16	60	60
17	44	51
18	68	63
19	28	45
20	57	52
21	52	55
22	61	67
23	68	65
24	76	73
25	45	42
26	58	53
27	69	63
28	59	54
29	45	41
30	35	32
Mean	**55**	**54.4**

1.   Plot the Geography results for males and females in a back to back
stem and leaf graph.   (3 marks)

2.   Find the median and upper and lower quartiles of Geography for the males.   (2 marks)

The Geography and Physics results are plotted on the following scatter diagram.

TO ANSWER QUESTIONS **3.** and **4.** USE THE SHEET PROVIDED AT THE END OF THIS EXAM.

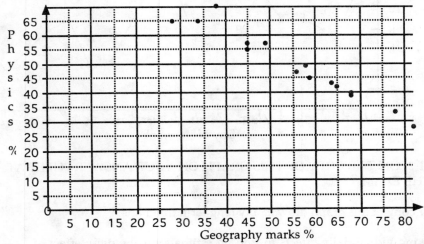

3.   On the copy of this diagram on your answer sheet, draw in the line of best
fit.   (1 mark)

4.   On the same graph plot the results for the females and draw in the line of
best fit.   (2 marks)

5.   What conclusions can you draw about the relationship between Geography and Physics marks for
the two groups?   (2 marks)

(b)   The data in the following table gives the number of staff reporting ill for a construction company for the last four weeks. The moving means for successive sets of five days in the time series, and individual daily effects are included.

Day	accidents	Moving mean	Individual daily effects
Mo 1	14		
Tu	9		
We	8	9.8	-1.8
Th	9	9.4	-0.4
Fr	9	9	0
Mo 2	12	8.6	3.4
Tu	7	8.2	-1.2
We	6	8.8	-2.8
Th	7	9	-2
Fr	12	9.4	2.6

Day continued	accidents	Moving mean	Individual daily effects
Mo 3	13	9.2	3.8
Tu	9	8.6	0.4
We	5	8	-3
Th	4	7	-3
Fr	9	6.4	2.6
Mo 4	8	6.2	1.8
Tu	6	6.8	-0.8
We	4	???	???
Th	7		
Fr	11		

1.   Explain why a FIVE point moving average was selected.   (1 mark)

2.   Calculate the missing mean for the last Wednesday and its individual daily effect.   (2 mark)

The raw data and moving mean is plotted in the graph below.

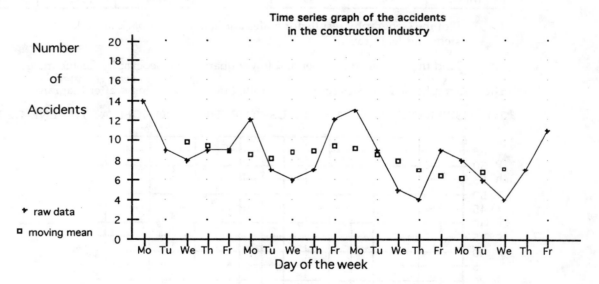

Time series graph of the accidents in the construction industry

ANSWER PART 3. ON THE COPY OF THIS GRAPH ON YOUR ANSWER SHEET AT THE END OF THE EXAM.

3.   On your copy of this graph draw in any long term trend line.   (1 mark)

4.   Use the individual daily effects to find an estimate for the daily effect of a Monday.   (2 marks)

5.   Use your trend line in 3. and your estimate of the daily effect of a Monday, to predict thenumber of accidents in one further weeks time on a Monday (Mo 6).   (2 marks)

Practice Exam Answers

Practice Exam Answers

Practice Exam Answers

Practice Exam Answers

QUESTION FOUR

(a) **1.**   Copy and complete the following table by adding the $\log_e$ of each value.

TEMP °C	4.6	7.2	11.2	17.8	23.3
$\log_e$ (TEMP)					
time sec	180	86	41	20	12
$\log_e$ (time)					

2. $\log_e$ (*time*) [y axis] vs TEMP [x axis]   **3.** $\log_e$ (*time*) [y axis] vs $\log_e$ (TEMP)[x axis]

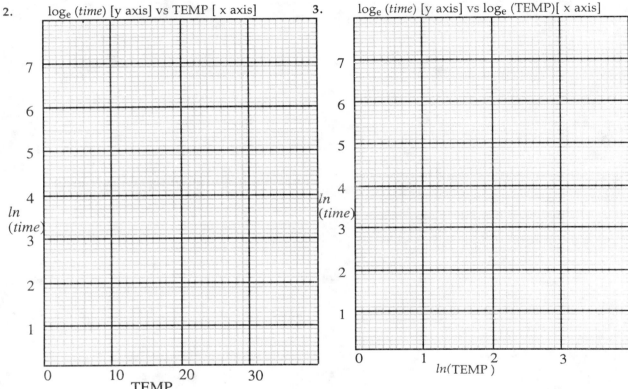

(b)   **1.**

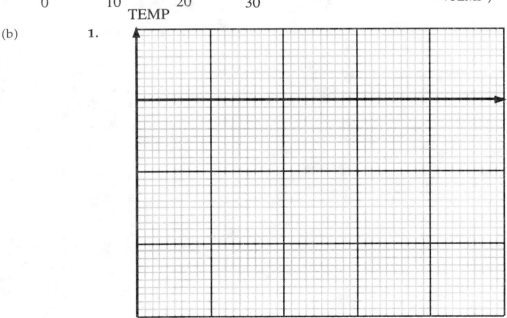

Practice Exam Answers

Practice Exam Answers

Practice Exam Answers

QUESTION SEVEN

(a)   **3.** and **4.**

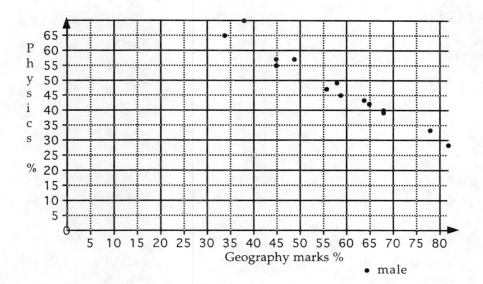

(b)   **3.**

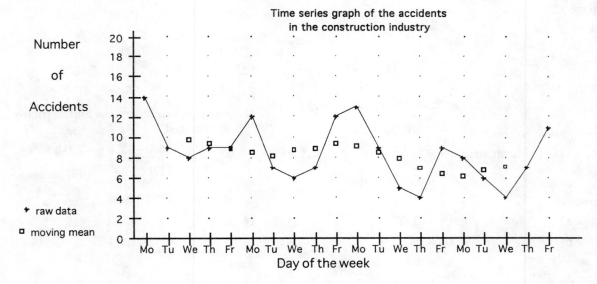

Answers

For some problems, one of the steps leading to the answer is given along with the answer so students with an incorrect answer can gain information as to where their error occurred. People only learn by making mistakes and finding out what caused the mistake or error.

Chapter 1
STATISTICS

page 14

1. a) $\bar{x}$ = 8.9   (1dp)
        s = 7.8   (1dp)
        (n divisor)

   b) $\bar{x}$ = 12.7   (1dp)
        s = 13.8   (1dp)
        (n divisor)

2. a) $\bar{x}$ = 6.6   (1dp)
        s = 2.9   (1dp)
        (n divisor)

   b) $\bar{x}$ = 67.7   (1dp)
        s = 17.7   (1dp)
        (n divisor)

3. $\bar{x}$ = 10.1   (1dp)
        s = 0.6   (1dp)
        (n divisor)

page 15

4. $\bar{x}$ = 43.2   (1dp)
        s = 20.4   (1dp)
        (n divisor)

5. $\bar{x}$ = 5.5   (1dp)
        s = 2.7   (1dp)
        (n divisor)

6.   mean height = $\dfrac{609.4}{360}$
        = 1.69m (2dp)

page 16

7. a) s^2 = 20.25
   b) $\bar{x}$ = 34.32
        s = 4.5
   c) $\bar{x}$ = 78.96
        s = 13.5
   d) $\bar{x}$ = 130.6
        s = 22.5

page 21

8. a) $E(\bar{X})$ = 40
        $Var(\bar{X})$ = 2.25
        $sd(\bar{X})$ = 1.5
   b) μ = 47
        σ = 17.8
        $sd(\bar{X})$ = 3.02
   c)   n = 16
        $E(\bar{X})$ = 613
        $Var(\bar{X})$ = 1089
   d) μ = 87
        n = 1444
        $Var(\bar{X})$ = 0.0025

9. a) $E(\bar{X})$ = 43
   b) $sd(\bar{X})$ = 1.93

page 22

10. a) $\dfrac{1}{6} \times 240$ = 40
    b)   0.024

11. a)   15
    b)   0.0013

12.   n = 272

page 24

13. a) samples independent and normally distributed
   b)   1600 – 1350 = 250 hours
   c) $\dfrac{120^2}{100} + \dfrac{80^2}{121}$ = 197 hours
   d)   14 hours

14. a)   6 ml
   b)   1.212ml   (4 sig figs)

page 27

15. a)   P(Z > 2.236)
        = 0.0127
   b)   P(Z < -3.578)
        = 0.0002
   c) P(-0.894 < Z < 3.130)
        = 0.8135

page 28

16. a) $\quad$ P(Z > 1.125)

$$= 0.1304$$

b) $\quad$ P(Z < -2.475)

$$= 0.0067$$

c) P(1.125 < Z < 3.375)

$$= 0.1300$$

d) $\quad$ P(Z < 0.8438)

$$= 0.8007$$

page 29

17. a) $\quad$ P(Z < -1.863)

$$= 0.0312$$

b) P(Z < -2.981) or P(Z > 1.118)

$$= 0.1333$$

18. P(-1.528 < Z < -0.306) $= 0.3165$

page 32

19. a) $\quad 300 \pm 1.96\frac{(45)}{\sqrt{100}}$

$$291.18 < \mu < 308.82 \quad (2dp)$$

b) $\quad 300 \pm 2.58\frac{(45)}{\sqrt{100}}$

$$288.39 < \mu < 311.61 \quad (2dp)$$

20. $\quad 68 \pm 1.96\frac{(10)}{\sqrt{25}}$

$$64.08 < \mu < 71.92 \quad (2dp)$$

21. $\quad 8.75 \pm 2.58\frac{(1.191)}{\sqrt{20}}$

using (n – 1) divisor for std dev.

$$8.06 < \mu < 9.44 \quad (2dp)$$

page 33

22. $\quad 7.38 \pm 1.96\frac{(3.842)}{\sqrt{20}}$

using (n – 1) divisor for std dev.

$$5.70 < \mu < 9.06 \quad (2dp)$$

23. $\quad 8.5 \pm 1.645\frac{(2)}{\sqrt{200}}$

$$8.27 < \mu < 8.73 \quad (2dp)$$

24. a) $\quad 27 \pm 2.58\frac{(2.5)}{\sqrt{50}}$

$$26.09 < \mu < 27.91 \quad (2dp)$$

b) $\qquad\qquad$ Yes

page 35

25. a) $0.125 \pm 1.96\sqrt{\dfrac{0.125(0.875)}{120}}$

$$0.066 < \pi < 0.184$$

b) $0.125 \pm 2.58\sqrt{\dfrac{0.125(0.875)}{120}}$

$$0.047 < \pi < 0.203$$

page 36

26. $0.7143 \pm 1.96\sqrt{\dfrac{0.7143(0.2857)}{210}}$

$$0.65 < \pi < 0.78$$

27. $0.8667 \pm 1.645\sqrt{\dfrac{0.8667(0.1333)}{450}}$

$$0.84 < \pi < 0.89$$

28. a) $0.25 \pm 2.58\sqrt{\dfrac{0.25(0.75)}{300}}$

$$0.19 < \pi < 0.31$$

b) $\qquad\qquad$ 16.67%

c) Biased, since expected proportion well outside 99% confidence interval.

page 38

29. $(270 - 200) \pm 1.96\sqrt{\dfrac{30^2}{200} + \dfrac{25^2}{150}}$

$$64.2 < \mu_1 - \mu_2 < 75.8 \quad (1dp)$$

page 39

30. $(25 - 16) \pm 2.58\sqrt{\dfrac{3^2}{20} + \dfrac{5^2}{32}}$

$$6.1 < \mu_1 - \mu_2 < 11.9 \quad (1\ dp)$$

31. a) $(42 - 35) \pm 1.96\sqrt{\dfrac{5^2}{30} + \dfrac{3^2}{30}}$

$$4.9 < \mu_1 - \mu_2 < 9.1 \quad (1dp)$$

b) samples are normally distributed and independent of one another and sufficiently large.

c) $\quad$ Yes

page 42

32. $\qquad\qquad$ n ≥ 323

33. $\qquad\qquad$ n ≥ 74

34. $\qquad\qquad$ n ≥ 999

page 43

35. $\qquad\qquad$ n ≥ 8

36. $\qquad\qquad$ n ≥ 383

37. $\qquad\qquad$ n ≥ 17

Chapter 2

TIME SERIES

page 51

1.

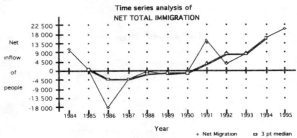

page 52

2.

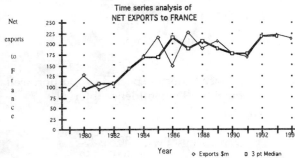

page 53

3.

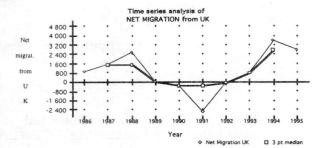

page 54

4.

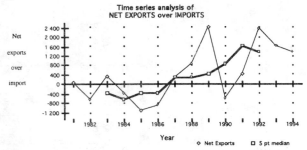

page 58

5.

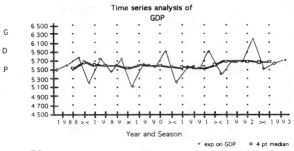

page 59

6.

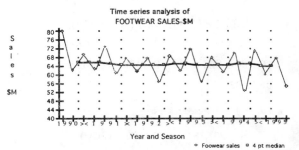

page 60

7.   Smoothed over 6 two monthly periods.

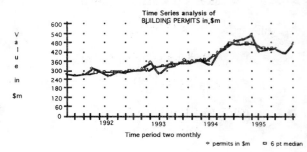

page 61

8.

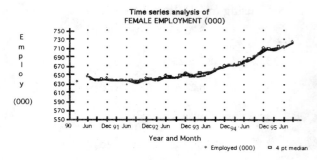

page 66

9.

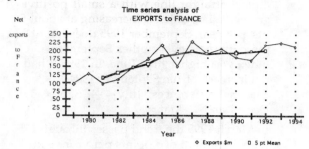

Time series analysis of
EXPORTS to FRANCE

◇ Exports $m   □ 5 pt Mean

page 67

10.

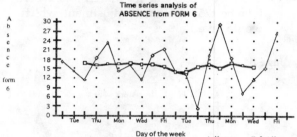

Time series analysis of
ABSENCE from FORM 6

◆ Absence   □ 5 pt Mean

page 68

11.

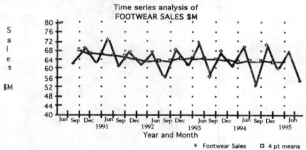

Time series analysis of
FOOTWEAR SALES $M

◇ Footwear Sales   □ 4 pt means

page 69

12.

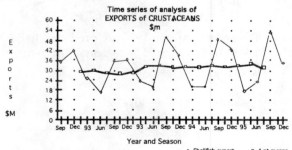

Time series of analysis of
EXPORTS of CRUSTACEANS
$m

• Shellfish export   □ 4 pt means

page 72

13.

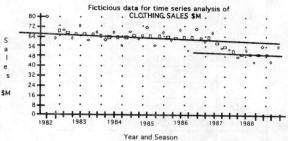

Ficticious data for time series analysis of
CLOTHING SALES $M

◇ sales/ season   □ 4 pt mean

The **Long Term Trend** was for the sales to decrease each year by about $m 1. The strong **Seasonal Cycle** had higher sales in March (autumn) and September (spring). In 1987 there is a downward **Step** of about $m 11 and then the **Long Term Trend** continued at the same rate.

page 73

14.

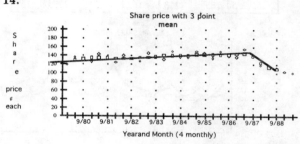

Share price with 3 point
mean

• share price   □ 3 point mean

The **Long Term Trend** of the share price was a steady climb of about 3¢/year (gradient of the straight line). There is a **Seasonal Cycle** with the shares selling more in September of each year. In 1987 (about October) the share price started to decline rapidly. This apparent **Ramp** is too short to be described accurately.

page 74

15.

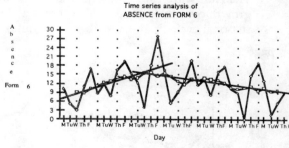

Time series analysis of
ABSENCE from FORM 6

◇ Raw data absence   □ 5 pt Mean

The **Seasonal Cycle** was for more students to be absent on Friday and fewer on Wednesday. The **Long Term Trend** was for 3 more students a week to be absent per week for the first three weeks and then for 2 fewer students absent for the last 4 weeks.

page 77

16.

Period	Food $m	Food Index	Hard ware $m	Hard ware Index	Dept store $m	Dept store Index
Dec	1800	107	187	113	397	138
92 Mar	1680	100	166	100	288	100
Jun	1650	98	156	94	337	117
Sep	1710	102	157	95	308	107
Dec	1855	110	217	131	429	149
93 Mar	1700	101	187	113	311	108
Jun	1690	101	178	107	359	125
Sep	1792	107	166	100	380	132
Dec	1949	116	216	130	560	194
94 Mar	1810	108	182	110	368	128
Jun	1817	108	175	105	430	149
Sep	1892	113	182	110	404	140
Dec	2081	124	224	135	609	211
95 Mar	1966	117	187	113	392	136
Jun	1928	115	173	104	437	152
Sep	1899	113	162	98	395	137

Time Series of
RETAIL SALES INDICES

The **Department store** sales shows a strong seasonal pattern with high sales every December. The December sales appear to be increasing at a higher rate than the sales for the rest of the year.

The **Food index** has changed less and shows a mild seasonal cycle. There are slightly higher sales in December.

The **Hardware Index** has shown little or no growth over the period. It also shows a seasonal cycle (high December - low June).

page 83

17.

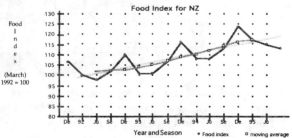

Food Index for NZ

17. continued

The smoothed index series shows an almost straight line with a small positive gradient. The index is increasing at about 5 pts. per year. September 1995 does not fit the pattern as every other September index was higher than June. In 1995 it had not increased from September 1994.
Seasonal differences; July = -4, Sept = -1, Dec = 7 and   Mar = -2

In March 1995 the trend passes through 115 with a gradient of 5 points per year so in March 1997 it would be expected to pass through 115+2*5 = 125.
The predicted value for March 1997 would then be 125 + seasonal adjustment which would give 123.

page 84

18.

Dept.store sales $m

Comment

The sales increased by about 50 million each season per annum. The December sales were a significant component of the total sales.
The smoothed data shows strong **approximately linear growth.** The seasonal differences are

$$July = -14, \qquad Sept = -39,$$
$$Dec = 121 \text{ and } \quad Mar = -62.$$

The sales in March 1996 are predicted to be = Trend line in Mar 96 + seasonal difference which gives

$$Sales = (460 + 50) - 62$$
$$= \$m \ 448.$$

page 85
19.

Hardware sales

Comment

There is a very strong pattern of high sales on Saturday (mean $138 above the trend line). The worst sale day is Monday. The smoothed data shows strong approximately linear decline of $3 per week. The seasonal differences are Sat = 138, Sun = -47, Mon = -63, Tue = -22, Wed = -32, Thu = -3 and Fri =24.

In three Saturdays time the expected sales are = Trend in 3 Saturdays + seasonal difference

$$= (135 - 3 \times 3) + 138$$
$$= \$ 264$$

page 86
20.

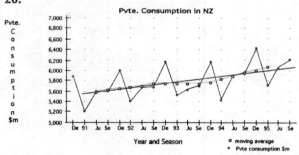

Pvte. Consumption in NZ

Comment

The consumption increased by about 110 million each season per annum. The December consumption was higher than any other season. The seasonal differences are June = $m -39, Sept = $m -39, Dec = $m 443 and Mar = $m -314.

The smoothed data shows strong approximately linear growth.

The consumption for December 1997 is predicted to be

$$= \text{long term trend (Dec 97)} + \text{seasonal difference}$$
$$= (5950 + 2 \times 110) + 443$$
$$= \$m\ 6613$$

Chapter 3
PROBABILITY

page 93

1. a)   P(Peter ∩ Susan) $= 0.15 \times 0.20$
          $= 0.03$

   b)   P(one is late) $= 0.15 \times 0.80 + 0.20 \times 0.85$
          $= 0.29$

   c) P(Peter' ∩ Susan') $= 0.85 \times 0.80$
          $= 0.68$

2. a)   P(2 G and 1 R)   = P(GGR) + P(GRG) + P(RGG)

          $= \left(\frac{6}{10} \times \frac{6}{10} \times \frac{4}{10}\right) \times 3$

          $= \frac{54}{125}$ (0.432)

   b)   P(2 G and 1 R)   = P(GGR) + P(GRG) + P(RGG)

          $= \left(\frac{6}{10} \times \frac{5}{9} \times \frac{4}{8}\right) \times 3$

          $= \frac{1}{2}$ (0.50)

page 94

3.   P(at least 1 solved) $= 1 - P(\text{none solved})$
          $= 1 - (0.8 \times 0.75 \times 0.6)$
          $= 0.64$

4.   P(both are faulty) $= \frac{4}{10} \times \frac{3}{9}$
          $= \frac{2}{15}$ (0.1333)

5. a) P(Green & 1st jar) $= \frac{1}{3} \times \frac{10}{50}$
          $= \frac{1}{15}$ (0.0667)

   b)   P(Green lolly) $= \frac{1}{3} \times \frac{10}{50} + \frac{1}{3} \times \frac{10}{30}$
          $+ \frac{1}{3} \times \frac{10}{20}$
          $= \frac{31}{90}$ (0.3444)

   c)   P(Green) $= \frac{n(G)}{n(L)}$
          $= \frac{3}{10}$ (0.30)

6.   P(Abe) $= \frac{1}{2} + \frac{1}{16} + \frac{1}{128} + ...$
          $= \frac{4}{7}$ (0.5714)

      P(Bernadette) $= \frac{1}{4} + \frac{1}{32} + \frac{1}{256} + ...$
          $= \frac{2}{7}$ (0.2857)

      P(Colin) $= \frac{1}{8} + \frac{1}{64} + \frac{1}{512} + ...$
          $= \frac{1}{7}$ (0.1429)

page 97

7. $\quad \frac{1}{2} \times \frac{2}{3} \times \frac{1}{2} + \frac{1}{2} \times \frac{2}{3} \times \frac{1}{2} \quad = \frac{1}{3}$

8.

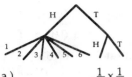

a) $\quad \frac{1}{2} \times \frac{1}{6} \quad = \frac{1}{12}$

b) $\quad = \frac{1}{2}$

page 98

9.

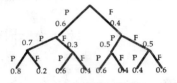

a) $\quad 0.6 \times 0.7 \times 0.8 \quad = 0.336$

b) $\quad 0.6 \times 0.3 \times 0.4$

$\quad + 0.4 \times 0.5 \times 0.4$

$\quad + 0.4 \times 0.5 \times 0.4 \quad = 0.232$

page 99

10.

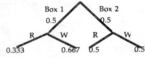

$P(\text{red drawn out}) \quad = \frac{1}{2} \times \frac{3}{9} + \frac{1}{2} \times \frac{4}{8}$

$\quad = \frac{5}{12} \quad (0.4167)$

page 100

11.

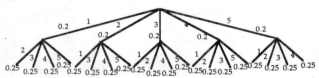

a) $\quad P(\text{sum} < 7) \quad = \frac{12}{20} \quad (0.6)$

b) $\quad P(\text{sum} \geq 5) \quad = \frac{4}{5} \quad (0.8)$

page 103

12. a) $\quad 0.20 + 0.15 - 0.08 \quad = 0.27$

b) $\quad \frac{0.08}{0.15} \quad = 0.533$

13. a) $\frac{7}{20} \times 0.6 + \frac{5}{20} \times 0.8 + \frac{8}{20} \times 0.4$

$\quad = 0.57$

b) $\quad \frac{\frac{5}{20} \times 0.8}{0.57} \quad = 0.35$

page 104

14. a) $\quad \frac{75}{200} \quad = 0.375$

b) $\quad \frac{\frac{40}{200}}{\frac{125}{200}} \quad = 0.32$

15. a) $\quad \frac{\frac{1}{36}}{\frac{11}{36}} \quad = \frac{1}{11}$

b) $\quad \frac{\frac{2}{36}}{\frac{11}{36}} \quad = \frac{2}{11}$

page 105

16. a) $\quad P(\text{choc}) \quad = \frac{x}{x + y}$

b) $\quad P(\text{1st two choc}) \quad = \frac{x}{x + y} \times \frac{(x - 1)}{x + y - 1}$

c) $P(\text{choc then caram}) \quad = \frac{x}{x + y} \times \frac{y}{x + y - 1}$

d) $P(\text{2nd carm | 1st choc})$

$\quad = \frac{\frac{x}{x + y} \times \frac{y}{x + y - 1}}{\frac{x}{x + y}}$

$\quad = \frac{y}{x + y - 1}$

e) $\quad P(\text{carm} \geq 2) \quad = \frac{y(y - 1)(y - 2) + 3xy(y - 1)}{(x + y)(x + y - 1)(x + y - 2)}$

f) $P(\text{carm} \geq 2 \text{ | 1st choc})$

$\quad = \frac{\frac{xy(y - 1)}{(x + y)(x + y - 1)(x + y - 2)}}{\frac{x}{(x + y)}}$

$\quad = \frac{y(y - 1)}{(x + y - 1)(x + y - 2)}$

page 108

17. a)

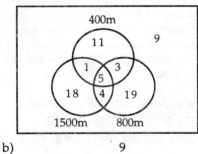

b) $\quad 9$

c) $\quad \frac{13}{70}$

d) $\quad \frac{28}{61}$

page 109

18. a)

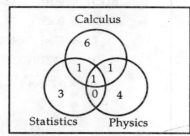

b) $\frac{10}{16}$

c) $\frac{3}{16}$

d) $\frac{13}{16}$ = 81.25%

e) $\frac{\frac{3}{16}}{\frac{9}{16}}$ = $\frac{1}{3}$

page 112

19. a)   E(X) = 5.55

b)   E(X) = $\frac{16}{11}$

page 113

20. a)

X	1	2	3	4
P(X=x)	$\frac{3}{50}$	$\frac{8}{50}$	$\frac{15}{50}$	$\frac{24}{50}$

E(X) = $3\frac{1}{5}$

b)   P(X > 2) = $\frac{39}{50}$

21. a) $13k^2$ = 1

k = 0.2774 $(\frac{1}{\sqrt{13}})$

b)   E(X) = $\frac{55}{13}$

c)   P(X ≤ 3) = $\frac{6}{13}$

page 114

22.

X	0.95	0.45	0.05	-0.05
P(X=x)	$\frac{1}{36}$	$\frac{5}{36}$	$\frac{6}{36}$	$\frac{24}{36}$

E(X) = 0.064 (gain of 6c)

23.

X	$1	$1.50	$2	$2.50	$3	$4
P(X=x)	$\frac{2}{42}$	$\frac{12}{42}$	$\frac{6}{42}$	$\frac{8}{42}$	$\frac{12}{42}$	$\frac{2}{42}$

E(X) = $2.29

24.   E(F) = 1.1 for fast post

E(S) = 1.85 for standard

E(X) = 0.4(1.1) + .6(1.85)

= 1.55 days

page 117

25. a)   Var(X) = 4.79

sd(X) = 2.19

b)   Var(X) = 0.7934

sd(X) = 0.8907

26. a)

X	3	4	5	6
P(X=x)	$\frac{6}{30}$	$\frac{7}{30}$	$\frac{8}{30}$	$\frac{9}{30}$

E(X) = 4.67

b)   Var(X) = 1.22

c)   sd(X) = 1.11

d)   P(X ≥ 3) = $\frac{24}{30}$

page 118

27. a)

X	$8	$3	-$2
P(X=x)	$\frac{1}{6}$	$\frac{1}{18}$	$\frac{7}{9}$

E(X) = -0.06 cents

b)   Var(X) = 14.27

c) $\frac{1}{6}(10-x) + \frac{1}{18}(5-x) + \frac{7}{9}(-x) = 0$

Cost = $1.94

28. a)

X	1	2	3	4
P(X=x)	$\frac{1}{4}$	$\frac{1}{4}$	$\frac{1}{4}$	$\frac{1}{4}$

b)   E(X) = 2.5

Var(X) = 1.25

page 119

29. a)

X	0	1	2	3
P(X=x)	0.45	0.27	0.19	0.09

b)   E(X) = 0.92

c)   Var(X) = 0.9936

sd(X) = 1.00

30. a)

X	$950	$150	$100	-$50
P(X=x)	$\frac{1}{52}$	$\frac{3}{52}$	$\frac{12}{52}$	$\frac{36}{52}$

E(X) = $15.38

b)   sd(X) = $149.85

page 123

31. a) mean = 22
        stdev = 4
    b) mean = 16
        stdev = 4
    c) mean = -13
        stdev = 4
    d) mean = 54
        stdev = 12
    e) mean = 74
        stdev = 16
    f) mean = -37
        stdev = 8

32. a) $E(W) = 3\frac{2}{7}$
    b) $E(W^2) = 15\frac{6}{7}$
    c) $Var(W) = 5\frac{3}{49}$ (5.061)
    d) $E(3W - 1) = 8\frac{6}{7}$ (8.857)
    e) $E[(3W - 1)^2] = 124$
    f) $Var(3W - 1) = 45\frac{27}{49}$ (45.55)

page 124

33. a)

X	0	1	2	3
P(X=x)	$\frac{1}{8}$	$\frac{3}{8}$	$\frac{3}{8}$	$\frac{1}{8}$

    b) $P(X < 2) = \frac{1}{2}$
    c) $E(X) = 1\frac{1}{2}$
    d) $Var(X) = \frac{3}{4}$
        $sd(X) = 0.8660$

34. a)

N	0	1	2	3	4	5	6	7	8	9
P(N=n)	$\frac{1}{10}$	$\frac{1}{10}$	$\frac{1}{10}$	$\frac{1}{10}$	$\frac{1}{10}$	$\frac{1}{10}$	$\frac{1}{10}$	$\frac{1}{10}$	$\frac{1}{10}$	$\frac{1}{10}$

    b) $E(X) = 4.5$
        $Var(X) = 8.25$
        $sd(X) = 2.87$
    c) $P(N^2 < 25) = \frac{2}{5}$ (0.4)

page 127

35. a) 14, 3, 1.73
    b) 13.6, 6.1, 2.47
    c) 102, 28, 5.29

page 128

36. a) $Z = S - R$
    b) $E(Z) = 0.10$
        $sd(Z) = 0.05$

37. a) $T = 15M + 35C$
    b) $sd(T) = \sqrt{225Var(M) + 1225Var(C)}$
        $= \sqrt{225(4^2) + 1225(10^2)}$
        $= \$355$

page 129

38. a) $P = 2A + 3B$
    b) $E(P) = 135$ secs
        $sd(P) = 18.97$
        ≈ 19 secs

39. a) $E(X) + E(Y) = 6.6$
    b) $Var(X + Y) = 1.3$
    c) $E(X) - E(Y) = -2.8$
    d) $Var(X - Y) = 1.3$
    e) $sd(X + Y) = 1.14$
    f) $sd(X - Y) = 1.14$

page 133

40. a) $P(X = 0) = 0.0576$
    b) $P(X = 4) = 0.1361$
    c) $P(X \leq 3) = 0.8059$
    d) $P(X \geq 6) = 0.0113$

41. a) $P(X = 5) = 0.0001$
    b) $P(X = 0) = 0.4437$
    c) $P(X > 3) = 0.0023$
    d) $P(X < 2) = 0.8352$

page 134

42. a) $P(X = 5) = 0.0591$
    b) $P(X \geq 5) = 0.0750$
    c) $P(X = 1) = 0.1721$
    d) $P(X \leq 4) = 0.9270$

43. a) $P(X = 12) = 0.1422$
    b) $P(X = 6) = 0.0040$
    c) $P(X > 10) = 0.4434$
    d) $P(X = 9) = 0.1720$

page 135

44. a) $P(X = 6) = 0.1762$
    b) $P(X < 5) = 0.0196$
    c) $P(3 \leq X \leq 7) = 0.5636$
    d) $P(X = 9) = 0.1342$

page 135 continued

45. a)   P(X = 2)   = 0.0229

      b)   P(X < 5)   = 0.2616

      c)   P(X = 0)   = 0.0003

      d)   P(X = 8)   = 0.0763

page 139

46. a)   P(X = 0)   = 0.0183

      b)   P(X = 2)   = 0.1465

      c)   P(X > 3)   = 0.5665

      d)   P(4 ≤ X ≤ 6)   = 0.4559

page 139

47. a)   P(X = 2)   = 0.0107

      b)   P(X > 3)   = 0.9577

      c)   P(4 ≤ X ≤ 7)   = 0.4106

      d)   P(X ≥ 6)   = 0.8088

page 140

48. a)   P(X = 0)   = 0.0334

      b)   P(X > 4)   = 0.2558

      c)   P(2 ≤ X ≤ 5)   = 0.7237

49. a)   P(X = 3)   = 0.0867

      b)   P(X = 0)   = 0.3012

      c)   0.3614 x 0.3614   = 0.1306

page 141

50. a)   P(X = 3)   = 0.0892

      b)   0.1339 x 0.1339   = 0.0179

51. a)   P(X = 0)   = 0.4724

      b)   P(X ≤ 2)   = 0.9596

      c)   0.4724 x 0.4724   = 0.2231

page 146

52. a)

      (i)   P(Z > 1.6)   = 0.0548

      (ii)   P(Z < -1)   = 0.1587

      (iii) P(-0.4 < Z < 1.4)   = 0.5746

      b)   159

page 147

53. a)

      (i)   P(Z < -1.333)   = 0.0913

      (ii)   P(Z > -2.667)   = 0.9962

      (iii) P(-1 < Z < 0.667   = 0.5890

      b)   61 days

page 148

54. a)   P(Z > 1.667)   = 0.0478

          50 x 0.0478   = 2.39   (2 years)

      b)   P(Z < -2.667)   = 0.0038

          50 x 0.0038   = 0.19   (0 years)

page 148 Q 54 continued

      c)

      P(0.333 < Z > 2.267)   = 0.3579

          50 x 0.3579   = 17.895 (18 years)

      d)

      P(-0.867 < Z < -0.133)   = 0.2541

          50 x 0.2541   = 12.71   (13 years)

page 149

55. a)   P(Z > 0.870)   = 0.1922

      b)   P(Z < -1.30)   = 0.0962

      c) P(1.739 < Z < 3.043)   = 0.0398

      d)   P(Z < -2.174)   = 0.0148

          460 x 0.0148   = 6.808   (7 TV's)

page 152

56.   74 metres

57.   17.4 mm

page 153

58.   Distinction   = 63 or better

          Merit   = 55 to 62

59.   lower   = 117

          upper   = 131

page 156

60 a)

      (i)   P(Z > 1.375)   = 0.0845

      (ii)   P(Z < -0.625)   = 0.2660

      (iii)

      P(-0.625 < Z < 0.375)   = 0.3802

      b)   0.0845 x 500   = 42.25   (43 sacks)

page 157

61. a)

      (i) P(0.125 < Z < 0.208)   = 0.0326

      (ii)   P(Z > 1.458)   = 0.0724

      (iii)

      P(-0.625 < Z < 0.958)   = 0.5649

      b)   lower quartile   = 40%

          upper quartile   = 56%

page 160

62.   P(Z > 1.376)   = 0.0843

page 161

63. a)   P(Z < -0.481)   = 0.3152

      b)   P(Z > 2.598)   = 0.0047

      c) P(-1.443 < Z < 0.674)   = 0.6754

64. a)   0.5511

      b)   0.0058

      c)   0.6047

Chapter 4
COMBINATIONS and the BINOMIAL THEOREM

page 164

1. Choice $= 4 \times 3 \times 4$
$= 48$ possibilities

2 a) items $= 5 \times 5 \times 5$
$= 125$ combinations

b) items $= 5 \times 4 \times 3$
$= 60$ combinations

3 a) numbers $= 4^3$
$= 64$

b) numbers $= 3 \times 4 \times 4$
$= 48$

4. plates $= 26 \times 26 \times (10 \times 10 \times 10 \times 10 - 1)$
$= 6759324$

leading 0's represented as blank
-1 for all zeros.

page 166

5. $\dfrac{(m+1)!}{(m-1)!} = m(m+1)$

6. $61!+62!+63! = 61! + 62 \times 61! + 63 \times 62 \times 61!$
$= 61! (1 + 62 + 63 \times 62)$
$= 3969 \times 61!$

page 167

7. $\dfrac{17!}{3! \cdot 14!} = 680$

8. $10! + (6!)^2 = 6! (10 \times 9 \times 8 \times 7 + 6!)$
$= 5760 \times 6!$
or $= 8 \times (6!)^2$
or $= 4147200$

9. $\dfrac{(m+4)!}{m(m+3)!} = \dfrac{(m+4)}{m}$

10! $\dfrac{70!}{3!.5!.65!} = 2017169$

page 170

11. ways $= 6!$
$= 720$

12. ways $= 8!$
$= 40320$

13.a) 12 @ table so 11 arranged relative to any individual $= 11!$
$= 39916800$

b) chairperson top so arrange other 11
$= 11!$
$= 39916800$

c) Compared to the fixed seat
$= 12!$
$= 479001600$

14. a) words $= 6!$
$= 720$

b) words $= 7!$
but each has two A's so each word repeated
answer $= 7! \div 2$
$= 2520$

c) words $= 11! \div (2 \times 2 \times 2)$
$= 4989600$

page 173

15. $^{30}P_6 = 427518000$

16. $^{10}P_3 = 720$

17. total $= {}^7P_4 + {}^7P_3 + {}^7P_2 + {}^7P_1$
$= 1099$

18. Horse placed could be in any of three positions. $^{16}P_2$ picks the other two
possibilities $= 3 \times {}^{16}P_2$
$= 720$

19. a) $^9P_5 = 15120$

b) Select 3 other letters in order and place IN in each of the four positions
$4 \times {}^7P_3 = 4 \times 210$
$= 840$

20. a) $^{15}P_3 = 2730$

b) select four and take into account the dead heat has no order.
$^{15}P_4 \div 2 = 32760 \div 2$
$= 16380$

page 177

21. hands of 5 = $^{52}C_5$

$\qquad$ = 2598960

22. $\qquad ^{40}C_6 = 3838380$

23. a) $^{10}C_5 = 252$

b) As the selection for the second waka is determined by filling the first the answer is still 252.

24. a) group = $^5C_2 \times {}^5C_2$

$\qquad$ = 100

b) no couples = $^5C_4 \times 2 \times 2 \times 2 \times 2$

$\qquad$ = 80

page 178

25. total = $(^{10}C_6 + {}^{10}C_2) + 5$ front etc.

$\qquad$ = 1419

26. 1st class = 13, 14, 15, 16 or 17

$\qquad$ total = $^{30}C_{13} + {}^{30}C_{14} + {}^{30}C_{15}$ etc

$\qquad$ = 685 482 570

27. a) $^{10}C_2 = 45$

b) $^{10}C_8 = 45$

c) gap = $45 - 9$

$\qquad$ = 36

28. $^nC_r + {}^nC_{r-1} = \dfrac{n!}{(n-r)!r!} + \dfrac{n!}{(n-(r-1))!(r-1)!}$

$\qquad = \dfrac{n!}{(n-r)!r!} + \dfrac{n!}{(n-r+1)!(r-1)!}$

$\qquad = \dfrac{(n-r+1).n! + r.n!}{(n-r+1)!r!}$

$\qquad = \dfrac{n!(n-r+1+r)}{(n+1-r)!r!}$

$\qquad = \dfrac{(n+1)!}{(n+1-r)!r!}$

$\qquad = {}^{n+1}C_r$

$\qquad$ = RHS

page 181

29. $\qquad ^{10}C_4 = 210$

30. a) $26^4 = 456976$

b) $^{26}P_4 = 358800$

31. a) Imagine the 30 coins in a row, there are 29 gaps between them and you have to insert 3 divisions.

$\qquad ^{29}C_3 = 3654$

b) If we add four coins to our 30 and divide them up as per part a) we get

$\qquad ^{33}C_3 = 5456$

we can now remove a coin from each of the four boxes getting us back to 30 and introducing the possibility that some boxes will be empty

32. $\qquad$ ways = all diff. + 1 repeat + 2 repeat

$\qquad = {}^8P_4 + 3$ of $^5C_2 \times 4! \div 2 + 3$ of $^4C_2$

$\qquad = 1680 + 360 + 18$

$\qquad = 2058$

page 182

33. $\qquad ^5C_2 = 10$

34. $\qquad r = 1$ or 3

page 185

35. $(3x - 5)^6 = 729x^6 - 7290x^5 + 30375x^4 - 67500x^3 + 84375x^2 - 56250x^1 + 15625$

36. $(\frac{2}{y} - 5y^2)^5 =$

$32y^{-5} - 400y^{-2} + 2000y^1 - 5000y^4 + 6250y^7 - 3125y^{10}$

37. x^5 term is $175000x^5$

38. independent term is $^-10240$

page 186

39. 5th term $1088640 \, x^{14}$

40. $x^4 y^3$ term is $^-90x^4 y^3$

41. coefficient is 2520000

42. using $1 + 11 \times 0.03 + 55 \times 0.03^2 + 165 \times 0.03^3$

= 1.383955

Chapter 5

CALCULUS

page 189

1. $\dfrac{2e^4 - 2e^{-3}}{7} = 15.6$ (3 sig fig)

2. $\dfrac{944 - 647}{4.25} = 69.9$ (3 sig fig)

page 192

3. $\displaystyle\lim_{h \to 0} \dfrac{x^2 + 2xh + h^2 - 5(x+h) - 1 - (x^2 - 5x - 1)}{h}$
    $= 2x - 5$

4. $f'(x) = 3x^2 - 4x$

page 194

5. $f'(x) = 3x^2 - 6$

6. $f'(x) = 9x^2 - 4x - 10x^{-3}$

page 195

7. $f'(x) = -8x^{-5} - 3x^{-0.5}$
    $= \dfrac{-8}{x^5} - \dfrac{3}{\sqrt{x}}$

8. $f'(x) = 6x - 12$

9. $f(x) = 3 + 5x^{-1} - 6x^{-2}$
    $f'(x) = -5x^{-2} + 12x^{-3}$
    $= \dfrac{-5}{x^2} + \dfrac{12}{x^3}$

10. $f'(x) = 2.5x^{1.5} + 3x^{-1.5}$

11. $f(x) = 4x^2 - 17x - 15$
     $f'(x) = 8x - 17$

12. $f(x) = x^{1.5} - x^{-1} + 3x^{-0.5}$
     $f'(x) = 1.5x^{0.5} + x^{-2} - 1.5x^{-1.5}$
     $f'(x) = \dfrac{3}{2}\sqrt{x} + \dfrac{1}{x^2} - \dfrac{3}{2\sqrt{x^3}}$

page 197

13. $f'(x) = 6e^{2x}$

14. $f'(x) = 6x - 4e^{2x} - 10e^{-2x}$

15. $f(x) = 5e^{-x}$
     $f'(x) = -5e^{-x}$
     $= \dfrac{-5}{e^x}$

16. $f(x) = e^{2x}$
     $f'(x) = 2e^{2x}$

page 199

17. $f'(x) = 2x + 5$
     $f'(-1) = 3$

18. $f'(x) = x^2 - 4x + 3$
     $f'(2) = -1$
     $f'(3) = 0$ as turning point.

page 200

19. $f'(x) = 8x - 8$
     $x = 0$ $f'(0) = -8$
     $x = 1$ $f'(1) = 0$

20. $f'(x) = x^2 - 6x + 8$
     at $x = 3$ $f'(3) = -1$
     and $f(3) = 7$
     ANS $y - 7 = -1(x - 3)$
              $y = -x + 10$

21. a) $s'(1) = 30$
            $s'(4) = 12$
            $s'(9) = -18$
     b) $t = 6$ weeks

22. a) $v'(5) = 1.125$
           $v'(12) = 0.95$
           $v'(25) = 0.625$
     b) $v(25) = 23.4$ (3 sig fig)

page 203

23. $f'(x) = 2x + 4$
     $2x + 4 = 0$
          $x = -2$
     $(-2, 1)$ is a minimum point

24. $f'(x) = x^2 - 4x + 3$
          $x = 1$ or 3
     $(1, 4\frac{1}{3})$ is a max. and $(3, 3)$ is a min. point

page 204

25. $f'(x) = 8 - 2x$
     $8 - 2x = 0$
          $x = 4$
     $(4, 16)$ is a maximum point

page 204 continued

26. ($^-$1, 8) is a maximum point

(3, $^-$24) is a minimum point

27. (2, 6) is a minimum point

($^-$2, $^-$2) is a maximum point

28. (2, 19) is a maximum point

($^-$2, $^-$13) is a minimum point

page 207

29. numbers both 15

product = 225

30. sides both 6.5

Area = 21.125 cm^2

31. $x = 500$ m

$y = 250$ m

32. $V = h(10 - 2h)^2$

$= 100h - 40h^2 + 4h^3$

$V' = 100 - 80h + 12h^2$

max and min at

$h = 5, \dfrac{5}{3}$

Min at $h = 5$, max at $h = \dfrac{5}{3}$

ANS $V = 74.074$

$= 74.1$ (3 sig fig)

page 209

33.

	f′(x)	f(x)
a)	$f'(x) = 5x^4 + 2x$	$f(x) = x^5 + x^2 + c$
b)	$f'(x) = 12x^2 + 4$	$f(x) = 4x^3 + 4x + k$
c)	$f'(x) = 12x^3 + 6x^2$	$f(x) = 3x^4 + 2x^3 + 11$
d)	$f'(x) = 12e^{-3x} + 4x^3$	$f(x) = {}^-4e^{-3x} + x^4 - 5$
e)	$f'(x) = 24e^{4x}$	$f(x) = 6e^{4x} + 9$

34.

a) $f'(x) = 8e^{2x}$ $f(x) = 4e^{2x} + k$

b) $f'(x) = 6e^{3x}$ $f(x) = 2e^{3x} + k$

c) $f'(x) = 4x^3 + 3x^2$ $f(x) = x^4 + x^3 + k$

d) $f'(x) = 12e^{-3x}$ $f(x) = {}^-4e^{-3x} + k$

e) $f'(x) = 15x^4 + 2$ $f(x) = 3x^5 + k$

f) $f'(x) = 24e^{4x} - 6x + 2$ $f(x) = 6e^{4x} - 3x^2 + 2x + k$

page 211

35. general solution

$y = Ae^{12x}$

36. general solution

$y = Ae^{-3x}$

37. general solution

$y = Ae^{0.5x}$

38. general solution

$y = Ae^{-0.45x}$

page 212

39. general solution

$y = Ae^{0.05t}$

specific solution

$y = 41.68e^{0.05t}$

40. general solution

$y = Ae^{-0.13t}$

specific solution

$3152 = Ae^{-0.26}$

$A = 4088$

$y = 4088\,e^{-0.13t}$

page 216

41. $y' = 0.025\,y$

ANS $y = 133000\,e^{0.025t}$

$t = 14$ $y = 133000\,e^{0.35}$

$= \$188736$

$= \$189000$ (3 sig fig)

42. $y' = 0.23y$

ANS $y = 6\,e^{0.23t}$

$t = 24$ $y = 6\,e^{5.52}$

$= 1497.8$

$= 1497$ truncated

43. $y = 1350\,e^{kt}$

$t = 125$ years $y = 675$

$675 = 1350\,e^{125k}$

$e^{125k} = 0.5$

$125k = ln\,0.5$

$k = {}^-0.00555$

$100 = 1350\,e^{-0.00555t}$

$e^{-0.00555t} = 0.07407$

$t = 469$ years

44. $P = 175000\,e^{0.025t}$

$t = {}^-10$ $P = \$136000$ (3 sig fig)

Chapter 6
SEQUENCES & SERIES

page 222

1. a) $t_n = 7n - 5$
          $t_{20} = 135$

    b) $t_n = 120\left(\frac{3}{5}\right)^{n-1}$
          $t_{20} = 0.007312$ (4 sig figs)

    c) $t_n = {}^-11n + 21$
          $t_{20} = {}^-199$

    d) $t_n = -3\left(2q^2\right)^{n-1}$
          $t_{20} = -1572864q^{38}$

2. a) $S_{25} = 2550$
    b) $S_{25} = 637534189$
    c) $S_{25} = -4350$
    d) $S_{25} = 27960$ (4 sig figs)

page 223

3. a) $T(1) = -5$
          $T(2) = 4$
          $T(3) = -27$
          $T(4) = -1462$
          $T(5) = -4274861$

    b) $T(1) = 4$
          $T(2) = {}^-4$
          $T(3) = 2$
          $T(4) = 1$
          $T(5) = {}^-1$

4. a)   10 waves (then it goes 10 m to the pool)
    b) $100 + 60 + 10 = 170$ m

5. a) $S_\infty = 200$ cm
    b) $n = 8$

page 225

6.   115

7. $\frac{-1}{9} + \frac{1}{11} - \frac{1}{13} + \frac{1}{15} - \frac{1}{17} = -0.08928$ (4 sig figs)

8. $\sum_{n=1}^{9} {}^-3n + 23$

9. $\sum_{n=1}^{8} 20\left(\frac{1}{2}\right)^{n-1}$

page 226

10. $3 + 20 + 49 + 90 + 143 = 305$

11. $4 + {}^-8 + 16 + {}^-32 = {}^-20$

12. $\sum_{n=1}^{24} \frac{1}{2n+3}$

13. $\sum_{n=1}^{8} (2n+1)2^n$

14. $(a+b) + (2a+b) + (3a+b) + (4a+b)$
          $= 10a + 4b$

15. $\sum_{n=1}^{\infty} \frac{3^{n-1}}{2^n}$

page 229

16.

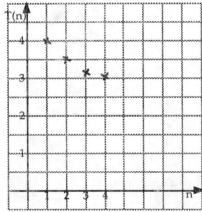

Strictly decreasing, bounded below by 3

17.

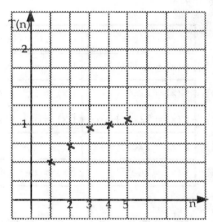

Strictly increasing, bounded above by 2

18. Oscillating as it converges to 4

page 231

19.   as $n \to \infty$, $\frac{1}{n^2} \to 0$
          $\therefore$ limit $= 0$

page 231 continued

20.   rewrite as $3 - \dfrac{7}{2n+3}$

as $n \rightarrow \infty$, $\dfrac{7}{2n+3} \rightarrow 0$

$\therefore$ limit $= 3$

21.   rewrite as $\dfrac{1}{2} + \dfrac{4.5}{2n-1}$

as $n \rightarrow \infty$, $\dfrac{4.5}{2n-1} \rightarrow 0$

$\therefore$ limit $= \dfrac{1}{2}$

22.   rewrite $\left(\dfrac{1}{2}\right)^n$ as $\dfrac{1}{2^n}$

as $n \rightarrow \infty$, $\dfrac{1}{2^n} \rightarrow 0$

$\therefore$ limit $= 3$

page 232

23. a) $S_1 = 7$

$S_2 = 6$

$S_3 = 5\dfrac{2}{3}$

$S_4 = 5\dfrac{1}{2}$

b) $7, -1, \dfrac{-1}{3}, \dfrac{-1}{6}$

c) To converge $\lim\limits_{n \rightarrow \infty} S_n$ must exist

as $n \rightarrow \infty$, $\dfrac{2}{n} \rightarrow 0$

$\therefore$ limit $= 5$

page 233

24. a) $1\dfrac{2}{3}, 2\dfrac{1}{5}, 2\dfrac{3}{7}, 2\dfrac{5}{9}$

b)   when $n = 1$ $T_1 = \dfrac{5}{3}$

when $n = 2$ $T_2 = \dfrac{11}{5}$

when $n = 3$ $T_3 = \dfrac{19}{7}$

when $n = 4$ $T_4 = \dfrac{23}{9}$

same as in part a) therefore T_n is nth term

c) rewrite as $3 - \dfrac{4}{2n+1}$

as $n \rightarrow \infty$, $\dfrac{4}{2n+1} \rightarrow 0$

$\therefore$ limit $= 3$

25. a) $t_1 = 2$

$t_2 = 1\dfrac{1}{4}$

$t_3 = 1$

$t_4 = \dfrac{7}{8}$

b)

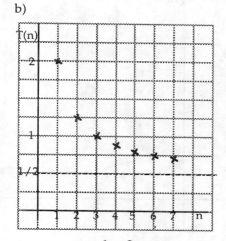

c)   rewrite as $\dfrac{1}{2} + \dfrac{3}{2n}$

as $n \rightarrow \infty$, $\dfrac{3}{2n} \rightarrow 0$

$\therefore$ limit $= \dfrac{1}{2}$

d) $S_1 = 2$

$S_2 = 3\dfrac{1}{4}$

$S_3 = 4\dfrac{1}{4}$

$S_4 = 5\dfrac{1}{8}$

e) No

page 236

26. $1 + 5x + \dfrac{25x^2}{2} + \dfrac{125x^3}{6}$

27. $1 + x^2 + \dfrac{x^4}{2} + \dfrac{x^6}{6}$

28. 0.3625

29. $2 + 7x + 10x^2 + \dfrac{26x^3}{3}$

30. $1 - x - \dfrac{15x^2}{2} - \dfrac{27x^3}{2}$

31. $1 - \dfrac{x^2}{2} + \dfrac{x^3}{3}$

Chapter 7
GRAPHS
page 241

1. $8x^8$

2. $\dfrac{1}{x^{13}}$

3.

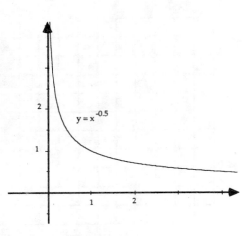

$y = x^{-0.5}$

4.

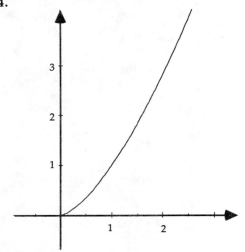

page 242

5.

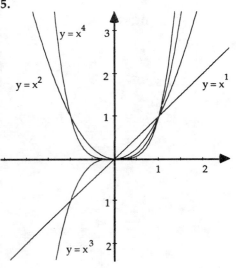

$y = x^4$

$y = x^2$

$y = x^1$

$y = x^3$

6.

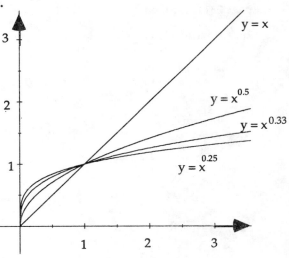

$y = x$

$y = x^{0.5}$

$y = x^{0.33}$

$y = x^{0.25}$

7. a)

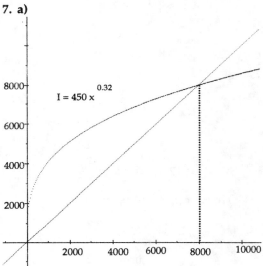

$I = 450 x^{0.32}$

b) Break even point is about \$8000.

page 245

8.

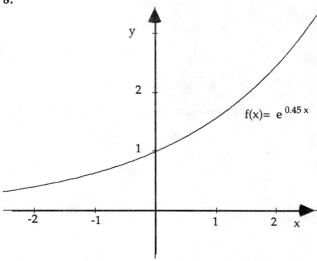

$f(x) = e^{0.45x}$

page 245

9.

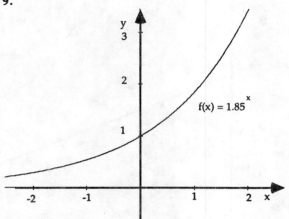

$f(x) = 1.85^x$

page 246

10.

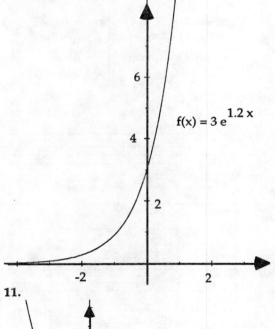

$f(x) = 3\,e^{1.2\,x}$

11.

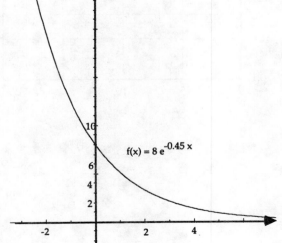

$f(x) = 8\,e^{-0.45\,x}$

12. a)

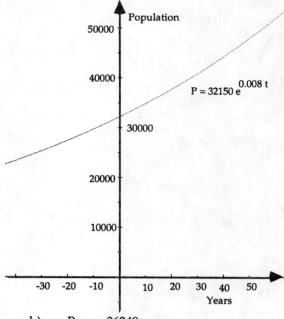

$P = 32150\,e^{0.008\,t}$

b) Pop = 36249
c) t = 27 years

page 249

13.

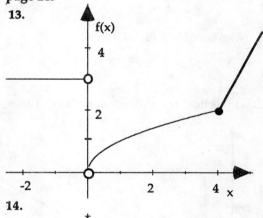

14.

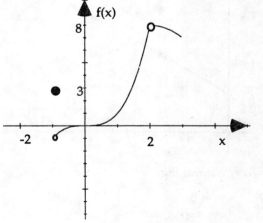

page 249

15. a) $f(4) = 2$

$f(^-1.5) = 2$

b) $x = ^-1, 1, 5$

c)

$$f(x) = \begin{cases} -2x - 1 & -3 < x < -1 \\ x^2 & -1 \le x < 2 \\ -x + 6 & 2 < x < 6 \end{cases}$$

page 251

16. $2y + 1 = e^{3x}$

17. $3 = \log_2 8$

18. $\log_e \frac{M}{45} = 2t$

$t = \frac{1}{2} \log_e \left(\frac{M}{45}\right)$

19. $y = \log_{10} 4x(x + 1)$

$10^y = 4x(x + 1)$

20. $t = \frac{1}{0.055} \log_e \left(\frac{R}{35500}\right)$

$= 6$ (3 sig fig)

21. $t{\times}\log_{10} 1.015 = \log_{10} 1.4167$

$= 23.4$ years   (3 sig fig)

page 254

22. a) (vertical scale different for base 10 logs)

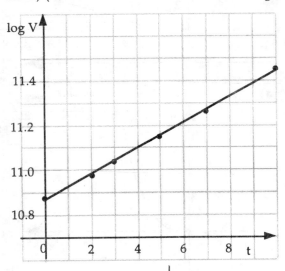

natural logs	base 10 logs
b) $m = 0.0584$	$m = 0.0253$
c) $V = 53000\, e^{0.0584\, t}$	$a = 10^{0.0253}$
	$= 1.06$
	$V = 53000 \times 1.06^t$

23. a) (vertical scale different for base 10 logs)

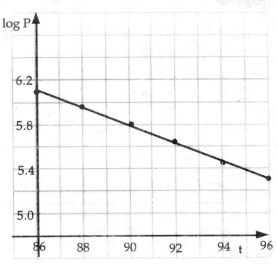

natural logs	base 10 logs
b) $m = = ^-0.085$	$m = ^-0.0368$
c) $P = 460\, e^{-0.085\,(t)}$	$a = 10^{-0.0368}$
where t is in years	$= 0.919$
since 1986	$V = 460 \times 0.919^t$

page 256

24.

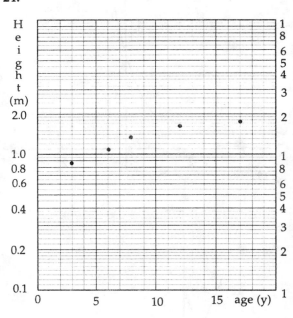

page 258
25.

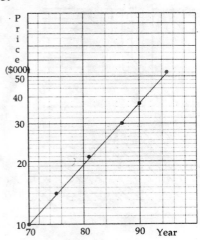

Rate = 0.07 (1 sig fig)

page 261
26. a)

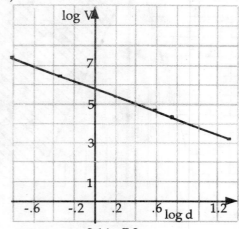

b)   grad $= \dfrac{3.14 - 7.3}{1.29 - {}^{-}0.79}$

         $= {}^{-}2$

c) $V = 300\, x^{-2}$

27. a)

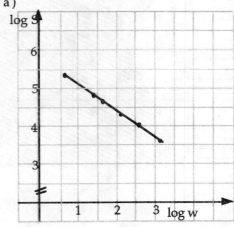

page 261 Q 27 continued

b)   grad $= \dfrac{3.56 - 5.35}{3.13 - 0.69}$

         $= {}^{-}0.734$

c) $S = 350\, x^{-0.73}$ (2 sig fig)

page 265
28. Semi-Log

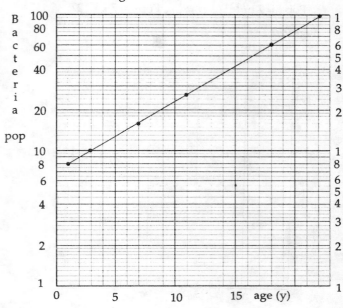

page 266
28. Log - Log

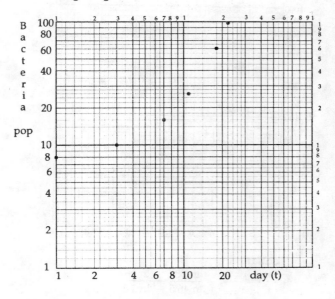

page 265/266 Q28 continued.
Equation

Using $P = k\,e^{at}$	Using $P = k\,c^t$
$a = \dfrac{\ln 98 - \ln 8}{22 - 1}$	$\log c = \dfrac{\log 98 - \log 8}{22 - 1}$
$= 0.12$	$c = 1.127$
$Pop = k\,e^{0.12\,t}$	$Pop = k \times 1.127^t$
$8 = k\,e^{0.12 \times 1}$	$8 = k \times 1.127$
$Pop = 7\,e^{0.12\,t}$	$Pop = 7 \times 1.127^t$

page 267
29. Semi-Log

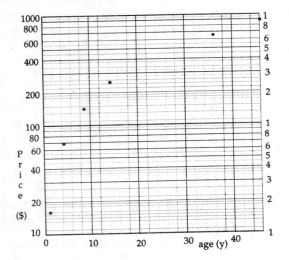

page 268 Log-Log

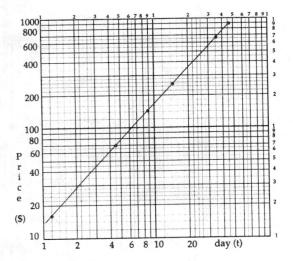

equation

$$k = \frac{\ln 887 - \ln 16}{\ln 46.5 - \ln 1.2}$$

$$= 1.10$$

$$\text{Price} = C\,x^{1.10\,t}$$

$$16 = C\,x^{1.10 \times 1.2}$$

$$\text{Price} = 13.1\,x^{1.10\,t}$$

page 272
30.

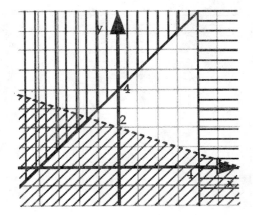

31.

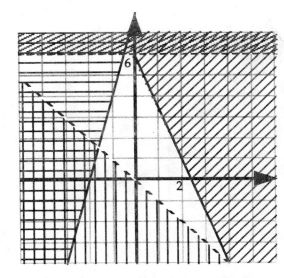

page 273
32.

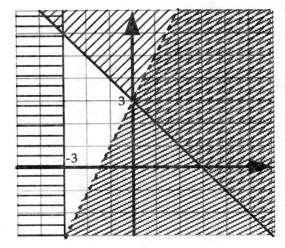

page 273
33.

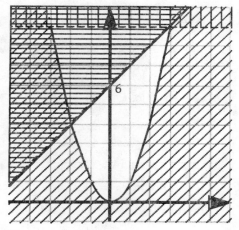

page 275
34.

let x = Ryder and y = Performa
x ≥ 4 and y ≥ 6
x + y ≤ 20 and 60x + 80y ≤ 1440

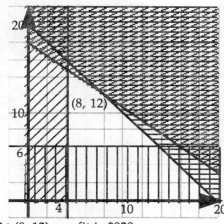

At (8, 12) profit is $920

35.

let x = Pinot and y = Sauv.
x ≥ 0 and y ≥ 0
x + y ≤ 10 and 40x + 10y ≤ 200

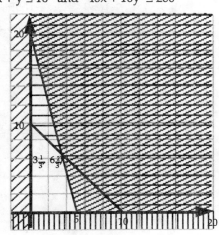

page 275 Q 35 continued

  a) At $(3\frac{1}{3}, 6\frac{2}{3})$ profit is $56667

  b) $3\frac{1}{3}$ of Pinot and $6\frac{2}{3}$ of Sauv.

page 276
36. a)

let x = small and y = large
x ≥ 25 and y ≥ 15
x + y ≤ 100 and 5x + 10y ≤ 800

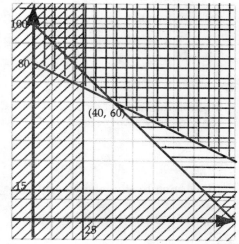

  b) At (40, 60) max profit is $1800
     At (25, 15) min profit is $675

37. a)

let x = Ha of corn and y = Ha of Pump.
x ≥ 0 and y ≥ 0
x + y ≤ 10 and 15x + 30y ≤ 240
125x + 75y ≤ 1125

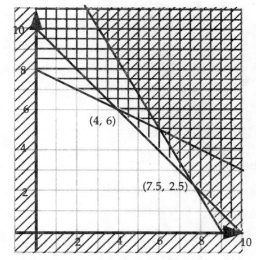

  b) At (4, 6) profit is $2760
      and at (7.5, 2.5) profit is $2550
      so 4 Ha of corn and 6 Ha of Pumpkin.

Chapter 8

EQUATIONS

page 280

1. $x = 2$

and $y = {}^-3$

2. $x = 2.20$ (3 sig fig)

and $y = {}^-1.52$ (3 sig fig)

3. $x = 2.18$ (3 sig fig)

and $y = 1.36$ (3 sig fig)

4. $x = 2.62$ (3 sig fig)

and $y = 2.24$ (3 sig fig)

page 282

5. Multiplying the first by 3 gives you a contradictory statement of

$$0 = 17$$

So equations are inconsistent

6. Attempting to eliminate x results in a statement that is always true which implies there is no unique solution.

page 285

7. step 1 $^-y - 2z = {}^-9$

$5y - 2z = 15$

∴ $^-12y = 30$

Ans $x = {}^-3, y = 4, z = 2.5$

8. A true statement so no unique solution.

9. $x = 6.23$ (3 sig fig)

$y = {}^-1.81$ (3 sig fig)

$z = {}^-2.57$ (3 sig fig)

10. $x = 1.06$ (3 sig fig)

$y = 1.46$ (3 sig fig)

$z = 0.96$ (3 sig fig)

page 288

11. $120L + 7.2S = 5000$

$0.013L + 0.0046S = 1.7$

Answer

Liver $= 23.5$ g

Spinach $= 303$ g

12. $11A + 16.5B + 4C = 134.55$

$6A + 21B + 7C = 138.75$

$4A + 27B + 12C = 172.50$

Answer

Job A $= \$5.10$ /hr

Job B $= \$3.70$ /hr

Job C $= \$4.35$ /hr

page 289

13.   Apples $= \$3.15$

Spinach $= \$7.04$

Potatoes $= \$1.27$

The fourth visit should cost $19.20 which it did so no increase.

14.   Runs at 17.1 km/hr

Cycles at 40.8 km/hr

Paddles at 23.4 km/hr

page 294

15. $x = 1.17$ (2 dp)

16. $x = 2.77$ (2 dp)

page 295

17. $x = 1.51$ (2 dp)

18. $x = 1.77$ (2 dp)

page 300

19.

step	x_0	x_1
1	1.0000	1.3105
2	1.3105	1.2239
3	1.2239	1.1760
4	1.1760	1.1659
5	1.1659	1.1655

Answer is $x = 1.166$ (3 dp)

20. a)

step	x_0	x_1
1	3.0000	2.7962
2	2.7962	2.7729
3	2.7729	2.7726

Answer is $x = 2.773$ (3 dp)

b) Because the tangent at x = 2 is almost parallel to the x axis.

page 301

21. $f'(x) = 2x - 3$ so iterations become

step	x_0	x_1
1	2.000	3.000
2	3.000	2.667
3	2.667	2.619
4	2.619	2.618

Answer is x = 2.62   (2 dp)

22. $f'(x) = e^x - 2x$ so iterations become

step	x_0	x_1
1	⁻1.0000	⁻0.7330
2	⁻0.7330	⁻0.7038
3	⁻0.7038	⁻0.70347
4	⁻0.70347	⁻0.70347

Answer is x = ⁻0.703   (3 dp)

23. $f'(x) = x + e^x - 9$

step	x_0	x_1
1	3.0000	3.17141
2	3.17141	3.15324
3	3.15324	3.15301
4	3.15301	3.15301

Answer is x = 3.1530   (4 dp)

24. $f'(x) = 4x^3 - 9x^2 + 2$

step	x_0	x_1
1	3.0000	2.79310
2	2.79310	2.73622
3	2.73622	2.73207
4	2.73207	2.73205
5	2.73205	2.73205

Answer is x = 2.7321   (4 dp)

Chapter 9
DISPLAY OF DATA

page 304

1. a)

Retail price of cars $

19	330, 450, 500
20	100, 900
21	300, 350, 800
22	000, 350, 400, 750, 800, 900
23	200, 400, 700, 750, 995
24	100, 220, 350, 950
25	100, 600, 750
26	000, 995
27	000, 500

b)   Lower Q   = 21800
       Median   = 23300
       Upper Q   = 24950
       Inter Q   = 3150

2. a)

Runs - Batsman 1		Runs - Batsman 2
1, 0	0	0, 0
3, 0	1	4
8, 4, 2, 1	2	0
7, 5, 5, 4, 4, 2	3	6, 6
5, 3, 1	4	2, 4, 5, 7
7	5	1, 3, 7, 8
2	6	1, 4
	7	3, 4
2	8	4, 7

b)Batsman 2 - higher median (49), greater concentration of scores at top end.

page 307

3. a)

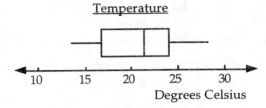

Temperature

Degrees Celsius

b)

Lower Q = 17

Median = 22

Upper Q = 24

50% of the temperatures range between 17 and 24 degrees with the maximum only 3 degrees hotter.

4. a)

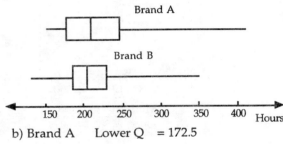

Life of light bulbs (hours)

Brand A

Brand B

Hours

b) Brand A   Lower Q = 172.5

Median = 207.5

Upper Q = 245

Brand B   Lower Q = 187.5

Median = 205

Upper Q = 225

No brand clearly better than the other in terms of life. Brand A has a greater range than Brand B.

page 310

5. a)

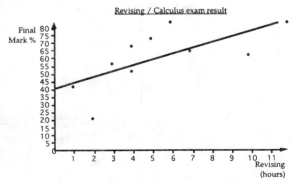

Revising / Calculus exam result

Final Mark %

Revising (hours)

b)   casual relationship between time spent revising and calculus result.

6. a)

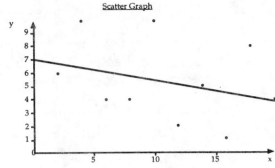

Scatter Graph

b)   No relationship between the two sets of data.

page 313

7.

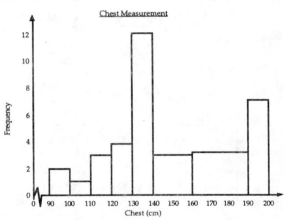

Chest Measurement

Frequency

Chest (cm)

8.

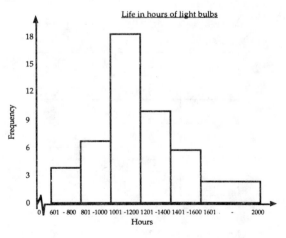

Life in hours of light bulbs

Frequency

Hours

page 315

9.

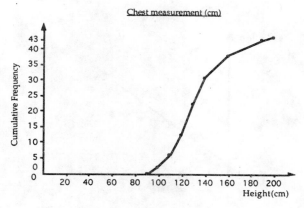

Chest measurement (cm)

b) Estimates from graph

Lower Q = 115
Median = 130
Upper Q = 145

10.

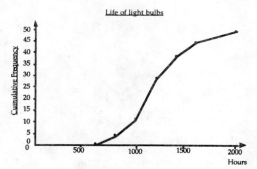

Life of light bulbs

b) Estimates from graph

Lower Q   = 1020
Median   = 1150
Upper Q = 1380

PRACTICE EXAM
ANSWERS

SECTION A (35 marks)

QUESTION ONE

(a) Upper Q = 43.5 cm   ✓✓

(b) **1.** $\dfrac{42}{132}\left(\dfrac{7}{22}\right)$ ✓✓

   2. $\dfrac{49}{144}$ ✓✓

(c)   0.1044   ✓✓

(d)   16128   ✓✓

(e) **1.**

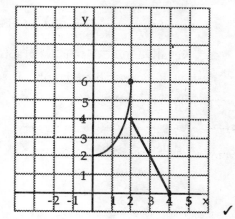

✓✓

   2.   f(2.3) = 3.4   ✓✓

(f)   a = 0.5825   ✓✓

(g) **1.**   E(X) = 5.679   ✓✓

   2.   SD(X) = 1.104   ✓✓

   3.   P(x ≠ 5) = $\dfrac{43}{56}$ ✓✓

(h)   f'(x) = $14x + 6e^{-2x}$ ✓✓

(i) **1.**   x = 2   ✓

             y = ⁻3   ✓

   2.   Any pair of parallel lines. ✓✓

(j) $\displaystyle\sum_{k=1}^{15}(-4k + 68)$ ✓✓

(k) **1.**   log 8   ✓✓
   2. $\dfrac{1}{4}$ ✓✓

(1) $\dfrac{n(n-1)}{2}$ ✓ ✓

(m) $\dfrac{7}{13}$ ✓ ✓

(n) **1.** $f(3) = 6$ ✓ ✓

2.   when $x = 4$ ✓ ✓

3. $x = 1$ and $x = 3.5$ ✓ ✓

(o) **1.** $\lambda = 0.2$ ✓ ✓

2.   0.0012   ✓ ✓

(p) a^2 ✓ ✓

(q) **1.** $f(1) = 2$ ✓

                $f(2) = {}^-1$ ✓

Change of sign means existence of root

2.   Negative indicates below graph

Positive indicates above graph. Therefore

        must cut x axis.   ✓ ✓

(r)   mean $= 27$ ✓

        std dev. $= 3.854$ ✓

SECTION B: (36 marks)

QUESTION TWO

(a)   **1.**

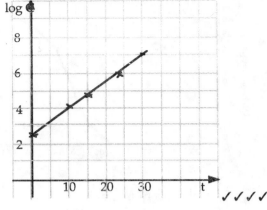

✓✓✓✓

2. $m = 0.1471$ ✓ ✓

3. $C = 14e^{0.1471t}$ ✓ ✓

4. $3850 = 14e^{0.1471t}$ ✓

        $275 = e^{0.1471t}$ ✓

    $\ln(275) = \ln(e^{0.1471t})$ ✓

        $t = 38.18$

        $t = 39$ days   ✓

(b) **1.** $f'(x) = 2 - e^x$ ✓

max point (0.693, 1.386)   ✓ ✓ ✓

2. $x_{n+1} =$
$x_n - \dfrac{2x - e^x + 2}{2 - e^x}$ ✓ ✓

        $x_0 = 1$ ✓ ✓

        $x_1 = 2.7844$ ✓ ✓

        $x_2 = 2.1768$ ✓ ✓

3.

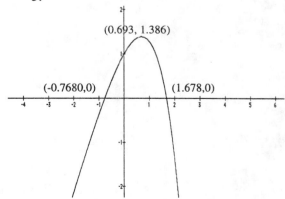

(0.693, 1.386)

(-0.7680,0)   (1.678,0)

Graph ✓ Turning pt ✓ +ve root ✓ -ve root ✓

4. Starting value needs to be greater than 0.693 else will converge to the -ve root. Situation occurs when a turning point is between two roots.
✓✓

(c) $P = ke^{-0.024t}$ ✓

when t = 0

$P = ke^0$

$P = k$ ✓

half population = 0.5k   ✓

$0.5k = ke^{-0.024t}$ ✓

$0.5 = e^{-0.024t}$

$\ln(0.5) = \ln(e^{-0.024t})$ ✓

$t = 28.9$ years   ✓

QUESTION THREE

(a) 1.
$$0.02r + 0.012p \le 1.2 \quad ✓✓$$
$$10r + 21p \le 1200 \quad ✓✓$$
$$r \ge 15 \quad ✓$$
$$p \ge 25 \quad ✓$$

2.

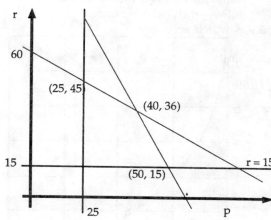

graphing each line ✓✓ + ✓✓ + ✓ + ✓
labels ignored

3.   (25,45)   profit = $618.75

(40, 36)   profit = $720.00

(50, 15)   profit = $675.00

40 Pohutakawa and 36 Radiata should be sent
working ✓✓   answer ✓✓ (CAO OK)

4.   max profit = $720.00   ✓✓

(b) 1. $\binom{11}{7} = 330$ ✓✓

2. $\binom{3}{2} \times \binom{4}{3} \times \binom{4}{2} = 72$ mult ✓✓ ans ✓✓

3. $^{11}P_3 = 990$ ✓✓

(c) 1.   Each is one half of the previous. ✓✓

2.   Area $= \dfrac{1}{8}$ the total   ✓✓

3. Sequence $= \left\langle \dfrac{1}{8}, \dfrac{1}{16}, \dfrac{1}{32}, \dfrac{1}{64}, \dots \right\rangle$
ignore + signs   ✓✓

4.   recognition of sum to infinity ✓✓

Total $= \dfrac{1}{4}$ ✓✓

QUESTION FOUR

(a) 1.

TEMP °C	4.6	7.2	11.2	18.0	23.3
$\log_e$ (TEMP)	1.5	2.0	2.4	2.9	3.1
time sec	180	86	41	20	12
$\log_e$ (time)	5.2	4.5	3.7	3.0	2.5

TEMP any two ✓ rest correct extra ✓
same for time ✓✓ total **2 marks.**
If $\log_{10}$ then penalise once.

2. ✓✓ watch accuracy

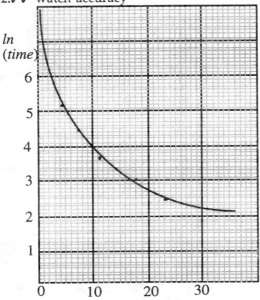

3. ✓✓ watch accuracy. str line optional

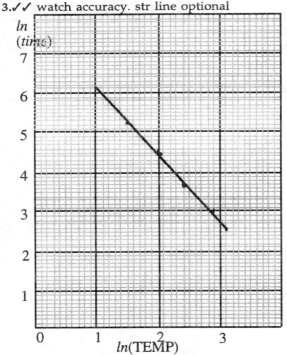

4. The log-log graph gives the best approximation of a straight line.   ✓

This implies the best model is a Power function of the form   ✓

$$time = A\,(TEMP)^k$$ ✓

as taking logs of both sides gives   ✓

$$\log_e (time) = \log_e (A\,(TEMP)^k)$$ ✓

which simplifies to

$$\log_e (time) = \log_e (A) + k\,\log_e (TEMP)$$

The form is of a straight line graph.   ✓
$y = c + mx$ the y intercept is $\log_e (A)$ and the gradient is k

5. Working must be seen for full marks

$$k = \frac{ln\,(time_2) - ln\,(time_1)}{ln\,(TEMP_2) - ln(TEMP_1)}$$ ✓

$$k = \frac{2.5 - 5.2}{3.1 - 1.5}$$ ✓

$$= {}^{-}1.69$$ ✓

sub. into $time = A\,(TEMP)^k$ ✓

gives $180 = A\,(4.6)^{-1.69}$ or equiv   ✓

$A = 2373$ ✓

rounding to 2 dp gives $k = {}^{-}1.7$ and $A = 2400$
Correct answer only 1 mark

6. When   TEMP $= 30$

$$time = 2400\,(30)^{-1.7}$$
$$= 7.4 \text{ seconds}$$ ✓✓

(b) 1.

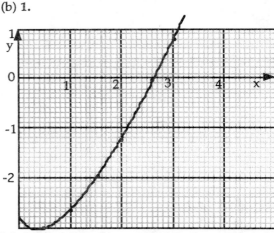

labels ✓ points ✓ curve joining ✓ accuracy ✓
Solution $x = 2.6$ ✓✓ must be from their graph.

2.

x_0	y_0	x_1	y_1	x_m	y_m
2.500	-0.192	3.000	0.874	2.750	0.329
2.500	-0.192	2.750	0.329	2.625	0.065
2.500	-0.192	2.625	0.065	2.563	-0.063
2.563	-0.063	2.625	0.065	2.594	0.000

starts with **2.5** and **3.** ✓ works to 3 dp ✓
method/working ✓✓✓✓ Answer 2.59 ✓✓

QUESTION FIVE

(a) **1.** $P(X < 115) = P(Z < \dfrac{115 - 140}{12})$ ✓

$= P(Z < -2.083)$ ✓

$= 0.5 - 0.4813$ ✓

$= 0.0187$ ✓

2. $P(X > 150) = P(Z > \dfrac{150 - 140}{12})$

$= P(Z > 0.833)$ ✓

$= 0.5 - 0.2975$

$= 0.2025$ ✓

so 430×0.2025 ✓

$= 87$ cups ✓

3. $\dfrac{150 - \mu}{12} = 1.645$ ✓✓

$\mu = 130.26$ ✓

so $\mu = 130$ ml ✓

4. $\dfrac{1.96(12)}{\sqrt{n}} < 2$ ✓

$\dfrac{553.1904..}{n} < 4$ ✓

$n > 138.3$ ✓

$n \geq 139$ ✓

(b) **1.** Mean $= 4$ ✓

Std. dev. $= 1.661$ ✓

$= P(X > 0)$

$= P(Z > \dfrac{0 - 4}{1.661})$ ✓

$= P(Z > -2.408)$ ✓

$= 0.5 + 0.4920$ ✓

$= 0.9920$ ✓

2.

$4 - 1.96(1.661) < \mu_1 - \mu_2 < 4 + 1.96(1.661)$ ✓✓

$0.7444 < \mu_1 - \mu_2 < 7.256$ ✓✓

3. There is a significant difference between the two machines. ✓✓

Assumptions - normally distributed and independent. ✓✓✓✓

4. More than two machines required (sample too small) ✓✓ and they should be tested in different environments ✓✓

QUESTION SIX

1. - Fixed number of events

- Independence is assumed

- same probability for each event

- only two possible outcomes. ✓✓

minus one tick per error.

2. $\pi = 0.15$, n $= 10$ and x $= 2$

$P(X = 1) = 0.3474$ ✓✓

3. $P(X \geq 2) = 1 - [P(X=0) + P(X=1)]$ ✓

$= 1 - [0.1969 + 0.3474]$ ✓✓

$= 0.4557$ ✓

4. $n\pi > 5$ and $n(1 - \pi) > 5$ ✓✓

5. $\mu = 27$ ✓

$\sigma = \sqrt{180 \times 0.15 \times 0.85}$

$= 4.79$ ✓

continuity correction X $= 29.5$ ✓

$P(X > 29.5) = P(Z > \dfrac{29.5 - 27}{4.79})$ ✓

$= 0.5 - P(0 < Z < 0.522)$ ✓

$= 0.5 - 0.1992$

$= 0.3008$ ✓

6. Poisson distribution ✓✓

7. x $= 4$, $\lambda = 4.4$ $P(X=4) = 0.1917$ ✓✓

8. x $= 2$, $\lambda = 2.2$

$P(X=2 \text{ for 2 hours}) = [P(X = 2)]^2$ ✓✓

$= 0.0719$ ✓

9. 15 min $\lambda = 0.55$ and $x > 0$ ✓

$P(X > 0) = 1 - P(X=0)$ ✓

$= 1 - 0.5769$ ✓

$= 0.4231$ ✓

[answer of 0.4512 ie used tables $\lambda = 0.6$ ✗✗✓✓]

10. claims $= 75$ ✓✓

11. $P(X=\text{claim}) = 0.55$ ✓✓

12. $P(Y2 \mid Y1) = \dfrac{P(Y2 \cap Y1)}{P(Y1)}$ ✓

$= \dfrac{0.1}{0.275}$ ✓

$= 0.3636$ (4 sf) ✓✓

QUESTION SEVEN

(a) **1.** Stem and leaf graph of female and male Geography results. **(title)** ✓

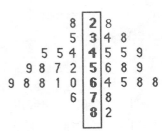

Female results %		Male results %
8	**2**	8
5	**3**	4 8
5 5 4	**4**	5 5 9
9 8 7 2	**5**	6 8 9
9 8 8 1 0	**6**	4 5 8 8
6	**7**	8
	8	2

males ✓✓ females ✓✓ back to back ✓

2. Median: = 58   ✓ ✓

Lower Q = 45   ✓

Upper Q = 68   ✓

3.

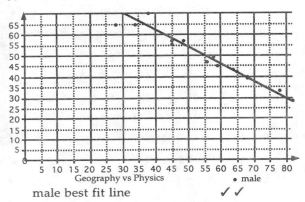

Geography vs Physics   • male

male best fit line   ✓ ✓

4.

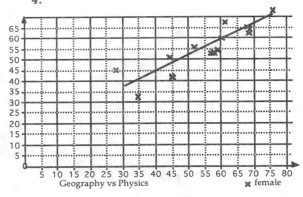

Geography vs Physics   ✗ female

plotting points okay   ✓ ✓
female best fit line   ✓ ✓

5. Males who do well in Geography tend to do poorly in Physics.   ✓ ✓
Females who do well in Geography also tend to do well in Physics (but the correlation is not as good)   ✓ ✓

(b) **1.** The natural period for our time series is the five week days.   ✓ ✓

2. mean = 7.2, ✓✓ difference = ⁻3.2   ✓ ✓

3.

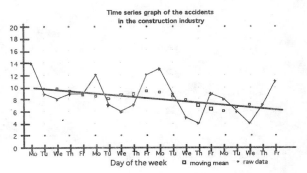

Straight trend line   ✓ ✓
(just joins moving means✗✓)

4. Seasonal effect Monday = 9.0 / 3 ✓✓
= 3.0   (1 dp) ✓✓

5. Long term trend is -1 per week so the trend line will be at approximately 6.   ✓ ✓

6th Monday = 6 + 3
= 9   ✓ ✓

Formulae

PROBABILITY

$$P(A \cup B) = P(A) + P(B) - P(A \cap B)$$

$$P(A \mid B) = \frac{P(A \cap B)}{P(B)}$$

SAMPLE MEAN AND SAMPLE VARIANCE

$$\bar{x} = \frac{\sum fx}{n}$$

$$s^2 = \frac{\sum fx^2 - \frac{(\sum fx)^2}{n}}{n}$$

MEAN AND VARIANCE OF A RANDOM VARIABLE

$$\mu = E(X)$$
$$= \sum x \cdot P(X = x)$$

$$\sigma^2 = Var(X)$$
$$= E(X^2) - [E(X)]^2$$

BINOMIAL DISTRIBUTION

$$P(X = x) = \binom{n}{x} \pi^x (1 - \pi)^{n-x}$$

$$\mu = n\pi, \qquad \sigma = \sqrt{n\pi(1 - \pi)}$$

POISSON DISTRIBUTION

$$P(X = x) = \frac{\lambda^x e^{-\lambda}}{x!}$$

$$\mu = \lambda, \qquad \sigma = \sqrt{\lambda}$$

DISTRIBUTION OF SAMPLE STATISTICS

Statistic	Mean	Standard Deviation
Sample Mean	$E(\bar{X}) = \mu$	$\sigma_{\bar{x}} = \frac{\sigma}{\sqrt{n}}$ (std error of mean)
Sample Proportion	$E(P) = \pi$	$\sigma_P = \sqrt{\frac{\pi(1 - \pi)}{n}}$ (std error of proportion)
Difference of Means (of two independent samples)	$E(\bar{X}_1 - \bar{X}_2) = \mu_1 - \mu_2$	$\sigma_{\bar{x}_1 - \bar{x}_2} = \sqrt{\frac{\sigma_1^2}{n_1} + \frac{\sigma_2^2}{n_2}}$

NUMERICAL METHODS

Bisection $\qquad x_2 = \frac{x_0 + x_1}{2}$

Newton Raphson $\qquad x_1 = x_0 - \frac{f(x_0)}{f'(x_0)}$

Formulae

SERIES

Arithmetic $t_n = a + (n-1)d$

$$S_n = \frac{n}{2}[\,2a + (n-1)d\,]$$

Exponential $e^x = 1 + x + \frac{x^2}{2!} + \frac{x^3}{3!} + \dots$ (for all x)

Geometric $t_n = ar^{n-1}$

$$S_n = \frac{a(1-r^n)}{1-r}, \; r \neq 1$$

$$S_\infty = \frac{a}{1-r} \text{ for } |r| < 1$$

DIFFERENTIATION

$y = f(x)$	$\dfrac{dy}{dx} = f'(x)$
x^n	nx^{n-1}
$\ln x$	$\frac{1}{x}$
e^{ax}	ae^{ax}

LOGARITHMS

If $y = b^x$ then $\log_b y = x$

$\log_b x + \log_b y = \log_b xy$

$\log_b x - \log_b y = \log_b \frac{x}{y}$

$\log_b x^a = a \log_b x$

If $y = e^x$ then $x = \log_e y \; (= \ln x)$

BINOMIAL THEOREM

$$(a+b)^n = \binom{n}{0}a^n + \binom{n}{1}a^{n-1}b^1 + \binom{n}{2}a^{n-2}b^2 + \dots + \binom{n}{r}a^{n-r}b^r + \dots + \binom{n}{n}b^n$$

where $\binom{n}{r} = {}^nC_r = \frac{n!}{(n-r)!\,r!}$ Note : ${}^nP_r = \frac{n!}{(n-r)!}$

BINOMIAL COEFFICIENTS

Some values of $\binom{n}{r}$ are given in the table below

n \ r	0	1	2	3	4	5	6	7	8	9	10
0	1										
1	1	1									
2	1	2	1								
3	1	3	3	1							
4	1	4	6	4	1						
5	1	5	10	10	5	1					
6	1	6	15	20	15	6	1				
7	1	7	21	35	35	21	7	1			
8	1	8	28	56	70	56	28	8	1		
9	1	9	36	84	126	126	84	36	9	1	
10	1	10	45	120	210	252	210	120	45	10	1
11	1	11	55	165	330	462	462	330	165	55	11
12	1	12	66	220	495	792	924	792	495	220	66
13	1	13	78	286	715	1287	1716	1716	1287	715	286
14	1	14	91	364	1001	2002	3003	3432	3003	2002	1001
15	1	15	105	455	1365	3003	5005	6435	6435	5005	3003

Statistical Tables

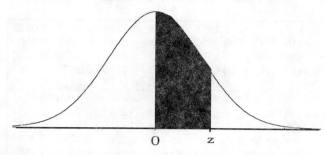

Normal Distribution

This table gives the probability that the standardised Normal variate Z lies between 0 and z.

Differences

z	0	1	2	3	4	5	6	7	8	9	1	2	3	4	5	6	7	8	9
0.0	0.0000	0.0040	0.0080	0.0120	0.0160	0.0199	0.0239	0.0279	0.0319	0.0359	4	8	12	16	20	24	28	32	36
0.1	0.0398	0.0438	0.0478	0.0517	0.0557	0.0596	0.0636	0.0675	0.0714	0.0753	4	8	12	16	20	24	28	32	35
0.2	0.0793	0.0832	0.0871	0.0910	0.0948	0.0987	0.1026	0.1064	0.1103	0.1141	4	8	12	15	19	23	27	31	35
0.3	0.1179	0.1217	0.1255	0.1293	0.1331	0.1368	0.1406	0.1443	0.1480	0.1517	4	8	11	15	19	23	26	30	34
0.4	0.1554	0.1591	0.1628	0.1664	0.1700	0.1736	0.1772	0.1808	0.1844	0.1879	4	7	11	14	18	22	25	29	32
0.5	0.1915	0.1950	0.1985	0.2019	0.2054	0.2088	0.2123	0.2157	0.2190	0.2224	3	7	10	14	17	21	24	27	31
0.6	0.2257	0.2291	0.2324	0.2357	0.2389	0.2422	0.2454	0.2486	0.2517	0.2549	3	6	10	13	16	19	23	26	29
0.7	0.2580	0.2611	0.2642	0.2673	0.2704	0.2734	0.2764	0.2793	0.2823	0.2852	3	6	9	12	15	18	21	24	27
0.8	0.2881	0.2910	0.2939	0.2967	0.2995	0.3023	0.3051	0.3078	0.3106	0.3133	3	6	8	11	14	17	19	22	25
0.9	0.3159	0.3186	0.3212	0.3238	0.3264	0.3289	0.3315	0.3340	0.3365	0.3389	3	5	8	10	13	15	18	20	23
1.0	0.3413	0.3438	0.3461	0.3485	0.3508	0.3531	0.3554	0.3577	0.3599	0.3621	2	5	7	9	12	14	16	18	21
1.1	0.3643	0.3665	0.3686	0.3708	0.3729	0.3749	0.3770	0.3790	0.3810	0.3830	2	4	6	8	10	12	14	16	19
1.2	0.3849	0.3869	0.3888	0.3907	0.3925	0.3944	0.3962	0.3980	0.3997	0.4015	2	4	6	7	9	11	13	15	16
1.3	0.4032	0.4049	0.4066	0.4082	0.4099	0.4115	0.4131	0.4147	0.4162	0.4177	2	3	5	6	8	10	11	13	14
1.4	0.4192	0.4207	0.4222	0.4236	0.4251	0.4265	0.4279	0.4292	0.4306	0.4319	1	3	4	6	7	8	10	11	13
1.5	0.4332	0.4345	0.4357	0.4370	0.4382	0.4394	0.4406	0.4418	0.4429	0.4441	1	2	4	5	6	7	8	10	11
1.6	0.4452	0.4463	0.4474	0.4484	0.4495	0.4505	0.4515	0.4525	0.4535	0.4545	1	2	3	4	5	6	7	8	9
1.7	0.4554	0.4564	0.4573	0.4582	0.4591	0.4599	0.4608	0.4616	0.4625	0.4633	1	2	3	3	4	5	6	7	8
1.8	0.4641	0.4649	0.4656	0.4664	0.4671	0.4678	0.4686	0.4693	0.4699	0.4706	1	1	2	3	4	4	5	6	6
1.9	0.4713	0.4719	0.4726	0.4732	0.4738	0.4744	0.4750	0.4756	0.4761	0.4767	1	1	2	2	3	4	4	5	5
2.0	0.4772	0.4778	0.4783	0.4788	0.4793	0.4798	0.4803	0.4808	0.4812	0.4817	0	1	1	2	2	3	3	4	4
2.1	0.4821	0.4826	0.4830	0.4834	0.4838	0.4842	0.4846	0.4850	0.4854	0.4857	0	1	1	2	2	2	3	3	4
2.2	0.4861	0.4864	0.4868	0.4871	0.4875	0.4878	0.4881	0.4884	0.4887	0.4890	0	1	1	1	2	2	2	3	3
2.3	0.4893	0.4896	0.4898	0.4901	0.4904	0.4906	0.4909	0.4911	0.4913	0.4916	0	1	1	1	1	2	2	2	2
2.4	0.4918	0.4920	0.4922	0.4925	0.4927	0.4929	0.4931	0.4932	0.4934	0.4936	0	0	1	1	1	1	1	2	2
2.5	0.4938	0.4940	0.4941	0.4943	0.4945	0.4946	0.4948	0.4949	0.4951	0.4952	0	0	0	1	1	1	1	1	1
2.6	0.4953	0.4955	0.4956	0.4957	0.4959	0.4960	0.4961	0.4962	0.4963	0.4964	0	0	0	0	1	1	1	1	1
2.7	0.4965	0.4966	0.4967	0.4968	0.4969	0.4970	0.4971	0.4972	0.4973	0.4974	0	0	0	0	0	1	1	1	1
2.8	0.4974	0.4975	0.4976	0.4977	0.4977	0.4978	0.4979	0.4979	0.4980	0.4981	0	0	0	0	0	0	0	1	1
2.9	0.4981	0.4982	0.4982	0.4983	0.4984	0.4984	0.4985	0.4985	0.4986	0.4986	0	0	0	0	0	0	0	0	0
3.0	0.4986	0.4987	0.4987	0.4988	0.4988	0.4989	0.4989	0.4989	0.4990	0.4990	0	0	0	0	0	0	0	0	0
3.1	0.4990	0.4991	0.4991	0.4991	0.4992	0.4992	0.4992	0.4992	0.4993	0.4993	0	0	0	0	0	0	0	0	0
3.2	0.4993	0.4993	0.4994	0.4994	0.4994	0.4994	0.4994	0.4995	0.4995	0.4995	0	0	0	0	0	0	0	0	0
3.3	0.4995	0.4995	0.4996	0.4996	0.4996	0.4996	0.4996	0.4996	0.4996	0.4997	0	0	0	0	0	0	0	0	0
3.4	0.4997	0.4997	0.4997	0.4997	0.4997	0.4997	0.4997	0.4997	0.4997	0.4998	0	0	0	0	0	0	0	0	0
3.5	0.4998	0.4998	0.4998	0.4998	0.4998	0.4998	0.4998	0.4998	0.4998	0.4998	0	0	0	0	0	0	0	0	0
3.6	0.4998	0.4998	0.4999	0.4999	0.4999	0.4999	0.4999	0.4999	0.4999	0.4999	0	0	0	0	0	0	0	0	0
3.7	0.4999	0.4999	0.4999	0.4999	0.4999	0.4999	0.4999	0.4999	0.4999	0.4999	0	0	0	0	0	0	0	0	0
3.8	0.4999	0.4999	0.4999	0.4999	0.4999	0.4999	0.4999	0.4999	0.4999	0.5000	0	0	0	0	0	0	0	0	0
3.9	0.5000	0.5000	0.5000	0.5000	0.5000	0.5000	0.5000	0.5000	0.5000	0.5000	0	0	0	0	0	0	0	0	0

Binomial Distribution

Each entry gives the probability that a Binomial random variable X, with the parameters n and π, has the value x.

n	x	0.05	0.1	0.15	$\frac{1}{6}$	0.2	0.25	0.3	$\frac{1}{3}$	0.35	0.4	0.45	0.5
4	0	0.8145	0.6561	0.5220	0.4822	0.4096	0.3164	0.2401	0.1976	0.1785	0.1296	0.0915	0.0625
	1	0.1715	0.2916	0.3685	0.3858	0.4096	0.4219	0.4116	0.3951	0.3845	0.3456	0.2995	0.2500
	2	0.0135	0.0486	0.0975	0.1158	0.1536	0.2109	0.2646	0.2963	0.3105	0.3456	0.3675	0.3750
	3	0.0005	0.0036	0.0115	0.0154	0.0256	0.0469	0.0756	0.0987	0.1115	0.1536	0.2005	0.2500
	4		0.0001	0.0005	0.0008	0.0016	0.0039	0.0081	0.0123	0.0150	0.0256	0.0410	0.0625
5	0	0.7738	0.5905	0.4437	0.4018	0.3277	0.2373	0.1681	0.1317	0.1160	0.0778	0.0503	0.0312
	1	0.2036	0.3280	0.3915	0.4019	0.4096	0.3955	0.3601	0.3293	0.3124	0.2592	0.2059	0.1562
	2	0.0214	0.0729	0.1382	0.1608	0.2048	0.2637	0.3087	0.3292	0.3364	0.3456	0.3369	0.3125
	3	0.0011	0.0081	0.0244	0.0322	0.0512	0.0879	0.1323	0.1646	0.1811	0.2304	0.2757	0.3125
	4		0.0004	0.0022	0.0032	0.0064	0.0146	0.0283	0.0411	0.0488	0.0768	0.1128	0.1562
	5			0.0001	0.0001	0.0003	0.0010	0.0024	0.0041	0.0053	0.0102	0.0185	0.0312
6	0	0.7351	0.5314	0.3771	0.3348	0.2621	0.1780	0.1176	0.0878	0.0754	0.0467	0.0277	0.0156
	1	0.2321	0.3543	0.3993	0.4019	0.3932	0.3560	0.3025	0.2634	0.2437	0.1866	0.1359	0.0938
	2	0.0305	0.0984	0.1762	0.2010	0.2458	0.2966	0.3241	0.3292	0.3280	0.3110	0.2780	0.2344
	3	0.0021	0.0146	0.0415	0.0536	0.0819	0.1318	0.1852	0.2194	0.2355	0.2765	0.3032	0.3125
	4	0.0001	0.0012	0.0055	0.0080	0.0154	0.0330	0.0595	0.0823	0.0951	0.1382	0.1861	0.2344
	5		0.0001	0.0004	0.0006	0.0015	0.0044	0.0102	0.0165	0.0205	0.0369	0.0609	0.0938
	6					0.0001	0.0002	0.0007	0.0014	0.0018	0.0041	0.0083	0.0156
7	0	0.6983	0.4783	0.3206	0.2790	0.2097	0.1335	0.0824	0.0585	0.0490	0.0280	0.0152	0.0078
	1	0.2573	0.3720	0.3960	0.3907	0.3670	0.3115	0.2471	0.2049	0.1848	0.1306	0.0872	0.0547
	2	0.0406	0.1240	0.2097	0.2345	0.2753	0.3115	0.3177	0.3073	0.2985	0.2613	0.2140	0.1641
	3	0.0036	0.0230	0.0617	0.0782	0.1147	0.1730	0.2269	0.2560	0.2679	0.2903	0.2918	0.2734
	4	0.0002	0.0026	0.0109	0.0156	0.0287	0.0577	0.0972	0.1280	0.1442	0.1935	0.2388	0.2734
	5		0.0002	0.0012	0.0019	0.0043	0.0115	0.0250	0.0384	0.0466	0.0774	0.1172	0.1641
	6			0.0001	0.0001	0.0004	0.0013	0.0036	0.0064	0.0084	0.0172	0.0320	0.0547
	7						0.0001	0.0002	0.0005	0.0006	0.0016	0.0037	0.0078
8	0	0.6634	0.4305	0.2725	0.2325	0.1678	0.1001	0.0576	0.0390	0.0319	0.0168	0.0084	0.0039
	1	0.2793	0.3826	0.3847	0.3721	0.3355	0.2670	0.1977	0.1561	0.1373	0.0896	0.0548	0.0312
	2	0.0515	0.1488	0.2376	0.2605	0.2936	0.3115	0.2965	0.2732	0.2587	0.2090	0.1569	0.1094
	3	0.0054	0.0331	0.0839	0.1042	0.1468	0.2076	0.2541	0.2731	0.2786	0.2787	0.2568	0.2188
	4	0.0004	0.0046	0.0185	0.0261	0.0459	0.0865	0.1361	0.1707	0.1875	0.2322	0.2627	0.2734
	5		0.0004	0.0026	0.0042	0.0092	0.0231	0.0467	0.0683	0.0808	0.1239	0.1719	0.2188
	6			0.0002	0.0004	0.0011	0.0038	0.0100	0.0171	0.0217	0.0413	0.0703	0.1094
	7					0.0001	0.0004	0.0012	0.0024	0.0033	0.0079	0.0164	0.0312
	8							0.0001	0.0002	0.0002	0.0007	0.0017	0.0039
9	0	0.6302	0.3874	0.2316	0.1937	0.1342	0.0751	0.0404	0.0260	0.0207	0.0101	0.0046	0.0020
	1	0.2985	0.3874	0.3679	0.3488	0.3020	0.2253	0.1556	0.1171	0.1004	0.0605	0.0339	0.0176
	2	0.0629	0.1722	0.2597	0.2791	0.3020	0.3003	0.2668	0.2341	0.2162	0.1612	0.1110	0.0703
	3	0.0077	0.0446	0.1069	0.1303	0.1762	0.2336	0.2668	0.2731	0.2716	0.2508	0.2119	0.1641
	4	0.0006	0.0074	0.0283	0.0391	0.0661	0.1168	0.1715	0.2048	0.2194	0.2508	0.2600	0.2461
	5		0.0008	0.0050	0.0078	0.0165	0.0389	0.0735	0.1024	0.1181	0.1672	0.2128	0.2461
	6		0.0001	0.0006	0.0010	0.0028	0.0087	0.0210	0.0341	0.0424	0.0743	0.1160	0.1641
	7			0.0001	0.0003	0.0003	0.0012	0.0039	0.0073	0.0098	0.0212	0.0407	0.0703
	8						0.0001	0.0004	0.0009	0.0013	0.0035	0.0083	0.0176
	9							0.0001	0.0001	0.0003	0.0008	0.0020
10	0	0.5987	0.3487	0.1969	0.1614	0.1074	0.0563	0.0282	0.0174	0.0135	0.0060	0.0025	0.0010
	1	0.3151	0.3874	0.3474	0.3230	0.2684	0.1877	0.1211	0.0867	0.0725	0.0403	0.0207	0.0098
	2	0.0746	0.1937	0.2759	0.2907	0.3020	0.2816	0.2335	0.1951	0.1757	0.1209	0.0763	0.0439
	3	0.0105	0.0574	0.1298	0.1551	0.2013	0.2503	0.2668	0.2601	0.2522	0.2150	0.1665	0.1172
	4	0.0010	0.0112	0.0401	0.0543	0.0881	0.1460	0.2001	0.2276	0.2377	0.2508	0.2384	0.2051
	5	0.0001	0.0015	0.0085	0.0130	0.0264	0.0584	0.1029	0.1365	0.1536	0.2007	0.2340	0.2461
	6		0.0001	0.0012	0.0022	0.0055	0.0162	0.0368	0.0569	0.0689	0.1115	0.1596	0.2051
	7			0.0001	0.0002	0.0008	0.0031	0.0090	0.0162	0.0212	0.0425	0.0746	0.1172
	8					0.0001	0.0004	0.0014	0.0030	0.0043	0.0106	0.0229	0.0439
	9							0.0001	0.0003	0.0005	0.0016	0.0042	0.0098
	10	(all other entries < 0.0001)									0.0001	0.0003	0.0010

© Robert Lakeland & Carl Nugent

Poisson Distribution

Each entry gives the probability that a Poisson random variable X, with the parameter λ, has the value x.

x \ λ	0.1	0.2	0.3	0.4	0.5	0.6	0.7	0.8	0.9	1.0
0	0.9048	0.8187	0.7408	0.6703	0.6065	0.5488	0.4966	0.4493	0.4066	0.3679
1	0.0905	0.1637	0.2222	0.2681	0.3033	0.3293	0.3476	0.3595	0.3659	0.3679
2	0.0045	0.0164	0.0333	0.0536	0.0758	0.0988	0.1217	0.1438	0.1647	0.1839
3	0.0002	0.0011	0.0033	0.0072	0.0126	0.0198	0.0284	0.0383	0.0494	0.0613
4		0.0001	0.0003	0.0007	0.0016	0.0030	0.0050	0.0077	0.0111	0.0153
5				0.0001	0.0002	0.0004	0.0007	0.0012	0.0020	0.0031
6							0.0001	0.0002	0.0003	0.0005
7										0.0001

x \ λ	1.1	1.2	1.3	1.4	1.5	1.6	1.7	1.8	1.9	2.0
0	0.3329	0.3012	0.2725	0.2466	0.2231	0.2019	0.1827	0.1653	0.1496	0.1353
1	0.3662	0.3614	0.3543	0.3452	0.3347	0.3230	0.3106	0.2975	0.2842	0.2707
2	0.2014	0.2169	0.2303	0.2417	0.2510	0.2584	0.2640	0.2678	0.2700	0.2707
3	0.0738	0.0867	0.0998	0.1128	0.1255	0.1378	0.1496	0.1607	0.1710	0.1804
4	0.0203	0.0260	0.0324	0.0395	0.0471	0.0551	0.0636	0.0723	0.0812	0.0902
5	0.0045	0.0062	0.0084	0.0111	0.0141	0.0176	0.0216	0.0260	0.0309	0.0361
6	0.0008	0.0012	0.0018	0.0026	0.0035	0.0047	0.0061	0.0078	0.0098	0.0120
7	0.0001	0.0002	0.0003	0.0005	0.0008	0.0011	0.0015	0.0020	0.0027	0.0034
8			0.0001	0.0001	0.0001	0.0002	0.0003	0.0005	0.0006	0.0009
9							0.0001	0.0001	0.0001	0.0002

x \ λ	2.2	2.4	2.6	2.8	3.0	3.2	3.4	3.6	3.8	4.0
0	0.1108	0.0907	0.0743	0.0608	0.0498	0.0408	0.0334	0.0273	0.0224	0.0183
1	0.2438	0.2177	0.1931	0.1703	0.1494	0.1304	0.1135	0.0984	0.0850	0.0733
2	0.2681	0.2613	0.2510	0.2384	0.2240	0.2087	0.1929	0.1771	0.1615	0.1465
3	0.1966	0.2090	0.2176	0.2225	0.2240	0.2226	0.2186	0.2125	0.2046	0.1954
4	0.1082	0.1254	0.1414	0.1557	0.1680	0.1781	0.1858	0.1912	0.1944	0.1954
5	0.0476	0.0602	0.0735	0.0872	0.1008	0.1140	0.1264	0.1377	0.1477	0.1563
6	0.0174	0.0241	0.0319	0.0407	0.0504	0.0608	0.0716	0.0826	0.0936	0.1042
7	0.0055	0.0083	0.0118	0.0163	0.0216	0.0278	0.0348	0.0425	0.0508	0.0595
8	0.0015	0.0025	0.0038	0.0057	0.0081	0.0111	0.0148	0.0191	0.0241	0.0298
9	0.0004	0.0007	0.0011	0.0018	0.0027	0.0040	0.0056	0.0076	0.0102	0.0132
10	0.0001	0.0002	0.0003	0.0005	0.0008	0.0013	0.0019	0.0028	0.0039	0.0053
11			0.0001	0.0001	0.0002	0.0004	0.0006	0.0009	0.0013	0.0019
12					0.0001	0.0001	0.0002	0.0003	0.0004	0.0006
13								0.0001	0.0001	0.0002
14										0.0001

x \ λ	4.2	4.4	4.6	4.8	5.0	5.2	5.4	5.6	5.8	6.0
0	0.0150	0.0123	0.0101	0.0082	0.0067	0.0055	0.0045	0.0037	0.0030	0.0025
1	0.0630	0.0540	0.0462	0.0395	0.0337	0.0287	0.0244	0.0207	0.0176	0.0149
2	0.1323	0.1188	0.1063	0.0948	0.0842	0.0746	0.0659	0.0580	0.0509	0.0446
3	0.1852	0.1743	0.1631	0.1517	0.1404	0.1293	0.1185	0.1082	0.0985	0.0892
4	0.1944	0.1917	0.1875	0.1820	0.1755	0.1681	0.1600	0.1515	0.1428	0.1339
5	0.1633	0.1687	0.1725	0.1747	0.1755	0.1748	0.1728	0.1697	0.1656	0.1606
6	0.1143	0.1237	0.1323	0.1398	0.1462	0.1515	0.1555	0.1584	0.1601	0.1606
7	0.0686	0.0778	0.0869	0.0959	0.1044	0.1125	0.1200	0.1267	0.1326	0.1377
8	0.0360	0.0428	0.0500	0.0575	0.0653	0.0731	0.0810	0.0887	0.0962	0.1033
9	0.0168	0.0209	0.0255	0.0307	0.0363	0.0423	0.0486	0.0552	0.0620	0.0688
10	0.0071	0.0092	0.0118	0.0147	0.0181	0.0220	0.0262	0.0309	0.0359	0.0413
11	0.0027	0.0037	0.0049	0.0064	0.0082	0.0104	0.0129	0.0157	0.0190	0.0225
12	0.0009	0.0013	0.0019	0.0026	0.0034	0.0045	0.0058	0.0073	0.0092	0.0113
13	0.0003	0.0005	0.0007	0.0009	0.0013	0.0018	0.0024	0.0032	0.0041	0.0052
14	0.0001	0.0001	0.0002	0.0003	0.0005	0.0007	0.0009	0.0013	0.0017	0.0022
15			0.0001	0.0001	0.0002	0.0002	0.0003	0.0005	0.0007	0.0009
16						0.0001	0.0001	0.0002	0.0002	0.0003
17	all other entries < 0.0001							0.0001	0.0001	0.0001

© Robert Lakeland & Carl Nugent

NuLake Texts ORDER FORM

P O Box 103
Wanganui

(06) 344 6066
(025) 240 3641

(06) 348 0194
(06) 344 6166

order@nulake.co.nz

Name

Address

Phone   number   **Fax   Number**

Quantity	Title	Price	Sub Total
	Fifth Form Maths Workbook	$21.95	
	Calculus Workbook	$21.95	
	Statistics Workbook	$21.95	
	Postage and handling if prepaid		$0.00
		TOTAL	

Method   of   Payment

I enclose a cheque for $ being full payment.

Visit our Web Site
http://www.nulake.co.nz

NuLake texts has a World Wide Web site where you can

- Find out what other books we have available.

- Give us feedback as to how you have found the *Workbooks*.

- Check if we have identified any errors in the *Workbooks* you are using.

- Order books (personal orders must be prepaid).

Or you can just email us questions and comments directly to **feedback@nulake.co.nz**

If you want to contact any individual our email addresses are

Carl Nugent   **cnugent@nulake.co.nz**

Doreen Nugent   **dnugent@nulake.co.nz**

Robert Lakeland **rlakeland@nulake.co.nz**